ECONOMIC GROWTH IN THEORY AND PRACTICE

Economic Growth in Theory and Practice

R.M. Sundrum

St. Martin's Press   New York

First published in the United States of America in 1991

Printed in Great Britain

ISBN 0–312–05301–0

Library of Congress Cataloging-in-Publication Data
Sundrum, R. M.
Economic growth in theory and practice / R.M. Sundrum.
p.   cm.
Includes bibliographical references and index.
ISBN 0–312–05301–0
1. Economic development.   2. Classical school of economics.
3. Keynesian economics.   I. Title.
HD75.S89   1991
338.9 — dc20   90–42646
                                                           CIP

To Soundra

Contents

Preface   x

PART I   GROWTH AND STRUCTURAL TRANSFORMATION

1   Introduction   3
1.1   Objectives of a Theory of Growth   3
1.2   History of Thought on Growth Theory   5
1.3   The Argument in Brief   7

2   Economic Growth in Historical Perspective   15
2.1   The Logistic Pattern   15
2.2   Episodes of Economic Growth   18

3   The Structural Determinants of Growth   27
3.1   Structural Transformation During Growth   27
3.2   A Model of Growth and Structural Transformation   35
3.3   Further Issues   49

PART II   SUPPLY FACTORS: THE CLASSICAL DETERMINANTS

4   Theories of Growth   53
4.1   Introduction   53
4.2   The Magnificent Dynamics of Ricardo   54
4.3   The Neo-classical Theory of Growth   60
4.4   The Dualistic Growth Model of Lewis   69
4.5   The Mechanisation Process of Butt   72

5   Growth in the Agricultural Sector   77
5.1   Patterns of Agricultural Growth   77
5.2   Technical Progress in Agriculture   89
5.3   The Mechanisation Process in Agriculture   93
5.4   The Historical Mission of Agriculture   98

6   Growth in the Industrial Sector   101
6.1   The Beginnings of Industrialisation   101
6.2   Sources of Industrial Growth   108
6.3   Causes of Technological Progress   125
6.4   De-industrialisation   131

7 **Growth in the Service Sector**   **136**
  7.1 Characteristics of Services   136
  7.2 The Demand for Services   139
  7.3 Labour Productivity in the Service Sector   142
  7.4 Services and Overall Growth   146

**PART III DEMAND FACTORS: THE KEYNESIAN
          DETERMINANTS**

8 **Investment**   **153**
  8.1 Role of Demand   153
  8.2 The Dual Role of Investment   161
  8.3 The Stability of Growth Equilibrium   165
  8.4 Supply and Demand Effects of Investment   172

9 **Government Expenditures**   **182**
  9.1 Variations in Government Expenditures   182
  9.2 Level of Government Expenditures and Growth
     of Income   188
  9.3 Growth of Government Expenditures and
     Growth of Income   191

10 **Exports**   **199**
  10.1 Variations in Export Ratios   199
  10.2 Exports and Growth of Income: The Statistical
      Evidence   201
  10.3 Exports and Growth of Income: Theoretical
      Explanations   207
  10.4 The Taiwan Experience   218

**PART IV INFLATION, INCOME DISTRIBUTION AND
          GROWTH**

11 **Inflation and Growth**   **233**
  11.1 The Statistical Evidence   233
  11.2 Causes of Inflation   237
  11.3 Inflation and Growth: Supply Factors   243
  11.4 Inflation and Growth: Demand Factors   247

12 **Income Distribution and Growth**   **257**
  12.1 Theoretical Arguments and Statistical Evidence   257
  12.2 Relationship Through the Rate of Saving   264
  12.3 Relationship Through the Structure of Production   265

13 Conclusions **271**
    13.1 Factors in Long-Term Growth 271
    13.2 Major Episodes of Economic Growth 274
    13.3 Implications for Growth Policy 280

Bibliography and Author Index 288
Subject Index 300

Preface

As a member of the Economics Department of the Research School of Pacific Studies in the Australian National University, I have been engaged in the past few years in studying the remarkable developments that have been taking place in the developing countries of Asia and the Pacific in the post-war period. The performance of these countries has varied all the way from the slow growth of countries like India to the spectacular growth of the newly industrialising countries, such as South Korea and Taiwan. There is a large literature on this story, most of which has tried to explain the wide range of growth performance according to the prevailing theories of growth, i.e. in terms of the supply factors related to the expansion of productive capacity and of the allocative efficiency with which productive capacity was being used.

But on considering the actual differences between countries and the changes that occurred over time, it soon became apparent that differences in allocative efficiency alone could not explain the great differences in growth performance, and to the extent that these differences in growth performance were due to differences in the expansion of productive capacity, the differences in growth of productivity capacity themselves needed to be explained. Therefore, it became necessary to go back to the prevailing theories of growth. What the literature revealed was a scandalous state of affairs. The theories with the greatest academic prestige were more concerned with purely logical, and often tediously mathematical, exercises about hypothetical models than with the events of the real world. In fact, students in the 1980s were still being taught the stale theories developed in the 1950s and 1960s, with little reference to the tremendous changes that have taken place since then. Theoretical explanations of the performance of particular countries went little beyond such tautological arguments as, for example, that where countries grew rapidly, it was because they had followed 'sound' economic policies, and conversely. There was a deep division of the subject according to geography, a branch of the subject known as 'growth theory' being applied to the developed countries, and another branch of the subject known as 'development economics' being applied to the less-developed countries. Although the process of structural transformation had been studied in great detail, it had no place in prevailing growth theories. Growth rates were being compared between countries differing greatly in their economic structure. And growth theory proceeded as if the Keynesian Revolution had never occurred.

Clearly a new approach to the subject is long overdue, one based on the actual experience of economic growth as it has occurred both in developed and less-developed countries, and presenting a unified theory of growth from the earliest stages all the way to the most advanced, based on actual experience rather than on assumptions chosen only for their analytical convenience. Such an approach should also be one which takes full account of the structural transformation which is intimately associated with the growth process. It should also take full account of the role of demand factors in influencing both the utilisation of existing productive capacity and the expansion of that capacity. It is such a new approach that is presented in this book.

Once the broad outline of the new approach became clear, it was found that valuable elements for spelling out this outline were already available in the literature. On the one hand, there were studies such as *Modern Capitalism* by John Cornwall which had already sketched out this approach, and only needed to be extended in more empirical detail, especially about the less-developed countries. On the other hand, a number of statistical studies have begun to appear dealing with the empirical material, which needed to be embedded into a more coherent analytical framework. The present work attempts to provide this analytical framework.

Any analytical framework for the study of economic growth must inevitably be based on almost all branches of economic theory, ranging from the explanation of prices and quantities in individual markets to the macroeconomic theories of the national income, monetary phenomena and the distribution of income. It is clearly not possible to deal with all these theories in detail within the compass of a single text on growth theory. Therefore, all that could be done was to discuss the main points of these theories, and the controversies surrounding them, from the point of view of the growth process. However, an attempt has been made to give ample references to the more detailed discussions of these points in the literature.

The work is primarily addressed to postgraduate and advanced undergraduate students interested in economic growth. It should also be useful to professional economists engaged in theoretical research on the subject, as well as to those researching the growth experience of particular countries. Finally, it should also be useful to policy makers in individual countries and in the international economic organisations concerned with one of the most serious problems facing the world economy at present.

In writing this book, my greatest debt has been to John Cornwall. I have not only benefited from his significant writings on the subject, but he has also been most generous with his time in reading the draft of the book in several versions. The final revision of the book was in fact carried out during the short period I spent with him in 1988 as a visiting professor in Dalhousie University. Anne Booth and Norm Gemmell of the Australian National University also read the complete draft of the book and gave many useful comments and suggestions which have greatly improved the present version. I remain responsible for all errors that have survived, but I am deeply grateful to them for having saved me from numerous others.

R.M. SUNDRUM

Part I
Growth and Structural Transformation

1 Introduction

1.1 OBJECTIVES OF A THEORY OF GROWTH

A remarkable feature of the world economic scene is the great variation in income levels among countries, ranging from a per capita income of less than US$200 in the least developed countries of Asia and Africa to over US$15 000 in the United States and some of the richer countries of Europe and the Middle East. Of course, countries differ so much in their location, populations, endowments of productive resources, cultural backgrounds, economic institutions and political circumstances, especially their commitment to economic development, that some differences in the per capita incomes are only to be expected. On the other hand, most countries have had close contact with each other for the greater part of the past two centuries, so that they have increasingly had access to the same body of productive technology; it may therefore have been expected that this contact would have led to some reduction in the differences in their per capita incomes. In view of this historical circumstance, it is remarkable that the differences between countries are still so great.

An even more remarkable feature is that these large differences in income levels are essentially a relatively modern phenomenon. There have always been differences in income levels between countries. Some rough and highly fragmentary estimates for the period about two centuries ago suggest that at that time the differences between countries were much smaller than we observe today. Therefore, a considerable part of the differences in income levels between countries that we observe nowadays must be attributed to large differences in their rates of growth in the past, especially in the last two centuries. It follows then that, to explain the great differences in levels of income between countries, we must explain the differences in their long-term growth rates.

The explanation of these differences in growth rates is the task of growth theory. There is already a large literature on the subject, but the studies that have been carried out vary greatly in their focus. One difference is that some studies are highly theoretical, mainly concerned with working out the logical implications of certain assumptions, while others are highly descriptive, giving detailed accounts of how growth has taken place in particular countries at particular

3

times. Another difference is that some studies deal with short-term fluctuations in growth rates, often the changes from year to year, mostly concerned with the effect of short-term factors, while others have been concerned with longer-term patterns of growth resulting from more basic factors. A third difference is that studies are often confined to particular groups of countries, especially countries at a particular level of development. Thus, for example, the subject is sharply divided between development economics dealing with economic growth in the less-developed countries (LDCs), generally at a highly descriptive level, and growth economics mainly dealing with the developed countries (DCs) generally at a highly theoretical level.

By contrast, the present study is concerned with economic growth as it has actually occurred in practice, but it also attempts to provide theoretical explanations of this experience. These theoretical explanations are based on the working of ordinary market forces; therefore the study is confined to economies in which market forces play a significant role, a group which includes most countries. The study is also specially concerned with long-term growth, rather than with short-term fluctuations in the growth rate. It is unlikely that the factors influencing such long-term growth have differed in different groups of countries as much as is implied in the present literature on growth theory. It is true that rates of economic growth in different countries may be greatly influenced by their initial conditions, but these initial conditions themselves are the result of their growth experiences in earlier periods. Therefore, what is needed is a unified theory of growth covering both DCs and LDCs, one which brings out the more basic factors affecting long-term growth at different phases of the growth process, which can then be combined with the particular circumstances of individual countries to explain their actual growth at different times. It is in this spirit that Lewis (1984, p. 4) suggested that

> the economist's dream would be a single theory of growth that took an economy from the lowest level of say $100 per capita, past the dividing line of $2000 up to the level of Western Europe and beyond. Or to have, since processes may differ at different stages, a set of theories growing out of each other longitudinally, and handing over to each other.

Once such a growth theory has been developed, it can be used as the basis for policy actions, both to address the problems of accelerating growth in the LDCs and to combat the problems of stagflation in the DCs.

But such a theory can only be developed on the basis of reliable statistical data about the actual process of growth. In the early stages of developing the theory, such data were extremely scarce and of limited reliability, and confined to a few countries, especially those which had already attained a high level of development. But since the end of the Second World War, the quantity and quality of such data provided by national statistical agencies have greatly improved, and such data have also become much more comparable as between countries, mainly due to the efforts of the United Nations statistical agencies. We now have a significant accumulation of data covering three or four decades of the post-war period, which reveals a wide range of growth experiences among countries. At the same time, there has been much historical research on the earlier episodes of economic growth for a large number of countries. Therefore, the time is now ripe for a basic reconsideration of growth theory. The present study is an attempt to provide such a reconsideration on the basis of the newly available data.

1.2 HISTORY OF THOUGHT ON GROWTH THEORY

Growth theory started with the writings of the British classical economists. They were writing at a time when modern economic growth was just starting in the western countries. Therefore, their growth theory was largely concerned with an agricultural economy, and examined the effects of population growth on limited resources of land. Under these conditions, the process of growth was dominated by the Law of Diminishing Returns. Therefore, the main conclusion of their theory was that there would be a steady decline in the rate of economic growth until it ceased completely in the classical Stationary State. (This theory is considered in more detail in section 4.2 below.)

But in subsequent decades, these predictions of the classical theory failed to materialise in the western countries as they raced their way through modern economic growth to their present high levels of affluence. The classical theory of growth has therefore largely fallen into disrepute, but it still has some relevance to the LDCs which are going through the earlier phases of growth. Further, the classical writings are distinguished for their pioneering work in studying economic growth in essentially dynamic terms.

The main reason why the predictions of the classical theory failed to materialise in the western countries was that these countries entered into a phase of rapid industrialisation. While the force of diminishing returns operates strongly in the agricultural sector due to land scarcity, it is much weaker in the industrial sector; instead a much stronger force operating in the industrial sector is the tendency to increasing returns. The development of the industrial sector in a capitalist economy was studied in great detail by Marx but because his theory was intertwined so strongly with his socialist ideas, it was not absorbed into mainstream economics. It survives only among Marx's followers, and there too in a highly ideological fashion.

After Marx, economics was dominated by the Marginal Revolution. During the long period of the hegemony of this approach, the attention of economists was largely concentrated on the static problems of the allocation of *given* resources under market forces to alternative uses to satisfy the *given* tastes and preferences of consumers. There was a comparative neglect of growth theory.

Interest in growth theory among mainstream economists, however, revived in the 1950s and 1960s. Most of the new theory, however, was addressed to the long-term growth experience of the DCs during the period of their modern economic growth. This experience was summarised into a few 'stylised facts' indicating a steady state path of economic growth. Starting from these stylised facts, the so-called modern theory of growth proceeded along purely theoretical lines, mainly concerned to work out the logical consequences of a few conveniently chosen assumptions, and largely devoted to work out the 'possibility of persistent growth equilibrium' (Morishima, 1969, ch. 2), rather than to explain growth as it had actually occurred. To the extent that the stylised facts were relevant at all, they were derived from the experience of a handful of countries in a particular phase of their development. But even for these countries, the stylised facts were not very realistic, and in particular, by assuming a pattern of balanced growth, they ignored the significant structural transformation that had taken place. As a result, a review of this literature after more than a decade of its development had to conclude that 'growth economics is guided much more by logical curiosity than by a taste for relevance' (Sen, 1970, p. 36), and that 'by abstracting from those factors that determine the growth rate of the economy, economic growth models of the vintage developed in this (period) are open to the charge of being irrelevant' (Krauss and Johnson, 1974, pp. 334–5).

After a period of intense development, interest in theories of long-term growth has again flagged, giving way to more concern with short-term macroeconomic problems in the developed market economies (DMEs). Current textbooks therefore give only a stale account of the theories developed two or three decades ago. In the meantime, some remarkable developments have taken place in the real world. Growth in the DMEs has slackened; and there has been a great diversity of growth performance among LDCs, including some cases of very rapid growth. These new developments together with more information on earlier developments call for a new approach to growth theory, one which is comprehensive enough to explain growth over a long period, and which covers both DCs and LDCs. This is the objective of the present study. The basic argument of the proposed theory is briefly outlined in the next section.

1.3 THE ARGUMENT IN BRIEF

Prevailing studies of economic growth have greatly simplified that process in order to provide theoretical explanations. This is especially true of theories couched in sophisticated mathematical terms. But economic growth as it occurs in practice is a very complex process, and therefore requires a complex analysis. In order that the reader may follow the analysis of this study, the main argument and its essential building blocks are briefly summarised here.

We start with the concept of a country's productive capacity, i.e. the maximum amount of goods and services that can be produced with the existing factors of production at the prevailing state of technology. The output of any particular commodity that can be produced with the available resources can be increased by reducing the output of other goods. Therefore, a convenient way of describing the productive capacity of a country is in terms of the maximum output of a given commodity that can be produced, for varying outputs of other commodities. The concept may be illustrated in the case where there are only two commodities, X and Y. Then the productive capacity of the economy may be represented by the transformation curve, shown in Figure 1.1, which represents the maximum quantity of one commodity that can be produced for a given quantity of the other. This concept is useful in considering different ways in which growth might occur.

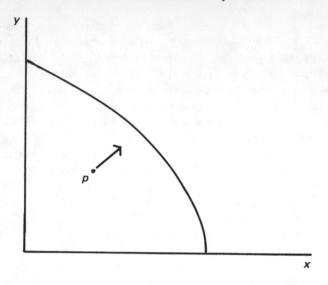

Figure 1.1

The first point to note is that growth theory is concerned with explaining the growth of the quantities of goods that are actually produced. These quantities may not necessarily be the maximum that can be produced with the available resources. For example, the quantities actually produced may be those indicated by the point p in Figure 1.1., i.e. less than what can be produced because some of the available resources are not fully utilised. If this is the case to begin with, then growth may occur by fuller utilisation of productive capacity, i.e. by a movement along the arrow marked in the figure starting at p, even if productive capacity is constant. The main reason why growth may occur in this way is if there is an increase in the demand for the goods and services than can be produced in the economy.

Next, we consider the case where the point p representing actual production lies on the transformation curve, as shown in Figure 1.2. But the combination of goods that is produced may not be such as will maximise the value of total output at prevailing prices. In this figure, the relative prices are shown by the line AA, and the point p' represents the combination of goods which maximises the value of goods at these prices. Then, another way in which growth might occur, even with a constant productive capacity, is by a movement along this transformation curve from p to p'. Growth occurring in this way may be said to be due to improvements in allocative efficiency.

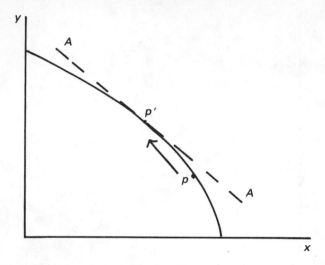

Figure 1.2

Finally, we consider the case where there is an increase in the productive capacity of the economy. This is shown in Figure 1.3 by an outward shift of the transformation curve. Then, there is a third way in which growth might occur, namely by a movement along the arrow from a point such as *p* on the first transformation curve to one such as *p'* on the second.

Most theories of growth have concentrated on explanations of the type illustrated in Figure 1.3, i.e. explanations in terms of the expansion of productive capacity, assuming that available resources are always efficiently allocated to maximise the value of output that can be produced at each point of time. Different theories have explained the growth of productive capacity in different ways to draw different conclusions about the rates of growth. Thus, for example, by concentrating on the growth of population on a given area of land, the classical economists derived their conclusion of a declining rate of growth. Later, on the basis of certain assumptions about capital accumulation and population growth, neo-classical economists produced a theory of a steady rate of growth. But contrary to these theories, the actual growth process leading from a low level of income in a traditional economy to the high level of affluence of the most developed, mature, economies of today has followed a logistic pattern of slow growth at low levels of income to begin with, faster growth at intermediate levels of income, falling back to slow growth

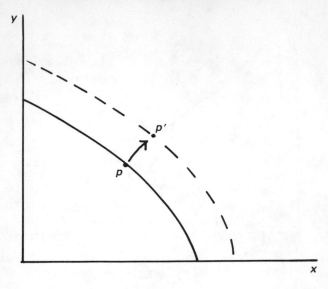

Figure 1.3

again at the highest levels of income. This pattern is observed both in the cross-section data describing growth of a large number of countries at different income levels in the post-war decades, and in the historical data of a few countries which have passed through some phases of this pattern in the past. This evidence is reviewed in Chapter 2.

The argument of the present study is that this logistic pattern has to be explained by a large number of factors, and the interactions among them. As a first step towards simplifying their analysis, these factors may be classified into three groups, as shown below:

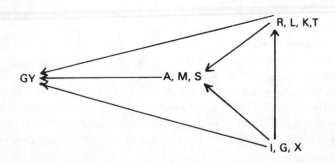

where

GY = growth of GDP

A,M,S = structure of the economy divided into sectors, such as agriculture (A), industry (M), and services (S);

R,L,K,T = supply factors of land (R), labour (L), capital (K) and technological progress (T); and

I,G,X = exogenous sources of demand such as investment (I), government expenditure (G) and exports (X).

The first group of factors (A,M,S) refers to the structure of the economy, as shown by the shares of the three major sectors in GDP and in employment. Most theories of growth tend to consider GDP as a single composite commodity and to concentrate on how the quantity of this commodity varies over time. But in fact GDP consists of a wide variety of commodities which differ greatly among themselves, both in the conditions of their supply (such as the intensity with which various factors of production are used) and in the conditions of their demand (such as the ways in which their consumption varies with changes in income and in prices). At the very least, we must distinguish the three major groups of commodities, generally classified as agricultural or primary commodities, industrial commodities, and services.

The division of the economy into these three sectors is particularly important because most economies undergo a significant structural transformation in terms of the relative importance of these sectors. In the initial stages of low income, agriculture is the most important sector both in terms of output shares and employment shares, and the dominance of this sector is an important reason for the low rate of growth in this phase. In the intermediate stage of growth, the centre of gravity shifts to the M-sector, accompanied by a significant acceleration of overall growth. In the later stages of growth, the centre of gravity shifts again to the S-sector, especially in terms of employment shares, and this shift is associated with a slackening of growth in this phase of the logistic pattern. These changes in the relative importance of the various sectors may therefore be described as the structural determinants of growth. Using some simple but highly plausible assumptions about the proximate causes of this structural transformation of the economy in terms of both supply and demand parameters, Chapter 3 shows how these structural determinants can be used to explain the logistic pattern of growth that we observe in practice.

This model raises two further issues. On the one hand, we must explain the proximate structural determinants in terms of more fundamental supply and demand factors. On the other hand, what Chapter 3 presents is only a basic model explaining a logistic pattern of growth in terms of the structural determinants of growth. While the experience of most countries corresponds to a logistic pattern in broad outline, they vary in detail. For example, certain phases of the logistic pattern may be squeezed in some countries which traverse those phases in a shorter time and therefore exhibit faster growth than the average, or may be stretched out taking a longer time to traverse those phases and therefore exhibiting slower than average growth.

Part of the solution of these issues lie in the second group of factors distinguished above, i.e. the role of the various factors of production – land (R), labour (L), capital (K) and technological progress (T). When the classical economists first essayed a theory of growth, they based it mainly on the growth of these factors of production. When neo-classical economists turned their attention to the subject, they emphasised the growth of these factors, but also considered the role of technological progress. Hence, these supply factors may be broadly described as the classical determinants of growth, discussed in Part II. This part of the book begins in Chapter 4 with brief summaries of some of the most important theories of growth in the literature, and an evaluation of some of their limitations. The first theory considered is the classical one which concentrates on the effects of population growth, taken as an endogenous variable itself, on a fixed stock of land – the 'original and indestructible properties of the soil' in Ricardo's immortal phrase. The second theory considered is the neo-classical theory of the interaction between an exogenous rate of population growth and the endogenous rate of capital accumulation. Two other models are also discussed which combine the above two approaches in various ways, namely Lewis's theory of development of a dualistic economy, and Butt's theory of capital accumulation in terms of a mechanisation process.

Later chapters then seek to modify these theories so that they are more useful to explain the process of growth as it has actually occurred in various countries. In particular, an attempt is made to relate them to the data on the growth process which have now become available. The theories considered in Chapter 4 were mostly concerned to explain the overall growth of the national income of countries. Although the classical theory was developed mainly in the context of the agricultural sector, that sector was generally taken as representing the economy as a whole. Similarly, the neo-classical theory was mainly concerned with the industrial sector, also taken to represent the entire economy. But in view of the important role of the structural determinants of growth noted in Chapter 3, especially their role in explaining the logistic pattern of growth, the various supply factors must be considered as they operate in different major sectors of the economy. Therefore, we consider the role of the supply factors in Chapter 5 for the agricultural sector, in Chapter 6 for the industrial sector and in Chapter 7 for the service sector.

The explanation of growth only in terms of the classical determinants is subject to two major limitations. One is that the supply factors which form the classical determinants of growth only determine the productive capacity of the economy. They do not determine the actual amount of production and how it varies over time. Classical and neo-classical economists assumed that supply would always create its own demand and therefore tended to neglect demand factors in explaining the level and growth of total production. Demand factors were invoked only to explain the composition of total production. But this argument is based on very special assumptions about the functioning of markets, which may not hold always. Hence, it cannot be assumed that supply creates its own demand, and therefore we must consider the role of demand factors in influencing the level and growth of production. The second limitation of the classical and neo-classical approach is that it assumes that supply and demand factors are independent of each other. This assumption is also not realistic. Therefore, we have to take fuller account of the interdependence of supply and demand factors, and in particular the long-term influence of demand factors on the growth of supply factors.

The crucial role of demand factors was first studied in a systematic way by Keynes. Keynes's work was mainly concerned with the influence of demand factors in the short run and only in highly developed countries, but it will be argued that these factors have a role in the LDCs also and have a significant impact on long-run growth, especially through their effects on the supply factors. Hence, these demand factors may be described as the Keynesian determinants of growth. They are discussed in Part III of the book.

Keynes's theory depends on a basic distinction between two types of demand, one which is endogenous in the sense that it depends on total income and cannot therefore explain overall income, and another which is exogenous in the sense that it does not depend on overall income. The theory is therefore an attempt to explain overall income in terms of the exogenous sources of demand. The endogenous sources of demand are usually classified as consumption, taxes and imports. Correspondingly, the exogenous sources of demand are usually classified as investment (I), government expenditure (G) and exports (X). These factors comprise the third group distinguished above. The role of investment both as a supply and a demand factor is discussed in Chapter 8. The role of government expenditure is discussed in Chapter 9 and that of exports in Chapter 10. In Keynes's own writings, and in most subsequent discussions of his theory, these demand factors are mostly discussed as they affect overall growth of the national product. But in view of the importance of the structural factors affecting growth, we must also consider how these demand factors operate in different sectors of the economy.

Then, we consider two other aspects of the economy which also influence the growth process, namely inflation and income distribution. The way these aspects influence the growth process has been discussed in the literature mainly in terms of their effects through various supply factors. In fact, they also have important effects through demand factors. These effects are discussed in Chapter 11 on inflation and in Chapter 12 on income distribution. In the final chapter, we bring together the threads of the argument of the preceding chapters, and use them to explain the various episodes of growth identified in Chapter 2.

2 Economic Growth in Historical Perspective

2.1 THE LOGISTIC PATTERN

The classical economists, who developed the first systematic theory of growth in the context of an agricultural economy, were so impressed with the force of diminishing returns in that sector that they predicted a steady decline of the rate of growth, due to the steady rise of the pressure of a growing population on a limited area of land. Later, in the early post-war years, neo-classical economists produced an alternative theory, referring mainly to an industrial economy, in which the main factor of production was fixed capital. The principal conclusion of this theory was that there would be a steady rate of growth of national income, with an endogenous rate of capital accumulation converging to a steady, exogenously given, rate of population growth. This theory of balanced growth was an attempt to explain what was assumed to be a stylised fact of the experience of the developed industrial countries over a long period of time.

The empirical basis of these theories, however, was very poor, being confined to the experience of a few countries in particular phases of their economic growth. In order to develop a more general theory applicable to a wider range of experience spanning all phases of economic growth, we must first consider the data from a larger sample of countries at different levels of development. Such data have now become available for nearly four decades of the period since the Second World War, and are summarised in Table 2.1.

This table shows that the growth experience of countries follows a somewhat different pattern from that assumed, either in the classical or in the neo-classical theories. The general pattern in one of a low rate of growth at low levels of income, a faster rate of growth at intermediate levels of income, and a slackening of growth at the highest levels of income. This pattern holds quite consistently for the first three decades of the post-war period, but to a lesser extent in the disturbed conditions of the 1980s. This pattern may be described as a logistic pattern of growth, and has been noted by a number of authors (e.g. Kristensen, 1974; Chenery, 1977; and Rostow, 1978, 1980). On the basis of an econometric analysis of post-war data from a large

Table 2.1   Rates of growth of GDP by level of per capita income

Per Capita Income (1981 US dollars)	Annual average growth rates of GDP			
	1950s	1960s	1970s	1980s
Below 250	3.5	4.2	3.9	3.2
250–500	4.7	4.2	4.2	2.2
500–750	4.3	5.5	3.5	1.0
750–1000	5.6	5.7	5.6	2.7
1000–2000	5.2	6.0	4.8	3.3
2000–4000	5.1	6.5	4.8	1.8
4000 & over	3.4	4.5	2.9	1.6
Total	4.3	4.9	4.2	2.3

Sources: World Bank (1984); OECD (1985) pp. 264–5, table XII–I.

Table 2.2   The logistic pattern of growth

Change in per capita income (1970 US$)	Time in years	Growth rate of GDP	Growth rate of population	Growth rate of per capita GDP
(0) 100–140	27	3.81	2.55	1.26
(1) 140–280	35	4.80	2.78	2.02
(2) 280–560	22	5.67	2.50	3.17
(3) 560–1120	17	6.30	2.20	4.10
(4) 1120–2100	14	6.58	2.00	4.58
(5) 2100–3360	10	6.21	1.50	4.71
(6) 3360–5040	9	5.60	1.00	4.60

Source: Chenery *et al.* (1986), table 8.2, p. 232.

sample of countries, Chenery *et al.* (1986) constructed a model of the growth process, summarised in Table 2.2.

On this pattern, there is a relationship flowing from the level of income to the rate of growth, which in turn affects the future level of income. Hence, following the logistic pattern, the level of income as a function of time may be described by an S-shaped curve. The two ways of describing the logistic pattern of growth are illustrated in Figure 2.1.

But the existence of a logistic pattern in the cross-section data does not necessarily establish that a similar pattern will also exist in the

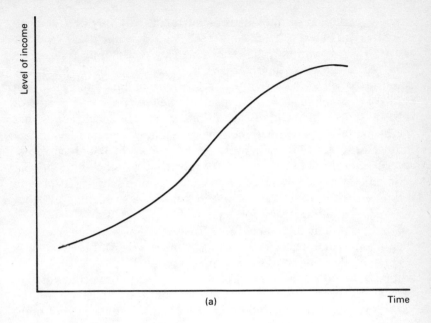

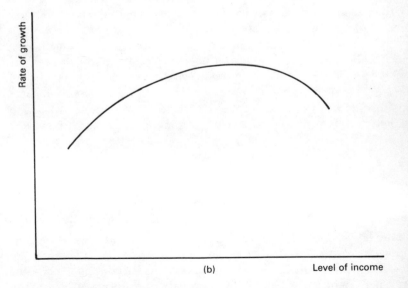

Figure 2.1

dynamic evolution of individual countries. It will only be true if all countries can be expected to follow the same dynamic path. Whether they did or not can only be determined by considering time series data. Although such time series data are not available for many countries covering sufficiently long periods of time, the historical record of economic growth has been studied over a longer period of time by economic historians. Their overwhelming conclusion is that the historical growth experience over such a long period has in fact followed the same logistic pattern as that shown by the above cross-section data, namely a tendency for growth to be slow in traditional economies with a low level of income, followed by rapid growth during a period of modernisation, and finally a slackening of economic growth in a mature economy.

Some economic historians (e.g. Rostow, 1960) have summarised their findings in terms of a stages theory of growth. This is valuable as a summary description of the historical record. But it is less useful as a theory of how this logistic pattern of growth occurred, mainly because of an underlying implication that the succession of the various stages is an inexorable function of the mere passage of time, and even then without any commanding hypothesis about the lengths of time needed for the transition from each stage to the next. A more useful theory would be one which places these events not on a calendar of historical time, but rather on a calendar of income levels. Such a theory will then lead to a deeper explanation of the various transitions in terms of more fundamental economic factors. Before developing such a theory, however, it is useful to consider some major episodes in the historical experience of economic growth, in order to see how these episodes fit into the logistic pattern of growth.

2.2 EPISODES OF ECONOMIC GROWTH

(a) Modern Economic Growth of DCs

In the later part of the eighteenth century, there was a sharp acceleration of growth in a small group of countries in western Europe, the so-called Industrial Revolution. Beginning in Britain, and spreading to other countries of Europe by a process of diffusion, it was taken over to European settlements in North America and Australia by the migration of Europeans, and finally it was established in Japan largely by a deliberate process of imitation. The quantitative aspects

Table 2.3   The rates of modern economic growth

Country	Period	Annual rate of growth of GDP (%)
United Kingdom	1770–1965	2.1
France	1830–1965	2.0
Belgium	1900–1965	1.9
Netherlands	1865–1965	2.5
West Germany	1855–1965	2.7
Switzerland	1910–1965	2.4
Denmark	1865–1965	2.9
Norway	1865–1965	2.8
Sweden	1865–1965	3.2
Italy	1900–1965	2.8
United States	1835–1965	3.6
Canada	1870–1965	3.5
Australia	1865–1965	3.2
Japan	1875–1965	4.0

Source: Kuznets (1971), table 1, pp. 11–14.

of the subsequent development have been intensively studied by Kuznets (1966, 1971), who has described it as 'modern economic growth'. It was also described as 'Prometheus Unbound' by Landes (1969), as a 'take off' by Rostow (1960), or simply as economic development by Schumpeter (1934).

Prior to this episode, economic growth occurred only at a snail's pace. Thus, Kuznets (1971, ch. 1) has estimated that per capita income may have increased only five fold over nearly nine and a half centuries, i.e. at an annual rate of less than 0.2 per cent. Using somewhat better data for Britain, per capita income in that country was estimated to have grown in the first seven decades of the eighteenth century at only about 0.17 per cent per annum. Similarly, he has estimated that per capita income in Italy grew in the last four decades of the nineteenth century at only about 0.12 per cent per annum.

Modern economic growth then represented a decisive break with the growth rates of traditional societies. In the words of Kuznets (1971, pp. 23–4, 28) 'the rates at which the economies of developed nations grew are little short of astounding', representing 'a striking acceleration of the growth rate in premodern times for Western Europe possibly by a factor of 10'. Some estimates for individual countries are summarised in Table 2.3.

This process of modern economic growth which started in Europe in the late eighteenth and early nineteenth centuries, however, affected only a small group of countries. Most other countries continued at the traditional low rates of growth. The question why only the countries of Western Europe and of European settlements overseas experienced modern economic growth in this period is still a great puzzle (see e.g. Rostow, 1975). Kuznets (1971, p. 28) has suggested that one reason why modern economic growth started in the countries of western Europe at the end of the eighteenth century was the higher level of income they had already attained by then. Extrapolating backwards from the data of 1965, he has estimated that 'the implied difference in initial levels a century ago is almost 4 to 1'. This argument is consistent with one aspect of the logistic pattern of growth, namely the tendency for countries which have reached an intermediate level of income to experience an acceleration of growth. The result was that, by 1965, the range of incomes between the two groups of countries was about 19 to 1.

Table 2.3 shows the average growth rate over long periods of time. The actual growth process, however, was not a smooth one. It was marked by fairly regular cyclical fluctuations, which were intensively studied in theories of the business cycle. However, these cycles were only fluctuations around a growing trend which is our main concern. More closely related to our hypothesis is that the process of modern economic growth was also accompanied by long cycles of about 40 years duration, which have come to be known as Kondratieff cycles after the Russian economist who first noted them (1935). Four such cycles have been identified in the period since the late eighteenth century (Mager, 1987), though the statistical basis of the earlier two cycles has been questioned (Cornwall, 1986). These long cycles also have a logistic pattern embedded in them. However, these long cycles must be distinguished from the logistic pattern of growth that we are concerned with in the present study. One reason is that they cover a shorter range, not only in terms of the time period involved, but also in the levels of income over which they occurred. Another reason is that the long cycles occurred only in a small sample of countries, especially those which had already undergone a considerable degree of industrialisation. Therefore, they are best considered as episodes within the process of modern economic growth. As such, they deal with the slow start of some major technological advances, their rapid development for a period, and a final phase of saturation of these innovations.

(b) Tropical Development of LDCs

The modern economic growth of the present-day DCs also coincided with a period of rapid growth of a number of other countries, especially those located in the tropical areas. But there were important differences between the two groups of countries. Firstly, the rapid growth of the tropical countries was not marked by any major technological progress; instead it was largely due to the more intensive exploitation of surplus resources of land and labour under a largely traditional technology. Secondly, it was not associated with any significant degree of industrialisation. Instead, it was based mainly on increased exports of primary products.

The foreign trade of these countries expanded rapidly for a number of reasons. First was a revolutionary change in ocean transport which halved transport costs in the second half of the nineteenth century, and led to a great expansion of world trade. Second was the growing demand for tropical products resulting from the growth of incomes and industrial production in the developed countries. Third were some of the policies followed by the colonial governments which ruled over most of these tropical countries. One of these policies was the establishment of a free trade regime, especially between each metropolitan country and its tropical dependencies, in line with the prevailing economic philosophy of the times. The other was the building of infrastructure and the development of institutions specifically for the purpose of promoting exports of primary products. The development of many tropical countries under such policies has been described as the 'colonial pattern of development' (Birnberg and Resnick, 1975). An important feature of this development was a great increase of exports, mainly of primary products, from these countries. The growth rates of the value of their exports in US dollars are shown in Table 2.4.

As a result of this growth of exports, the tropical countries experienced an acceleration of economic growth. However, the rapid growth of GDP could not be sustained when the surplus resources of land and labour were exhausted, and when the expansion of world trade slackened with the Great Depression of the 1930s. The result was that these tropical countries, even those which had participated intensively in world trade, emerged at the end of the Second World War as typical LDCs with a low level of per capita income.

Table 2.4   Growth rates of exports of tropical countries: 1883–1913

Countries	Growth rate of exports (per cent per annum)
Africa	
Egypt	3.2
British colonies	4.9
French colonies	6.7
Portuguese colonies	3.7
Others	2.2
Latin America	
Brazil	4.5
Colombia	4.1
Cuba	2.9
Mexico	4.3
Peru	3.7
Venezuela	1.3
Others	3.8
Asia	
Ceylon	5.7
India	2.9
Indo-China	4.9
Indonesia	3.9
Malaya	3.3
Philippines	2.5
Thailand	5.8
Others	3.6

Source: Lewis (1969), table 9, p. 48.

(c) Rapid Growth of DCs: 1950–73

Modern economic growth of the DCs faltered in the 1930s during the Great Depression and was interrupted in the Second World War. But after the Second World War, the DCs resumed another phase of rapid growth, faster even than before the Great Depression. The average rates of growth achieved until 1973 are summarised in Table 2.5.

This was also a period of rapid growth of industry and associated technological progress, but the underlying driving force was a rapid growth of international trade. While the rapid growth of international trade in the nineteenth century was largely based on the traditional pattern of exchange of manufactures for primary products, in the post-war period, it was much more an exchange of

Table 2.5   Rapid growth of developed countries: 1950–73

Country	Annual rate of growth of GDP (%)
Australia	4.8
Austria	5.3
Belgium	4.4
Canada	5.0
Denmark	4.3
Finland	4.7
France	5.2
West Germany	5.7
Italy	5.5
Japan	9.8
Netherlands	4.9
Norway	4.0
Sweden	4.0
Switzerland	4.6
UK	2.9
USA	3.6
Average of 16 countries	4.9

Source: Maddison (1982), appendix table, A8, pp. 176–7.

manufactures for manufactures, to a great extent of the same type of commodities. Further, much of the expansion of world trade consisted of trade amongst the developed industrial countries themselves.

(d) Growth Acceleration of LDCs: 1950–90

The post-war period also saw an acceleration of economic growth in the LDCs. The poverty of these countries emerged as one of the major problems confronting the world economy, leading to efforts to improve the situation by national policies and by international action, especially through the flow of aid from the affluent to the poor countries. As a result, the LDCs generally achieved a higher rate of growth than in pre-war periods. These growth rates of LDCs were higher even than that of the DCs, illustrating one aspect of the logistic pattern of growth. However, unlike the case of the DCs, growth rates were very uneven among the LDCs. In particular, countries in the middle income range tended to grow faster than countries in the lower income range, illustrating another aspect of the logistic pattern.

Table 2.6   Growth rates of LDCs

Annual growth rates of GDP (%)	Number of countries in		
	1950s	*1960s*	*1970s*
Below 3	15	15	21
3–4	14	12	14
4–5	9	19	11
5–6	9	11	10
6–7	6	10	9
7–8	1	4	7
8 and over	5	10	11
Total	59	81	83
Below 5	38	46	46
5 and over	21	35	37
Average growth rate	4.4	4.9	4.4

Source: World Bank (1984): OECD (1985), table XII–I, pp. 264–5.

The available data are summarised in Table 2.6; they cover all countries with a population of over one million, for which estimates have been made by the secretariat of the World Bank and the OECD (*World Tables, 1984, and Twenty-five Years of Development Co-operation*).

To some extent, the variations in growth rates were associated with different rates of investment, but as we argue in a later chapter, the relationship is not very strong. Even if the relationship had been stronger, we would have to explain why investment rates have varied so much. A more powerful explanation of differences in growth rates of LDCs is given by differences in growth rates of exports. To this extent, the post-war experience of LDCs is similar to the experience under the colonial pattern of development. But there is an important difference. While the growth of exports of the tropical countries in the nineteenth and early twentieth centuries related mainly to primary products, the LDCs with the fastest growth of national incomes in the post-war period were those whose export growth consisted largely of manufactures.

The most spectacular case of this relationship occurred in the newly industrialising countries (NICs), especially those in Asia. They experienced the highest rates of growth ever recorded over such long periods. For example, the average rates of growth of GDP during

Table 2.7   Growth rates of DCs: 1973–86

Country	Average annual rate of growth of GDP (%)
Australia	2.47
Austria	2.48
Belgium	1.74
Canada	3.13
Denmark	2.15
Finland	2.83
France	2.07
West Germany	1.98
Italy	2.07
Japan	3.92
Netherlands	1.54
Norway	3.82
Sweden	1.11
Switzerland	1.01
UK	1.03
USA	2.68
Average	2.25

Source: World Bank (1987).

1965–86 were 9.9 per cent per annum in Singapore, 7.8 per cent in Hong Kong, 8.9 per cent in Taiwan and 9.1 per cent in South Korea (*World Development Report, 1988*; and *Taiwan Statistical Yearbook, 1987*). The relationship between these high growth rates and the rapid growth of exports is discussed in detail in Chapter 10.

(e) Slackening Growth of DCs: 1973–86

After nearly a quarter century of rapid growth, economic growth has slackened in the DCs (Table 2.7). The average rate of growth of these 16 countries is less than half what they achieved during the period 1950–73. The causes of this slackening of growth are currently being debated in the literature. The fact that this slackening of growth is accompanied by high rates of unemployment, unprecedented in the DCs, suggests the crucial role of a shortfall of aggregate demand below aggregate supply, the problem which gave rise to the Keynesian theory at the time of the Great Depression. But this time, high levels of unemployment have also been associated with unusually high rates of inflation, unlike the 1930s. Therefore, the validity of the Keynesian analysis itself is being questioned in some quarters. However, it is more likely, as Cornwall (1983) has suggested, that the problem is due to the difficulties of following the Keynesian policies for dealing with unemployment in countries with a pronounced inflationary bias, which are in turn due to a variety of political and institutional factors affecting the labour market. These difficulties are further compounded by the fact that the mature DCs have largely become service economies, with the service sector employing the highest share of the labour force. A high proportion of service workers are employed in the public sector. But whatever the explanation, the slackening of growth currently in the DCs fits in with the growth deceleration at high income levels postulated in the logistic pattern of growth.

3 The Structural Determinants of Growth

3.1 STRUCTURAL TRANSFORMATION DURING GROWTH

Economic growth as it occurs in the real world is an extremely complex process, influenced by a wide variety of causal factors. We cannot therefore hope to explain it in all its details right from the start. Instead, a better procedure would be to follow the method of successive approximations. Therefore, to begin with, we consider the factors that lead to the logistic pattern of growth, which seems to be the general pattern underlying the growth process in all countries, and then consider the factors which explain deviations from this pattern in particular countries or groups of countries. Our first task thus is to explain the logistic pattern of growth. However, even this pattern can be explained by a variety of causal factors. In order to identify the more basic of these causes, we first consider the minimum set of factors which can generate this pattern of growth. This is not to say that other factors may not also be influential; rather it is just a method of applying Occam's Razor to our present problem. This is the objective of the present chapter.

(b) Changing Composition of GDP

Any explanation of the logistic pattern of growth must be based on one of the most striking features of the growth process, namely the systematic structural transformation of the economy that occurs during the growth process. This has now been well established by the historical researches of Kuznets for the developed countries (for a recent summary, see Cornwall, 1977, ch. 2). The principal form of this structural transformation is the changing composition of GDP originating in the three major sectors of the economy – agriculture, industry and services. Over long periods of time, there is a fall in the share of the agricultural sector and a rise in the shares of industry and services. The rise in the share of the industrial sector is accompanied by a significant acceleration of overall growth in the middle phase of this process. This gave rise to the view of manufacturing as the engine of growth. In the later phase, growth is less rapid, and the share of

Table 3.1   Composition of GDP (%) by level of per capita income

Sector	Per capita income in 1981 US dollars:						
	Below 250	250–500	500–750	750–1000	1000–2000	2000–4000	4000 & over
				A. 1950s			
A	49.5	41.4	29.9	18.9	12.5	10.6	7.4
M	14.6	19.4	23.7	25.8	34.0	43.6	37.1
S	35.9	39.2	46.4	55.3	53.5	45.8	55.5
				B. 1960s			
A	48.9	37.7	29.4	21.6	11.6	10.1	6.6
M	14.7	20.1	24.8	28.7	35.6	38.4	38.7
S	36.4	42.2	45.8	49.7	52.8	51.5	54.7
				C. 1970s			
A	44.2	35.7	28.0	22.8	13.3	8.3	5.2
M	18.2	23.2	27.0	30.7	36.5	37.7	36.8
S	37.6	41.1	45.0	46.5	50.2	54.0	58.0

Sources: World Bank, (1984).

the industrial sector stagnates or even falls. This in turn led to the concept of 'de-industrialisation'. In this phase, it is the service sector which grows most rapidly.

This is the pattern which Kuznets (1971) observed in the historical experience of a few developed countries. Sufficiently long time series data are not available for many other countries. Therefore, we consider instead the pattern shown by cross-section data of the shares of GDP originating in the three major sectors of countries at different income levels. Such data are summarised in Table 3.1 for each of the three post-war decades.

Another way of describing the structural transformation of the economy is in terms of the growth rates of output in the different sectors. The data for the period 1965–80 are summarised in Table 3.2, showing the averages for groups of countries at different income levels. The typical pattern is for the growth rate to be highest in the M-sector and lowest in the A-sector, leading to a steady rise in the share of the M-sector and a steady decline in the share of the A-sector.

The above tables show the data in the form of averages for groups of countries at different income levels. Chenery *et al.* (1986) have carried out a more elaborate econometric analysis of data from the post-war period, and summarised the results in the form of a cross-section model. The changing composition of GDP at different income levels according to this model is summarised in Table 3.3.

Table 3.2   Average growth rate of GDP by sectors and income level

Countries by per capita GDP (1980 US$) (No. of countries)		Average growth rate of GDP:			
		Total	Agriculture	Industry	Services
LDCs					
Less than 500	(15)	4.07	2.61	5.18	4.92
500–1000	(14)	5.38	3.72	7.13	5.39
1000–2000	(13)	7.18	3.87	9.91	7.56
2000 & over	(6)	6.35	2.68	6.70	6.72
All LDCs	(48)	5.58	3.29	7.22	6.00
DCs	(18)	4.15	1.57	4.36	4.37

Source: World Bank (1988).

Table 3.3   GDP shares of A,M,S sectors by per capita income

Per capita income (1970 US$)	GDP shares (%) of:		
	A	M	S
100	47	10	43
140	38	14	48
280	29	19	52
560	21	24	55
1120	14	31	55
2100	9	36	55
3360	7	36	57
5040	6	34	60

Source: Derived from Chenery *et al.* (1986), table 8.1, p. 231.

The corresponding growth rates are summarised in Table 3.4. The main difference between these estimates and the observed growth rates shown in Table 3.2 is that the growth rate of the S-sector is greater than that of the M-sector at the highest income levels.

(b) Changing Allocation of Labour

Another aspect of the structural transformation that occurs during the growth process is the changing allocation of the labour force to

Table 3.4   GDP growth rates by sector

| Growth period | GDP growth rates (%): | | | |
	Total	Agriculture	Industry	Services
0	3.81	3.03	5.35	4.15
1	4.80	3.98	5.65	5.07
2	5.67	4.13	6.79	5.90
3	6.30	4.11	7.57	6.30
4	6.58	3.66	7.84	6.45
5	6.21	3.16	6.18	6.67
6	5.60	3.24	4.95	6.23

Source: Chenery *et al.* (1986). Tables 8.4, p. 236.

the three sectors. The historical experience of some DCs is summarised in Table 3.5.

Similar data are not available for other countries for any long period. Therefore, their experience is summarised in Table 3.6 showing the data for 1960 and 1980 for groups of countries classified according to their per capita incomes. The corresponding growth rates of employment are shown in Table 3.7.

The proportionate allocation of labour to the three sectors is generally different from the relative sectoral shares of GDP. This is because labour productivity varies widely from sector to sector. The most recent data are summarised in Table 3.8 in terms of relative labour productivities, i.e. the labour productivity in each sector as a ratio of labour productivity in the economy as a whole. This is calculated simply by dividing each sector's share in GDP by its share in total employment.

From such data, we can calculate the growth rates of labour productivity in the various sectors by subtracting the growth rate of employment from the growth rate of GDP in each sector. The results for the period 1965–80 are summarised in Table 3.9.

From these data, we see that the structure of the economy, both in terms of output shares and employment shares, varies systematically at different levels of income. But in the logistic pattern of growth identified in the last chapter, we saw that the growth rate of total output and per capita output also vary systematically with the level of income. This suggests that there must be a relationship between the overall growth rates at different income levels and the dominance of

Table 3.5   Historical changes in sectoral allocation of labour in DCs

| Country/year | | Percentage share of employment in | | |
		Agriculture	Industry	Services
France:	1866	52.0	29.0	20.0
	1950	33.0	34.0	33.0
	1973	12.2	39.3	48.5
West Germany	1882	42.0	36.0	22.0
	1933	29.0	41.0	30.0
	1973	7.5	49.5	43.0
Italy	1871	62.0	24.0	14.0
	1954	41.0	31.0	28.0
	1973	17.4	44.0	38.6
Japan	1877	83.0	6.0	11.0
	1950	49.0	21.0	30.0
	1973	13.4	37.2	49.4
Netherlands	1849	45.4	29.4	25.2
	1909	28.0	35.0	37.0
	1947	19.0	33.0	48.0
	1973	6.8	36.2	57.0
Sweden	1910	46.0	26.0	28.0
	1950	20.0	41.0	39.0
	1973	7.1	36.8	56.1
UK	1901/11	34.4	30.0	35.6
	1851/61	20.2	43.2	36.6
	1911	12.0	43.0	45.0
	1950	5.0	47.0	48.0
	1973	2.9	42.6	54.5
USA	1870	50.0	25.0	25.0
	1950	12.0	35.0	53.0
	1973	4.1	31.7	64.2

Sources: Kuznets (1957, 1971); OECD *Labour Forces Statistics* (various issues) cited in Cornwall (1977), table 2.6, p. 17.

different sectors in the economy at those income levels. That is, the lowest income levels are characterised both by the dominance of the A-sector and a lower rate of growth. The intermediate levels of income are characterised by the dominance of the M-sector and a high rate of growth. The highest levels of income are characterised by the dominance of the S-sector and a lower rate of growth.

The logistic pattern has also been noted with reference to particular sectors. For example, a UNIDO study (UN, 1983, pp. 86–7) commented on the relationship between overall growth and industrial development as follows:

Table 3.6   Allocation of labour force by level of per capita income

Per capita income (1981 US$)	Percentage of labour force: 1960			1980		
	A	M	S	A	M	S
Below 250	83.4	6.0	10.6	80.9	7.8	11.3
250–500	77.6	8.5	13.9	72.0	11.7	16.3
500–750	66.5	13.2	20.3	60.1	17.1	22.8
750–1000	54.7	17.9	27.4	63.1	13.6	23.3
1000–2000	37.9	25.0	37.1	41.6	20.3	38.1
2000–4000	28.3	33.0	38.7	24.1	29.5	46.4
4000 & over	15.2	41.3	43.5	8.5	38.6	52.9

Sources: World Bank, (1983).

Table 3.7   Sectoral growth rates of employment: 1965–80

Per capita 1980 income in (US$) (No. of countries)	Growth rates of labour in: Agriculture	Industry	Services	Total
LDCs				
Less than 500 (15)	1.67	4.04	4.19	2.31
500–1000 (14)	1.39	4.54	4.87	2.55
1000–2000 (13)	0.51	4.67	4.67	2.67
2000 & over (2)	–0.83	4.36	3.86	2.98
All LDCs (48)	0.96	4.40	4.48	2.56
DCs (18)	–2.71	0.51	2.91	1.09

Source: World Bank (1988).

Growth begins with manufacturing having a relatively small share in GDP at low levels of per capita income. Changes in the composition of GDP become extensive, however, once per capita income reaches the intermediate range ($460–$1320). At this stage, manufacturing expands rapidly and provides the impetus for structural change. As income rises, the sector's share continues to grow. This growth slows down, however, when the country reaches what might be termed an advanced stage of its development. The growth pattern of the manufacturing sector is sometimes represented by an S-shaped curve, known to statisticians as a logistic. The shape of

Table 3.8   Relative labour productivity by income level

1980 per capita income in (US$) (No. of countries)		Relative labour productivity in:		
		Agriculture	Industry	Services
LDCs				
Below 300	(12)	0.63	2.67	2.95
300–600	(20)	0.48	2.55	3.02
600–1000	(12)	0.39	2.00	2.22
1000–2000	(16)	0.42	1.94	1.37
2000 & Over	(9)	0.39	1.49	1.01
All LDCs	(69)	0.47	2.20	2.22
DCs	(18)	0.67	1.00	1.11

Source: World Bank (1988).

Table 3.9   Growth rates of labour productivity by sector and income

1980 per capita income in (US$) (No. of countries)		Growth rate of labour productivity in:			
		Agriculture	Industry	Services	Total
LDCs					
Below 500	(15)	0.94	1.14	0.73	1.76
500–1000	(14)	1.33	2.59	0.52	1.83
1000–2000	(13)	3.36	5.24	2.89	4.51
2000 & Over	(6)	4.51	2.34	2.86	3.37
All LDCs	(48)	2.33	2.82	1.52	3.02
DCs	(18)	4.28	3.85	1.46	3.06

Source: World Bank (1988).

this curve suggests that, during some period in the development process, industrial growth is the overriding determinant of structural change. Once economies have reached an advanced stage, the dynamic role played by manufacturing wanes.

This logistic pattern has also been observed in the agricultural sector with regard to the rate at which the labour force share of that sector declines over time. Using data from 131 countries, arranged

Table 3.10   Agriculture share (%) of labour: level and decline

Group	1950	1960	Decline 1950–60	1970	Decline 1960–70
1	92.9	90.1	2.8	86.9	3.3
2	84.3	80.5	3.8	76.7	3.8
3	76.3	71.3	5.0	65.3	6.0
4	66.8	61.7	5.1	54.7	7.0
5	55.4	48.9	6.5	40.3	8.6
6	46.1	37.3	8.8	28.0	9.3
7	33.2	27.4	5.8	20.4	7.0
8	23.2	17.6	5.6	12.0	5.6
9	16.7	12.0	4.7	8.0	3.9

Source: Kuznets (1982).

into nine groups according to income level, Kuznets (1982) found the pattern shown in Table 3.10. Here, we see that the rate of decline in the agricultural share of employment rises with increases in income level up to a point, and falls thereafter, again confirming the logistic pattern. With respect to this pattern, Kuznets (1982, p. 48) makes the interesting suggestion:

> Given the close negative association between the share of labour force and per capita product of the country or group of countries, it seems reasonable to argue that a more *moderate* decline in the labour share in the A sector characterizing the groups with the initially high share implies a *smaller* rise in per capita product than that for less developed economies with initially lower shares of the labour force in agriculture.

As partial, yet significant, support for this inference, he offers the data shown in Table 3.11.

The fact that economies undergo a systematic structural transformation in the course of their economic growth both in terms of the sectoral composition of GDP and the sectoral allocation of employment is, of course, well known. The statistical data both in terms of cross section patterns and historical trends have been assembled here to show the quantitative magnitudes involved, especially regarding the productivity of labour in the various sectors and the rates of growth of these sectoral labour productivities at various stages of the growth process. What is perhaps not so well appreciated is the effect of this structural transformation on the growth process. In particular,

Table 3.11   Agricultural labour shares and GNP growth rates

Income	Agricultural share labour		GNP growth rate (%):
	1960	Decline 1960–70	1960–76
1	92.7	3.0	0.94
2	87.7	3.7	1.52
3	83.8	3.6	1.37
4	76.5	5.0	2.22
5	70.6	6.1	2.12
6	64.3	8.8	3.26
7	57.3	4.7	3.07
8	39.9	9.2	3.17

Source: Kuznets (1982).

it was observed in the last chapter that the rate of growth of GDP itself varies at different income levels in a logistic pattern. In view of these relationships, therefore, it is highly likely that the logistic pattern of growth is intimately related to the structural transformation of the economy. A model is presented in the next section to provide an explanatiõn of the logistic pattern of growth on this basis.

3.2 A MODEL OF GROWTH AND STRUCTURAL TRANSFORMATION

(a) A Preliminary Model

Some theories have already been advanced in the literature to explain the logistic pattern of growth. For example, according to Kristensen (1974) economic growth depends on two sources of technological progress, one based on absorbing advanced technology already existing in other countries, and the other on the unfolding of new technology. At the lower end of the scale are countries which do not have sufficient capital or technological manpower even to absorb technology from other countries, and so have a low rate of growth. Countries in the middle range have a larger stock of both capital and trained manpower, and will therefore be able to absorb existing technology more fully; as such absorption occurs quite rapidly, these countries will experience high rates of growth. At the upper end of the scale are countries, whose further growth depends on the invention of new technology; as the development of new technology is a slow affair, these countries will only have a low rate of growth. Hence, cross-section studies will show a logistic pattern of growth.

Rostow (1978, 1980) adopts a similar position, with the additional hypothesis that, in the advanced countries, there is a slackening of the desire for further growth on the one hand, and a tendency for people to demand more and more capital-intensive goods at the high level of income on the other. Chenery (1977) also explains the logistic pattern largely on technological grounds, arguing that the high growth rates of the middle income countries are due to their transition from the under-developed to the more developed stages, and therefore calls them the 'transitional' countries.

These arguments are certainly plausible, especially for the industrialisation process, and are clearly part of the explanation of the logistic pattern. However, they cannot explain that pattern fully. Some of the difficulties have been pointed out by Solow (1977) in commenting on Chenery's paper. First, Chenery's calculations about the role of manufacturing depend on a particular sequence in which the overall rate of growth is decomposed into various components according to sectors. Somewhat different results emerge when the decomposition into sectoral components is carried out in a different sequence. Therefore, the method used must be such that the results are invariant with respect to the order of decomposition (for an example, see section 5.1). Secondly, Chenery's analysis is heavily focused on the industrial sector, and does not take full account of the important role played by the service sector. Thirdly, Solow also argues that more account should be taken of the 'malleable' income elasticities of demand.

In order to develop an alternative explanation of the logistic pattern more specifically involving the structural transformation that occurs during growth, one possible approach is to consider the equation:

$$G_y = k_a G_a + k_m G_m + k_s G_s \tag{3.1}$$

where

k_i = GDP share of sector i;

G_i = growth rate of GDP in sector i; and

G_y = growth rate of total GDP.

To use this equation as the basis of a theory of growth, the simplest assumption we can make is that the growth rates of the various sectors are constant, and that these constant growth rates satisfy the condition $G_m < G_s < G_a$. How well such an assumption agrees with actual experience may be judged by seeing how closely a regression of G_y on the output shares, k_a, k_m and k_s fits the observed data. In fitting such a regression, we must of course remember that the three sector shares are not independent, being subject to the condition $k_a + k_m + k_s = 1$. Taking this condition into account, the results for a large number of DCs and LDCs in the three post-war decades are as follows:

1950s

$$G_y = -0.31k_a + 8.19k_m + 0.71k_s(R^2 = 0.32; n = 54)$$

1960s

$$G_y = -0.15k_a + 12.54k_m - 0.64k_s(R^2 = 0.33; n = 88)$$

1970s

$$G_y = -1.51k_a + 5.15k_m + 2.24k_s(R^2 = 0.11; n = 94)$$

In these regressions, the coefficients of the ks have the interpretation of the corresponding sectoral growth rates on the assumption that these growth rates are constant for all countries in each decade. The results show that G_m is the highest, consistent with observed experience; G_s is higher than G_a in two of the three decades. The R^2s are reasonable for such cross-section analysis in the first two decades, although not very high.

However, there is a serious problem with this approach, namely that the ks and the Gs are not independent of each other over time. In fact, if the sectoral growth rates differ from each other, then there will be a steady rise in the output share of the sector with the highest growth rate, and that share will steadily have more and more weight in determining G_y. Therefore, there will be a monotonic rise in G_y until it reaches the maximum sectoral growth rate.

This can be shown rigorously as follows. From the definition of k_a as the share of the A-sector in total output, we get,

$$\frac{dk_a}{dt} = k_a(G_a - G_y)$$

$$= k_a[G_a - k_aG_a - k_mG_m - k_sG_s]$$
$$= k_a[k_mG_a + k_sG_a - k_mG_m - k_sG_s]$$
$$= k_ak_m(G_a - G_m) + k_ak_s(G_a - G_s) \tag{3.2}$$

Similarly, we have

$$\frac{dk_m}{dt} = k_ak_m(G_m - G_a) + k_mk_s(G_m - G_s); \text{ and} \tag{3.3}$$

$$\frac{dk_s}{dt} = k_ak_s(G_s - G_a) + k_mk_s(G_s - G_m) \tag{3.4}$$

Thus, we see from (3.3) that if $G_m > G_a$, G_s, then k_m will increase steadily towards the value one. Differentiating (3.1) with respect to time, and substituting (3.2) into (3.4), we then easily get

$$\frac{dG_y}{dt} = k_ak_m(G_m - G_a)^2 + k_mk_s(G_m - G_s)^2$$

$$+ k_ak_s(G_a - G_s)^2 > 0 \tag{3.5}$$

Hence, so long as the sectoral growth rates are constant and different from each other, there will be a steady acceleration of the overall growth rate.

But this result is contrary to the logistic pattern; therefore we cannot use this model to explain that pattern. This model has another unfortunate consequence, namely that it completely determines the underlying income elasticities of demand. Thus, defining the income elasticity of demand for the product of the i-th sector as $\epsilon_i = G_i/G_y$ we see that in the case where G_m is the highest sectoral growth rate, ϵ_m will tend to the value 1, while ϵ_a tends to G_a/G_m and ϵ_s to G_s/G_m. It is clearly implausible that the behavioural parameters move in this rigid fashion.

(b) The Basic Model

In order to develop a more satisfactory model, we must consider the causes of the structural transformation in more detail. In the previous model, we only considered the growth rates of output in the various sectors, and the consequent changing composition of GDP. The main reason for the changing composition of GDP is the Engel effect, i.e. the fact that the income elasticity of demand for agricultural output is typically less than one, while the income elasticities of demand for industrial output and services are typically greater than one. Hence, as income rises, the demand for agriculture grows less than proportionately, leading to a smaller share of that sector.

But while the Engel effect explains the changing composition of GDP, it does not explain the changing allocation of labour to the various sectors. That depends on the productivity of labour in these sectors. Therefore, we must consider the productivity of labour in the different sectors explicitly. It is only then that the historical changes in the productivity of labour in the economy as a whole can be explained in terms of the structural determinants of growth. The importance of these factors has, of course, been long recognised (see e.g. Kindleberger, 1965, ch. 10, esp. pp. 180–1), but they need to be incorporated in a systematic model of growth and structural transformation.

It is for this purpose that we construct an alternative model in terms of the proportions of the labour force employed in the various sectors, and the productivity of labour in these sectors. Hence, we may assume a constant labour force without loss of generality, but greatly simplifying the analysis. We shall also assume that labour productivity grows over time at a constant rate in each sector, though the rate varies from sector to sector. Hence, instead of assuming that the growth rate of output is constant in each sector, we shall in fact be explaining it in terms of a varying allocation of labour, and a constant growth rate of labour productivity.

For this analysis, we define:

λ_i = proportion of labour force in sector i;
q_i = per worker output in sector i;
q = per worker output in the economy as a whole;
k_i = share of sector i in total GDP.

A prime is used to distinguish final from initial values, and a dot over a variable indicates its rate of growth. Then, it follows from these definitions that

$$q = \sum \lambda_i q_i \tag{3.6}$$

and further that

$$\dot{q} = \sum k_i \dot{q}_i + \sum (\lambda'_i - \lambda_i) \frac{q'_i}{q} \tag{3.7}$$

Using the fact that $\Sigma(\lambda'_i - \lambda_i) = 0$, equation (3.7) can also be written in a more useful form as

$$\dot{q} = \sum k_i \dot{q}_i + (\lambda'_m - \lambda_m) \frac{(q'_m - q'_a)}{q} + (\lambda'_s - \lambda_s) \frac{(q'_s - q'_a)}{q} \tag{3.8}$$

The first term on the right hand side of this equation represents the component of overall growth that is due to the growth of labour productivity within sectors. The remaining terms then represent the effect of the re-allocation of labour between sectors of unequal productivity. It will be seen that this re-allocation effect is an important component of overall growth, and one closely related to the logistic pattern of growth.

If so, it is all the more important to explain why such a re-allocation of labour occurs in practice. One of the most important reasons for this labour re-allocation is the varying demand for the output of the various sectors, as determined by the respective income elasticities of demand. From their definition, these income elasticities can be written as:

$$\epsilon_i = \frac{(\lambda'_i q'_i - \lambda_i q_i)}{\lambda_i q_i \dot{q}} \tag{3.9}$$

from which we get

$$\lambda'_i - \lambda_i = \frac{\lambda_i (\dot{q} \epsilon_i - \dot{q}_i)}{1 + \dot{q}_i} \tag{3.10}$$

Equation (3.10) thus gives us an expression for labour shifts in each sector in terms of the income elasticity of demand for that sector.

But unfortunately, the value of $(\lambda'_i - \lambda_i)$ in equation (3.10) depends on $\dot{q}$, while the value of $\dot{q}$ in equation (3.8) depends on the labour shifts. Therefore, these two equations must be solved simultaneously to express both $\dot{q}$ and $(\lambda'_i - \lambda_i)$ in terms of the initial parameters ϵ_i and $\dot{q}_i$.

The simplest way to solve these simultaneous equations is best illustrated for the case of two sectors A and B. As the productivity of labour in sector A grows, the quantity of labour needed to produce the initial quantity of output in that sector will decline by

$$\lambda_a - \frac{\lambda_a q_a}{q'_a} = \frac{\lambda_a \dot{q}_a}{1 + \dot{q}_a} \tag{3.11}$$

and similarly for sector B. Therefore, the total labour required to produce the initial quantities in sectors A and B will decline by

$$\frac{\lambda_a \dot{q}_a}{1 + \dot{q}_a} + \frac{\lambda_b \dot{q}_b}{1 + \dot{q}_b} \tag{3.12}$$

But as per capita income rises, the output of the various sectors will also rise. Thus, for a growth of per capita income, given by the average productivity of labour, at the rate $\dot{q}$, and for an income elasticity of demand, ϵ_i, in sector i, the quantity of output in that sector will rise by the amount $\dot{q}\,\epsilon_i\lambda_i q_i$. Therefore, the increase in the amount of labour required to produce these extra quantities will be

$$\dot{q}\left[\frac{\lambda_a \epsilon_a}{1 + \dot{q}_a} + \frac{\lambda_b \epsilon_b}{1 + \dot{q}_b}\right] \tag{3.13}$$

As the labour force is assumed to be constant, the reduction in labour required to produce the initial quantities must equal the increase in labour required to produce the additional quantities. Hence, by equating (3.12) and (3.13) we get an expression for $\dot{q}$ in terms of the initial parameters:

$$\dot{q} = \frac{\dfrac{\lambda_a \dot{q}_a}{1 + \dot{q}_a} + \dfrac{\lambda_b \dot{q}_b}{1 + \dot{q}_b}}{\dfrac{\lambda_a \epsilon_a}{1 + \dot{q}_a} + \dfrac{\lambda_b \epsilon_b}{1 + \dot{q}_b}} \tag{3.14}$$

Substituting this expression for $\dot{q}$ into (3.10), we get

$$(\lambda'_a - \lambda_a) = \frac{\lambda_a \lambda_b(\dot{q}_b \epsilon_a - \dot{q}_a \epsilon_b)}{\lambda_a \epsilon_a(1 + \dot{q}_b) + \lambda_b \epsilon_b(1 + \dot{q}_a)} \tag{3.15}$$

that is

$$\lambda_a' \gtreqless \lambda_a \quad \text{according as} \quad \frac{\epsilon_a}{\dot{q}_a} \gtreqless \frac{\epsilon_b}{\dot{q}_b} \tag{3.16}$$

This is a very interesting result. As may be expected, the re-allocation of labour between sectors is partly due to demand factors represented by the income elasticities of demand ϵ_i and partly due to supply factors represented by the rates of growth of labour productivity $\dot{q}_i$. What is particularly interesting about the above result is that the interaction between these two sets of factors is neatly represented by the ratio of the two parameters. In other words, whether a sector gains or loses labour depends on whether the ratio $(\epsilon_i/\dot{q}_i)$ in that sector is greater or less than that in the other sector.

Using the same approach, the extension to three sectors is straightforward:

$$\dot{q} = \frac{\dfrac{\lambda_a \dot{q}_a}{1 + \dot{q}_a} + \dfrac{\lambda_m \dot{q}_m}{1 + \dot{q}_m} + \dfrac{\lambda_s \dot{q}_s}{1 + \dot{q}_s}}{\dfrac{\lambda_a \epsilon_a}{1 + \dot{q}_a} + \dfrac{\lambda_m \epsilon_m}{1 + \dot{q}_m} + \dfrac{\lambda_s \epsilon_s}{1 + \dot{q}_s}} \tag{3.17}$$

and

$$\lambda_a' - \lambda_a = \frac{\dfrac{\lambda_a \dot{q}_a}{1 + \dot{q}_a} \left[\dfrac{\lambda_m \dot{q}_m}{1 + \dot{q}_m} \left\{ \dfrac{\epsilon_a}{\dot{q}_a} - \dfrac{\epsilon_m}{\dot{q}_m} \right\} + \dfrac{\lambda_s \dot{q}_s}{1 + \dot{q}_s} \left\{ \dfrac{\epsilon_a}{\dot{q}_a} - \dfrac{\epsilon_s}{\dot{q}_s} \right\} \right]}{\dfrac{\lambda_a \epsilon_a}{1 + \dot{q}_a} + \dfrac{\lambda_m \epsilon_m}{1 + \dot{q}_m} + \dfrac{\lambda_s \epsilon_s}{1 + \dot{q}_s}} \tag{3.18}$$

and similarly for the other two sectors.

To illustrate the implications of the above equations for the shift of labour, consider the case where the demand and supply parameters have the following values:

Parameters	Sector A	Sector M	Sector S
ϵ	0.6	1.5	1.3
$\dot{q}$	0.3	0.6	0.5
$\epsilon/\dot{q}$	2.0	2.5	2.6

Then, the pattern of re-allocation of labour will be:

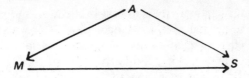

The important point to note is that the shift of labour does not depend only on the income elasticities, but on their ratios to the growth rates of labour productivity. Thus, labour is attracted to the S-sector, although it has a lower income elasticity than the M-sector.

Let us next consider the implications for the overall growth rate. Unlike equation (3.1), the overall growth rate in the present model depends on two terms as shown in equation (3.7) or (3.8). The first term is $\Sigma k_i \dot{q}_i$ a weighted average of the $\dot{q}_i$s, the weights being the output shares of the various sectors. Generally, the output share of the A-sector declines, while the output share of the M-sector rises in the intermediate stage and that of the S-sector in the final stage. As the growth rate of labour productivity is highest in the M-sector, the rise in the output share of that sector in the intermediate stages of growth is part of the explanation of the growth acceleration which occurs during that phase. Similarly, the rise of the output share of the S-sector at the expense of the M-sector in the final stages of growth is part of the explanation for the growth deceleration in that stage.

Although this term looks like the term $\Sigma k_i G_i$ in equation (3.1), there is one difference which is quite important. The difference is that, while the assumed values of the G_i's have a decisive influence on the ks over time, the assumed values of the $\dot{q}_i$s do not have such a direct influence. This is because the ks may vary both through differences in the $\dot{q}_i$s and through variations in the λs. Hence, there is an extra degree of freedom for the variation of the ks. This extra degree of freedom enables us to introduce the influence of the income elasticities of demand, ϵs, on the structural transformation of the economy.

The second term in the expression (3.7) or (3.8) for $\dot{q}$ refers to the effect of the re-allocation of labour. As argued above, labour shifts from the sector with a low value of $(\epsilon_i \dot{q}_i)$ to sectors with a higher value of the ratio. If the shift is from a sector with low labour productivity to a sector with a higher labour productivity, this re-allocation of labour makes a contribution to overall growth, over and above that due to the growth of labour productivity within sectors.

Generally, labour productivity is lowest in the agricultural sector and highest in the industrial sector. Hence, part of the acceleration of growth in the early stages is due to the shift of labour out of the A-sector to the other sectors. Similarly, part of the deceleration of growth in the later stages is due to the shift of labour from the M-sector to the S-sector.

(c) The Hierarchy of Commodities

We thus have a model of growth and structural transformation, based on both the demand parameters of income elasticities of demand and the supply parameters of growth rates of labour productivity. The simplest assumption to make is that these parameters are constant over time. But this is not a satisfactory assumption. One reason is that, if we assume these demand and supply parameters to be constant, then labour will shift continuously to the sector with the highest value of the $(\epsilon_i/\dot{q}_i)$ ratio, and the overall growth rate will tend continuously to the ratio $(\dot{q}_i/\epsilon_i)$ of that sector, as the entire labour force gets concentrated in that sector.

But there is a more important reason. While the supply parameters (growth rates of labour productivity) may be assumed to be constant, it is logically impossible for the income elasticities of demand to remain constant. These income elasticities will remain constant while there is structural transformation only if they are all equal to one. This can be seen most simply in the case of two sectors, A and B. Because the ϵs have to satisfy the condition

$$k_a\epsilon_a + k_b\epsilon_b = 1 \tag{3.19}$$

it follows that

$$k_a = \frac{\epsilon_b - 1}{\epsilon_b - \epsilon_a} \; ; k_b = \frac{1 - \epsilon_a}{\epsilon_b - \epsilon_a} \tag{3.20}$$

Hence, constant ϵs mean constant ks. Even if the structural transformation of the economy consists only of a changing sectoral allocation of labour with constant sectoral shares of output, we must have

$$\frac{\lambda_a}{\lambda_b} = \frac{\lambda_a'(1 + \dot{q}_a)}{\lambda_b'(1 + \dot{q}_b)} = \frac{\lambda_a(1 + \dot{q}\,\epsilon_a)}{\lambda_b(1 + \dot{q}\,\epsilon_b)} \tag{3.21}$$

from which it follows that the ∈s must be equal to each other, and therefore equal to one.

In fact, the empirical evidence about consumer behaviour from many countries shows clearly that income elasticities of demand for various commodities vary in a systematic way during the process of growth (Cornwall, 1972, pp. 61–2; 1977, pp. 100–2; Pasinetti, 1982, pp. 71–5). According to this evidence, the income elasticity of demand for each commodity goes through various phases as per capita income rises, being high to begin with when the commodity is a 'luxury', steadily declining as the commodity becomes a 'necessity' until it reaches zero when demand is satiated. Further, different commodities go through these phases at different income levels, so that all commodities can be arranged in a hierarchical pattern depending on the income levels at which they go through these phases. At the bottom of this hierarchy is food; then come various manufactured goods; and at the top of the hierarchy are many forms of services. The demand for the various commodities will also depend on relative prices, but as Pasinetti (1982, p. 73) argues 'price changes cannot but flatten out or steepen these relations; they cannot affect their basic shapes. In other words, price changes can only postpone or anticipate a time path which, if real income increases, is going to take place anyhow'.

(d) A Simulation Exercise

Stripped down to its essentials, the basic model consists of three key parameters: the allocation of labour to the various sectors, the growth rates of labour productivity over time, and the changing income elasticities of demand. These are just too many parameters to attempt an analytical solution. Therefore, we study the behaviour of the basic model only by means of a simulation exercise.

For this simulation exercise, we assume that the growth rates of labour productivity in the various sectors are constant over time, having the values $\dot{q}_a = 0.2$, $\dot{q}_m = 0.4$ and $\dot{q}_s = 0.3$.

In addition to these growth rates of labour productivity, we need some pattern of change of income elasticities of demand. Although the general pattern of these changes at different income levels has been recognised, different authors have used different mathematical forms to describe the equations of their demand systems. For the simulation exercise, it is assumed that the income elasticities of

Table 3.12 Simulation I: income levels, labour allocation and income elasticities

Period	$\dot{q}$	λ_a	λ_m	λ_s	ε_a	ε_m	ε_s
0	100	.700	.100	.200	0.70	1.56	1.23
1	127	.693	.102	.205	0.65	1.54	1.24
2	163	.684	.104	.212	0.61	1.52	1.22
3	210	.671	.107	.222	0.56	1.50	1.19
4	274	.656	.112	.232	0.52	1.48	1.14
5	363	.637	.118	.245	0.47	1.46	1.08
6	486	.617	.126	.257	0.43	1.43	1.02
7	662	.593	.137	.270	0.38	1.40	0.95
8	915	.566	.150	.284	0.34	1.37	0.88
9	1289	.537	.167	.296	0.29	1.33	0.81
10	1848	.504	.188	.308	0.25	1.29	0.74
11	2698	.468	.215	.317	0.21	1.25	0.69
12	3998	.430	.246	.324	0.17	1.20	0.66
13	5978	.389	.280	.331	0.14	1.15	0.69
14	8921	.346	.313	.341	0.11	1.10	0.78
15	13 104	.303	.338	.359	0.08	1.04	0.95
16	18 720	.261	.350	.389	0.06	0.99	1.17
17	25 873	.223	.344	.433	0.05	0.94	1.36
18	34 654	.189	.325	.487	0.04	0.90	1.50
19	45 220	.160	.295	.545	0.03	0.85	1.58
20	57 830	.134	.261	.605	0.03	0.81	1.62

demand for the three sectors vary during the process of growth according to the following relationships:

$$\epsilon_a = 0.075 (5 - \log y)^2 + 0.025 \tag{3.22}$$

$$\epsilon_m = 1.72 - 0.04(\log y)^2 \tag{3.23}$$

where y is per capita income. With ϵ_a and ϵ_m described by these functions, the value of ϵ_s may be derived from the condition

$$k_a\epsilon_a + k_m\epsilon_m + k_s\epsilon_s = 1 \tag{3.24}$$

that the ϵs must satisfy.

We can start the simulation exercise with some initial values of labour productivity and labour allocation. For our first simulation, let us assume $\lambda_a = 0.7$, $\lambda_m = 0.1$ and $\lambda_s = 0.2$; and $q_a = 80$; $q_m = 200$ and $q_s = 120$. From these initial values, the basic model leads to the levels of income, the changing labour allocation and the changing income elasticities of demand as shown in Table 3.12.

Table 3.13 Simulation I: growth rate, intra-sectoral productivity growth
effect and labour re-allocation effect

Period	Growth rate $\dot{q}$	Intra-sectoral productivity growth effect: $\Sigma k_i \dot{q}_i$	Re-allocation effect
0	.270	.264	.006
1	.280	.270	.010
2	.292	.276	.016
3	.306	.284	.022
4	.322	.292	.030
5	.340	.300	.040
6	.361	.309	.052
7	.383	.318	.065
8	.408	.327	.081
9	.434	.336	.098
10	.460	.346	.114
11	.482	.354	.128
12	.495	.362	.133
13	.492	.369	.123
14	.469	.374	.095
15	.429	.378	.051
16	.382	.379	.003
17	.339	.379	−.040
18	.305	.379	−.074
19	.279	.377	−.098
20	.260	.375	−.115

We see the labour-share of the A-sector declining steadily, that of
the M-sector rising up to period 16 and falling thereafter, and that of
the S-sector rising steadily throughout the whole period. The income
elasticities of demand for A and M sectors decline steadily because of
the particular formulae we have chosen, but the income elasticity of
demand of the S-sector falls up to period 12 and rises rapidly thereafter.

Table 3.13 then shows the growth rate of per capita labour productivity corresponding to per capita income, broken down into that
component due to the growth of labour productivity within sectors
and that component due to re-allocation of labour between sectors.
First, we note that the growth rate accelerates until period 12 and
declines thereafter, corresponding to the logistic pattern observed in
actual experience. Secondly, we note that this pattern is also observed in the intra-sectoral component. The growth rate corresponding to this component increases until period 17 and declines

Table 3.14 Simulation II: labour allocation, income elasticities and growth rate

Period	λ_a	λ_m	λ_s	ε_a	ε_m	ε_s	$\dot{q}$
0	.700	.100	.200	0.70	1.56	1.23	.336
1	.665	.117	.218	0.64	1.54	1.24	.341
2	.624	.138	.238	0.59	1.52	1.22	.346
3	.578	.161	.261	0.54	1.49	1.17	.350
4	.529	.189	.282	0.49	1.47	1.12	.353
5	.477	.220	.303	0.44	1.44	1.05	.354
6	.424	.256	.320	0.40	1.41	0.98	.355
7	.372	.296	.332	0.35	1.38	0.92	.355
8	.322	.340	.338	0.31	1.35	0.85	.354
9	.275	.386	.339	0.28	1.32	0.79	.352
10	.232	.435	.333	0.24	1.28	0.73	.349
11	.194	.484	.322	0.21	1.25	0.69	.346
12	.160	.534	.306	0.18	1.21	0.67	.341
13	.131	.580	.289	0.15	1.18	0.66	.335
14	.106	.622	.272	0.13	1.14	0.70	.329
15	.085	.658	.257	0.11	1.10	0.77	.322
16	.068	.685	.247	0.09	1.06	0.88	.315
17	.053	.704	.243	0.08	1.02	1.03	.308
18	.042	.712	.246	0.06	0.98	1.19	.301
19	.033	.710	.246	0.06	0.98	1.19	.301
20	.025	.698	.277	0.04	0.90	1.47	.289

thereafter. Thirdly, we note that there is a similar pattern in the growth rate due to the re-allocation effect, which increases until period 12 and declines rapidly thereafter. Because the intra-sectoral component is the weighted average of the sectoral growth rates of labour productivity, it cannot exceed the highest of the sectoral rates, namely 0.4 for the M-sector. But the overall growth rate exceeds 0.4 in several periods; this is because of the contribution from the re-allocation effect.

Thus we see that the re-allocation effect is a very significant source of the logistic pattern of overall growth. In fact, the re-allocation effect alone can produce the logistic pattern. This can be seen by considering a second simulation exercise in which we assume that labour productivity grows at the same rate, say 0.3 per period in all sectors. Table 3.14 shows the income levels, changing labour force shares and changing income elasticities of demand (again using the above relationships) for the second simulation.

We see that the labour shares of the three sectors, and their income elasticities behave as in the previous simulation. We also see that the growth rate of average labour productivity rises up to period 7 and declines thereafter. Because the growth of labour productivity in each sector is assumed to be the same, 0.3, the intra-sectoral component of overall growth is constant at that value throughout. Therefore, the excess of the overall growth rate over 0.3 and its logistic variation is entirely due to the re-allocation effect. While this exercise shows how the re-allocation effect alone can produce the logistic pattern of growth, it is likely that in practice, this pattern depends also on the intra-sectoral component due to differences in growth rates of labour productivity in different sectors, particularly their relationship according to $\dot{q}_a < \dot{q}_s < \dot{q}_m$. The main reason why this relationship may be expected to hold in practice is because agricultural productivity is subject to diminishing returns due to the limitation of land, while industrial productivity can grow faster both through capital accumulation and increasing returns to scale.

3.3 FURTHER ISSUES

In the previous section, we constructed a basic model which was able to explain both the logistic pattern that obtains during growth viewed as a single long-drawn out process, and the structural transformation that usually accompanies that process, using a minimum set of highly plausible assumptions about various demand and supply parameters. Further, it explains the logistic pattern of growth in terms of the structural transformation of the economy. For example, it shows the acceleration of growth at the middle levels of income as the consequence of the industrialisation that occurs during that phase, both because the intra-sectoral component of growth increases as the rising output share of the M-sector increases the weight attached to the high growth rate of labour productivity in that sector, and because the re-allocation effect increases, as labour shifts from the low productivity A-sector to the high productivity M-sector. Similarly, it shows the deceleration of growth that occurs at high levels of income as the consequence of the de-industrialisation that occurs during that phase, both because the intra-sectoral component falls as the rising output share of the S-sector increases the weight attached to the relatively smaller growth rate of labour productivity in that sector, and because the reallocation effect also falls as labour shifts from the high productivity M-sector to the lower productivity S-sector.

The different sectoral parameters of demand and supply may therefore be considered the structural determinants of growth, especially of the logistic pattern that growth generally follows. However, these parameters are only the proximate factors underlying that growth pattern. They need to be explained further in terms of more fundamental forces working in the economy. In particular, we have to explain why labour productivities and their growth rates differ from sector to sector, as assumed in the basic model. This is one question that must be addressed in the rest of the book.

Further, the basic model uses particular constant values of the underlying parameters to produce a particular logistic pattern of growth, i.e. growth along a particular S-curve. But the S-curve of growth varies from country to country, because different countries have different values of these parameters, and these parameters also change over time. Therefore, another question that must be addressed in the rest of the book is why these parameter values differ between countries and change over time. The answer to these questions will help to explain why the growth experience of individual countries differs from the average pattern we have tried to capture in our basic model.

To deal with these issues, we consider other factors underlying the structural determinants of growth. For convenience of exposition, these factors are separated into those dealing with supply factors, discussed in Part II, and with demand factors, discussed in Part III.

Part II
Supply Factors: the Classical Determinants

4 Theories of Growth

4.1 INTRODUCTION

There is already a large literature on growth theory. In much of this literature, the growth of the national income of countries is mainly explained in terms of the stocks of various factors of production – namely, land, labour, capital and the state of technology, and their variation over time. These are the theories developed by classical and neo-classical writers on the subject. Hence, these factors may be described as the classical determinants of growth. Their main distinguishing feature is that they deal primarily with the supply factors. Part II of the book deals with the extent to which these supply factors are able to explain growth as it has actually taken place.

Obviously, certain stocks of the factors of production are necessary to produce output, and an increase in these stocks is necessary for a growth of output. But for a complete theory of growth, there are two further questions to be considered. One relates to the question of why the stocks of these factors of production vary over time in different ways in different countries. The other relates to the question of how fully the available factors of production are utilised at any time. On the first question, the classical and neo-classical theories assumed that in the case of some factors of production, such as land and labour, their growth rate over time is given exogenously, while in the case of other factors of production, especially capital, their growth rate is determined by some simple assumptions, such as assumptions about savings behaviour. In the case of technological progress, some of the earlier theories assumed it also to be given exogenously, while more recent theories explain it as an endogenous process. These assumptions must be examined critically in the light of actual experience.

On the second question, the classical and neo-classical writers recognise that the stock of the various factors of production in a country only determines its productive capacity, and that the actual volume of production is determined by the extent to which productive capacity is actually utilised and depends on the strength of demand. But these authors generally neglect the role of such demand factors, because of a profound belief in Say's Law that supply creates its own demand. This belief in Say's Law is ultimately derived from a

53

view of market performance, namely the view that markets function efficiently and competitively so that the prices of all factors and goods speedily adjust to their equilibrium level at which demand equals supply. In particular, wages adjust speedily in the labour market to ensure full employment of the available labour force, and the rate of interest adjusts speedily in the capital market to ensure that savings equals investment. On these assumptions, all factors of production are fully utilised. Further, market forces allocate the resources available at any time in such an optimal manner that the total value of all the goods and services produced in an economy is the maximum that can be attained with the country's factor endowment. Hence, these theories of growth tend to be global theories purporting to explain the overall growth of national income by supply factors alone, with demand factors coming in only to explain the allocation of resources to, and the growth of output in, different sectors according to the varying patterns of demand at rising levels of income.

The role of demand factors is discussed in Part III. In Part II of the book, we address the role of supply factors in explaining economic growth. As an introduction to this analysis, the present chapter reviews the literature on classical and neo-classical theories of growth. Because the literature on this subject is so vast, we will only consider the major theories that have been advanced. Most of these theories deal with the overall growth of the economy. But in view of the importance of the structural determinants of growth, considered in Chapter 3, we also consider the role of the supply factors in each of the three major sectors of the economy. This is done in the next three chapters.

4.2 THE MAGNIFICENT DYNAMICS OF RICARDO

(a) Summary

The high point of the classical theories of growth was attained in Ricardo's formulation, which has justly been acclaimed as the 'magnificent dynamics' considering how thoroughly he explored the question he set himself, so early in the development of economics as a science. We shall therefore concentrate on the theory as formulated by Ricardo.

The locus of the Ricardian model is in the agricultural sector. The two main factors of production are therefore taken as land and labour. Land being the 'original and indestructible properties of the soil' is considered as fixed in supply. But the quality of land varies from place to place. At a given point of time, there is also a fixed supply of labour. Labour is always fully employed, and hired by capitalists for a wage. Competition among capitalists ensures that labour is allocated to different farms so as to equalise its marginal product on all farms, for if the marginal product of labour is lower in farm A than in farm B, it will profit capitalists to shift labour from A to B; then, under the influence of the Law of Diminishing Returns, the marginal product of labour will rise in A and fall in B until the two are equal. Consequently, the more fertile farms will be cultivated more intensively. The margin of cultivation will be extended to that farm which is just worth cultivating, in the sense that its average product of labour is just equal to the common level of the marginal product of labour on all cultivated farms. Farms less fertile than the marginal farm with an average product of labour less than the marginal product will be left uncultivated.

The distribution of income among workers, capitalists and land-lords plays an important role in this theory of growth. At any point of time, there is a fixed stock of corn, known as the Wage Fund, owned by capitalists and used to hire labour during the growing season. The rate of wages per worker is then determined by the size of the Wage Fund in relation to the labour force, i.e. it is just equal to the Wage Fund divided by the labour force. The wage rate is therefore independent of the marginal product of labour. In fact, the marginal product of labour is higher than the wage rate; the difference between these two quantities is the profit that capitalist earn per worker employed. The marginal product of labour is itself less than the average product on all intra-marginal farms. The difference between the average and the marginal products of labour, multiplied by the number of workers employed on a farm, then accrues to the landlord as rent of the land. More fertile land earns a higher rent because the average product of labour is higher and because more workers are employed. The marginal farm does not earn any rent.

This is the picture at a point of time. It is then set in historical motion by two dynamic forces, namely population growth and the increase of the Wage Fund. Landlords as a class spend the bulk of their rent incomes on 'unproductive consumption', the phrase used by classical writers to indicate that they do not save any part of their income for investment. Capitalists, however, save a high proportion of their profit incomes and add to the Wage Fund. This is one of the two main dynamic forces propelling the economy upward. The other dynamic force is the growth of population. This follows the Malthusian theory of demographic behaviour. According to this theory, population growth is an endogenous variable. If the wage rate determined by the relation between the Wage Fund and the size of the labour force leads to a standard of living of workers above a certain level, known as the 'subsistence level', then population will increase in size. Conversely, if the wage rate is such that the standard of living is below the subsistence level, there will be a decline in population size. The next result is that the steady expansion of the Wage Fund will lead to a steady growth of population. In this process, the wage rate will fluctuate around the subsistence level; the marginal product of labour will fall steadily, both through the more intensive cultivation of intra-marginal farms and the outward movement of the extensive margin of cultivation to less and less fertile farms; the rate of profit per worker employed will fall; the profit incomes of capitalists may rise for a time but will eventually decline, while all the time there will be a continuous rise in the rent incomes of landlords. Ultimately, the rate of profit will fall to zero, the Wage Fund will stop expanding, and the economy will reach the classical Stationary State.

(b) Critique

Although this theory of growth represents a major achievement as a piece of technical dynamic analysis, even by modern standards, it must be noted that it was developed by the classical economists as part of their advocacy of free enterprise and free trade. This was especially so with regard to the policy of the free import of food from other countries with a comparative advantage in food production, which was thought to be a way of slowing down the movement towards the Stationary State. The policy was also thought to be a way of slowing down the rise in the rent incomes of the landlords, most of which was assumed to be spent in unproductive consumption, at the expense of the profit incomes of capitalists, which provided the savings for the accumulation of capital.

But in the present context, we shall be evaluating the theory mainly from the point of view of its contribution to the explanation of economic growth. The main weakness of the theory will be examined under three heads – the assumptions about demographic behaviour, the treatment of technological progress, and the emphasis on capital in its circulating form rather than as fixed investment. These three aspects of the theory are the main reasons why its predictions have largely failed to materialise in subseqent history, especially in the present-day DCs.

(c) Demographic Behaviour

The classical hypothesis about demographic behaviour was based mainly on the relationship between the standard of living of workers and the subsistence level. But the concept of the subsistence level was left unclear. There is still a continuing controversy as to whether it was meant to be a physiological concept, in which case one would expect it to be fairly uniform over all regions, or to be a psychological or conventional concept, which allows for some variation in different regions. Although Marx generally followed the classical lead in his own positive analysis, he explicitly allowed a 'historical and moral element' to enter into the subsistence level, mainly to reconcile the concept with the higher level of wages in North America compared with Europe. The two interpretations of the subsistence concept are in turn related to whether the endogenous changes in population size were mainly due to changes on the mortality side or to changes on the fertility side, another question which was left unclear in the classical writings and has left room for much controversy. Some authors, like O'Brien (1975, 1981) tend to the physiological interpretation of the subsistence concept influencing population growth through the mechanism of mortality, while others like Hollander (1979) lean towards the psychological interpretation, influencing population growth through such fertility factors as the rate and age of marriage.

But whatever the classical writers may have meant, the Malthusian theory of demographic behaviour was decisively disproved in the subsequent history of the present-day developed countries. Contrary to that theory, the rate of population growth rose for a time with a fall in mortality while fertility remained high at a traditional level, but declined thereafter as fertility also fell to a level little above the level of mortality. The classical theory of population growth therefore gave way to an alternative theory, known as the demographic transition theory. This theory also treats population growth as an endogenous variable, with changes in mortality and fertility being influenced by the progress of something called development. But the concept of development was not fully explained. In particular, it was not made clear whether it was mainly an economic phenomenon reflected in rising levels of per capita income and industrialisation, or whether it was a social phenomenon reflected in rising levels of education and urbanisation, and the breakdown of traditional social systems based on the extended family institution. All that the demographic transition theory did was to take the diagram showing the actual historical experience of DCs in the form of time series, and to re-label the horizontal axis from one measuring the passage of historical time to one measuring something called development in order to produce an endogenous theory of population growth.

In fact, population growth is the result of complex forces, some of which are due to the official actions of public authorities and others which are determined by the personal circumstances of individuals. Thus, as Lewis (1955, p. 307) argued 'the truth is rather that that part of the fall in the death rate which is due to medical improvements is even more spectacular than that part which is due to improvements in food supply'. Also as Demeny (1968) has pointed out, the decline of fertility has been due more to the spread of contraceptive practices, largely following cultural and even linguistic lines, which brought fertility behaviour within the calculus of conscious decision-making than to changes in economic conditions *per se*. As a result, population growth in DCs has largely been exogenous of economic conditions.

In the LDCs, however, the Malthusian model of demographic behaviour appears to have held more closely, at least until recent times. For a long time, fertility remained at a high level, sometimes described as 'natural fertility' maintained at that level not only by biological factors but also by traditional customs of early marriage and large families, supported by institutions such as the extended family. It has even been argued (see e.g., Caldwell, 1976) that this was in fact a rational behaviour to ensure adequate support of parents in their old age under conditions of high infant mortality. Mortality, on the other hand, was largely determined by food supply. Hence, there was a steady growth of population associated with improvements in agricultural technology, leading in fact to the great concentrations of population in countries like China and India even in early historical times. In fact, it was even thought by Adam Smith himself that a country like China was already close to the classical Stationary State, if it was not already there. Some support for the view that many Asian countries have reached this position has been advanced by Ishikawa, whose conclusions are discussed in the next chapter.

But in recent times, the Malthusian process seems to have broken down even in the LDCs. This is shown by the sharp acceleration of population growth in these countries after the Second World War, due not so much to any significant rise in per capita incomes, but rather to considerable improvements in public health and advances in medical science. Thus, there was a sharp reduction in mortality levels due to the control of epidemic diseases such as cholera and malaria with the expenditure of modest resources by public authorities. Fertility also is declining but at a much slower pace, except in a few countries, where it has been greatly influenced by official family planning campaigns. The result is that population has grown rapidly in most of these countries, faster indeed than the rate needed to maintain the average income of workers at the subsistence level, leading to the emergence of absolute poverty on a mass scale. Thus, we have to conclude that population growth has not been influenced as tightly by economic conditions as assumed in the classical theory, but has tended to vary in a much more exogenous manner.

(d) Technological Progress

The classical theory of growth was also worked out assuming a constant state of agricultural technology. The result was that the growth of agricultural output under the influence of population growth was assumed to be subject to the full force of diminishing returns. But in historical fact, not only in the developed countries but also in the less-developed countries, there has been a steady progress of agricultural technology. We consider some of these technological advances in agriculture in the next chapter. But one type of technical innovation may be referred to here, namely the trend towards a steady rise in the yield of land by the invention of more and more labour intensive techniques of cultivation. The importance of these innovations has been stressed by Boserup (1965). Further, she has argued that many of these innovations were in fact induced by an exogenous growth of population. The result was therefore to stave off the full force of the Law of Diminishing Returns, if not completely, at least for a longer time than envisaged in the classical theory.

(e) Capital

The third and final aspect of the classical theory that we have to note critically is its concept of capital entirely as circulating capital. Even at that early stage of modern economic growth in the European countries when they were writing, the classical writers were aware of the importance of fixed capital in the form of machinery, especially in the industrial sector. But to a great extent, the classicals explained the accumulation of such capital in the industrial sector as being determined by the rate of return that capitalists earned from the accumulation of circulating capital in the agricultural sector in the form of the Wage Fund. But even in the agricultural sector, more and more fixed capital came to be applied in such forms as agricultural machinery, irrigation works and the use of chemical fertilisers. The use of capital in these forms was an important source of the rapid growth of agricultural productivity of both land and labour in the DCs, and an important reason why the predictions of the classical theory failed to materialise in those countries. The classical theory has therefore been modified by the explicit introduction of fixed capital in Butt's theory of the mechanisation process summarised in sections 4.5 and 5.3 below.

4.3 THE NEO-CLASSICAL THEORY OF GROWTH

(a) Summary

By about 1870, the classical writings on economic theory were superseded by the rise of the marginal revolution. As we have seen, the classical economists had already been applying the techniques of marginal analysis to the production side, to explain, for example, the allocation of labour to different farms so as to equalise its marginal product, and the trends in the rate of profit. What the marginal revolution did, however, was to apply the same techniques on the demand side, in particular to use the notions of the marginal utility that consumers derived from commodities and hence to explain the prices of commodities in terms of their marginal utilities. Following from this, there was an intense development of neo-classical theory for nearly a century, mainly developing the consequences of the equilibrium functioning of efficient and competitive product and factor markets in an elegant theoretical structure. In the process, however, there was a pronounced shift of attention to the static problems of resource allocation away from the dynamic problems of economic growth, which had been a major concern of the classical economists.

In the early days after the Second World War, there was a revival of interest in problems of growth on the part of neo-classical economists. A number of factors contributed to this renewal of interest. On the one hand, the problems of promoting a faster development of the LDCs came to occupy the forefront of world attention. On the other hand, more detailed data about the past experience of growth in the DCs had been accumulated by historical research. The result was increasing curiosity about how growth takes place and how it can be accelerated. The result was the neo-classical theory of growth, developed by mainstream economists, who attacked this new problem with the analytical techniques that had been perfected for the static analysis of the problems of resource allocation in competitive market economies. The same tools were being applied to a different problem.

But the particular form that the neo-classical theory of growth took turned out to have been influenced by an almost accidental circumstance (see e.g. Solow, 1988, p. 307). This was the fact that in a series of writings starting in 1939, Harrod and later Domar applied some of the ideas of the new Keynesian theory in a dynamic context to argue that economic growth was a highly unstable phenomenon. This theory is discussed in more detail in chapter 8 (especially section 8.3). Here we only note that, apart from relying heavily on the Keynesian theory that investment was largely exogenous, and that the *ex post* equality of savings and investment was brought about by changes in income rather than by changes in such prices as the rate of interest, their theory was also based on certain highly simplifying assumptions such as a constant incremental capital–output ratio (ICOR). This created a challenge to neo-classical economists to produce an alternative theory which allowed for continuous variations in the capital–labour ratio leading to a growth process which was dynamically stable. Therefore, the main concern of the neo-classical theory of growth has been with questions of the dynamic stability of the growth process.

The neo-classical theory of growth was developed primarily to explain economic growth of the DCs, and is therefore set mainly in the context of an industrial economy. In such an economy, the two main factors of production are capital – 'the produced means of production' and labour. The theory is therefore primarily concerned with the way growth of output is influenced by the growth of labour, assumed to be given exogenously, and the growth of capital stock due to investment. It is based on the following chain of causation:

Income → Savings = Investment → Growth of Income

Let us start with the last link of this chain of causation. To explain this link in the argument, the theory assumes an aggregate production function of the form

$$Y = F(L,K) \tag{4.1}$$

showing aggregate output Y as a smooth (i.e. continuous) function of the quantities of the two factors of production, namely labour L and capital K. More for its analytical convenience than for its realism, this function is assumed to be linear homogeneous, i.e. subject to constant returns to scale. This assumption is chosen particularly because it enables total output to be distributed to the two factors at rates corresponding to their marginal products, relying on the Euler's Theorem property of such functions. Because of this assumption, the production function can be written in intensive form

$$y = f(k); \quad f'(k) > O; \quad f''(k) < O. \tag{4.2}$$

where y is output per worker and k is capital per worker. The function $f(k)$ is assumed to be subject to diminishing returns. The immediate implication of this assumption is that the growth of per capita income is due to the growth of capital per worker brought about by investment. Investment has therefore to perform two functions. On the one hand, it has to expand the capital stock in line with the growth of labour supply, assumed to be at an exogenously given constant rate n; this is known as the widening of capital. On the other hand, it has to expand the amount of capital that each labourer has to work with; this is known as the deepening of capital. It is the deepening of capital which leads to the growth of per capita income.

In the second link in the above chain of causation, it is assumed that the amount of investment undertaken in an economy will be equal to the amount of savings. In line with the neo-classical theory of the functioning of markets in general and of the capital market in particular, it is assumed that this equality of savings and investment is brought about by the flexibility of the rate of interest.

Finally, the way the volume of savings itself is determined is explained in the first link of the chain of causation in terms of savings behaviour in which savings are determined by the level of per capita income. In the simplest versions of the neo-classical theory of growth, the relationship between savings and income is assumed to be given by a constant rate of savings s. Hence, the investment per worker is just equal to $sf(k)$.

These three links in the chain of causation are then used to develop the neo-classical theory of growth. The main concern of the theory is to derive the endogenous rate of capital accumulation from the exogenous rate of growth of population and labour. An economy is said to be dynamically stable if the endogenous rate of capital accumulation converges to the exogenous rate of population growth. It then turns out that, on these assumptions, the one-sector model is dynamically stable (Solow, 1956; Swan, 1956). This follows quite simply from the following diagram (Figure 4.1), where $sf(k)$ represents investment per worker, while nk represents the investment per worker needed for capital widening at the capital–labour ratio k and the rate of population growth n. Hence $sf(k)$–nk represents the rate of capital deepening.

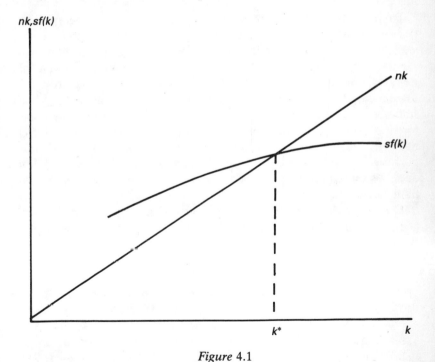

Figure 4.1

Given some simple assumptions about the production function, there is one level k^* of capital-intensity at which the two curves intersect. To the left of this point, $sf(k)>nk$ so that there is deepening of capital, tending to raise k towards k^*. To the right, $sf(k)<nk$ so that there is negative deepening of capital, tending to reduce k towards k^*. Hence, the economy tends towards the capital intensity k^* at which the rate of capital accumulation is just equal to the given rate of population growth. Hence, we get the fantastic result that the rate of capital accumulation and with it the rate of growth of GDP is tied to the rate of population growth, so that the brunt of explaining any growth of per capita income that may occur is thrown entirely on the rate of technological progress. In particular, the rate of growth of GDP does not depend at all on the rate of savings; the rate of savings only enters the model in determining the capital-intensity at which the model is dynamically stable, i.e. it only determines the level of income on the steady growth path rather than the rate of growth on this path.

There is also a two-sector version of the neo-classical theory. The two sectors are taken as those producing a composite consumer good and capital goods, a distinction first made by Marx. It has been shown that, on the usual neo-classical assumptions about the working of markets, this two-sector model is also dynamically stable provided certain conditions are fulfilled. One condition is that there should be sufficient substitutability between capital and labour in the two sectors (Uzawa, 1963). But this is not necessary. As Shinkai (1960) showed, the model may be dynamically stable even if factor proportions in the two sectors are fixed; in this case, dynamic stability depends on the consumer goods sector being more capital-intensive than the capital goods sector.

This theory has even been applied to explain the tendency that has been observed for income levels in the DCs to converge. For example, Barro (1984, pp. 288–9) has argued:

> Suppose that these countries are basically similar in terms of production functions, natural resources, and preferences. But at the starting date, which we take to be 1950, there are major differences across countries in the levels of capital stock per person. The countries that start with more capital per head should have higher initial values of output and consumption per head. But capital's marginal product is greater in the countries with less capital. Hence, these countries would invest a larger fraction of their output and, thereby, experience higher growth rates of capi-

tal, output, and consumption. Eventually, we predict that each country approaches the same path of steady-state growth. As predicted, the countries with the lower starting values of output (and capital) per person are the ones that tend to grow faster.

In this argument, the whole burden of the explanation of convergence is thrown on the capital accumulation process. (For an alternative explanation in terms of technological progress, see section 6.3 below.)

(b) Critique

Although there has been a lot of elaboration of the theory, the basic model is still the one that was developed in the 1950s and 1960s. The same model is discussed in the growth section of countless textbooks on macroeconomics to this day. It is therefore necessary to examine its weaknesses in some detail.

The first point to note is that the development of this theory has been based largely on logical curiosity, in particular about the possibility of steady growth equilibria rather than on explaining observed growth experiences. By restricting the analysis to the case of linear homogeneous production functions, it ignores the case of increasing returns which has played an important role in economic growth, especially in the industrial sector (see Chapter 5). To the extent that it refers to actual data at all, it is an attempt to explain 'the broad facts about the growth of advanced industrial economies' (Solow, 1970 p. 2). Because such economies were thought to have experienced some steady rates of growth, Solow (1970, p. 7) suggested that 'the steady state is at least not a bad place for the theory of growth to start'; however, he also went on to say that 'it may be a dangerous place for it to end'. In particular, the theory has little to contribute to the explanation of the tendency for some deceleration of growth that has been observed even in these advanced industrial economies.

Even in the case of the advanced industrial economies, the theory is based on a few 'stylised facts'. According to Kaldor (1961, p. 178), there were six such 'remarkable historical constancies', namely:

1. growth of output and labour productivity 'at a steady trend rate' with 'no recorded tendency for a falling rate of growth of productivity';
2. a continued increase in the amount of capital per worker;

3. a 'steady' rate of profit on capital;
4. 'steady capital-output ratios over long periods';
5. a steady share of profits and of wages; and mainly on theoretical grounds;
6. little deviation, over the long term, from full employment of labour.

These facts were also identified as the six basic trends of economic development by Samuelson (1980, p. 691). But after carefully checking these claims against historical statistics from some of the advanced industrial countries, especially Britain, and considering some serious conceptual problems involved in the statistical estimates, Hacche (1979, p. 254) has suggested that these 'stylised facts may turn out to be more stylised than factual'. In addition, one of the most important stylised facts of economic growth has been neglected in the development of the theory. As Hahn and Matthews (1964, p. 39) say in their survey article, 'Inasmuch as economic growth in practice is observed to be intimately associated with changes in the structure of production, this reduces the real-life applicability of the steady growth concept'.

The reasons why the theory does not explain the actual experience of economic growth may be examined by considering the three links of the chain of causation referred to above. In the first place, the relationship between investment and growth of output in practice is not as strong as postulated in the third link of the argument. Instead, a much more important influence on economic growth seems to be that due to technological progress. Secondly, the assumption that it is savings that determines investment is contrary to the entire Keynesian theory.

The third problem with this theory is the assumption that savings are determined by the level of income, as postulated in the first link of the argument of the neo-classical model. Instead of this relationship, it is more likely that savings are determined by investment opportunities. For example, an important reason for the low rate of savings in some of the poor countries is the lack of profitable opportunities to invest. If such opportunities exist, the required savings would generally be forthcoming. This is because the rate of savings depends not so much on the average level of income as on its distribution. This point has been particularly stressed by Lewis (1955, p. 236):

No nation is so poor that it could not save 12 per cent of its national income if it wanted to; poverty had never prevented nations from launching upon wars, or from wasting their substance in other ways. Least of all can those nations plead poverty as an excuse for not saving, in which 40 per cent or so of the national income is squandered by the top 10 per cent of income receivers, living luxuriously on rents. In such countries, productive investment is not small because there is no surplus; it is small because the surplus is used to maintain unproductive hordes of retainers, and to build pyramids, temples and other durable consumer goods, instead of to create productive capital.

He has repeated this argument again on a later occasion (Lewis, 1982, pp. 105–6):

The savings ratio is not an obstacle. It depends endogenously on the rate of growth; it is low when the growth rate is low, as in contemporary USA, and high when the growth rate is high, as in contemporary Japan. In a mature economy, productive investment gets the first call on savings, in the sense that entrepreneurs can always raise the money needed to finance productive investment. As Phelps Brown (1968) has suggested, in a mature economy the supply of savings to business enterprise becomes infinitely elastic at some modest rate of return (say a real rate of around 12 per cent net of tax). If there is not enough saving for all the intended projects, public and private, it is the public sector which runs short. The country then borrows from abroad – fast growers can always borrow. In any case, fast growth changes the relative share of profits, by increasing government receipts faster than government expenditures, and by mobilising private savings that would otherwise not occur.

Apart from these considerations, entrepreneurs finance their investments not so much by drawing directly on savings, but rather by borrowing from banks. Banks can lend for investment more than the amount of voluntary savings, because they not only lend the savings deposited with them but can also create credit. This is why Schumpeter (1934) assigned a key role to banks in the development process, and Gerschenkron (1962, p. 14) spoke of their 'truly momentous role as specific agents of industrialisation in a backward country'. If banks lend more than the voluntary savings of households, there may be inflation but this leads to 'forced' savings sufficient to finance investment. Even more important, individual countries may finance their investment by borrowing from other countries with surplus funds to lend. Contrary to the traditional assumption of trade theory, there was a considerable international flow of capital in the nineteenth and twentieth centuries.

In view of these sources of funds for investment, we may conclude that countries, both developed and less-developed, usually have a quite elastic supply of capital with which to finance their investment. In fact, Nurkse (1958, cited in Meier, 1976, p. 642) even argued that 'In my presentation, balanced growth is an exercise in economic development with unlimited supplies of capital, analogous to Professor Lewis's celebrated exercise in development with unlimited labour supplies'.

Given such an elastic supply of funds for investment, it is not the domestic rate of savings which determines the level of investment in a country. Instead, it is more likely to be determined by the expectations that entrepreneurs hold about the future profitability of their investments. Apart from this, another important influence on investment is technological progress, which makes investment profitable. As Lewis has argued:

> Civilisations in which there is rapid growth of technical knowledge or expansion of other opportunities present more profitable outlets for investment than do technologically stagnant civilisations, and tempt capital into productive channels than into the building of monuments (1954, p. 416). Not having new technology to invest shows up as a low propensity to save. Underdeveloped countries have plenty of rich people who have traditionally spent their incomes on hordes of servants, courtiers, armies and entertainers. Saving is a function of the opportunity to invest (1978, p. 155).

Similarly, Bauer and Yamey (1957, p. 12) argued that 'it is often nearer the truth to say that capital is created in the process of development than that development is a function of capital accumulation'. This is also what Hicks meant when he described modern economic growth as a process in which capital accumulation was continually racing to catch up with advancing technology.

4.4 THE DUALISTIC GROWTH MODEL OF LEWIS

(a) Summary

The neo-classical theory discussed in the last section was an attempt to explain economic growth primarily in terms of capital accumulation resulting from some simple assumptions about savings behaviour. Apart from the weaknesses pointed out above, this theory does not seem able to account for the high rate of growth that was actually achieved by the developed countries during the period of their modern economic growth. Another problem with the theory is that it does not distinguish between different sectors of the economy; therefore, it does not take account of the extent to which the acceleration of growth during this period was associated with a rapid rate of industrialisation. Further, it also assumes that labour is always fully employed; therefore it does not take account of the reserves of under-employed labour with which the process of modern economic growth began in the developed countries.

We therefore consider the theory of dualistic development advanced by Lewis (1954), which attempts to remedy these weaknesses of the neo-classical theory, by incorporating some features of the classical model of growth. Lewis's theory is also an attempt to explain economic growth primarily in terms of capital accumulation, but it is particularly concerned to explain a rapid rise in the savings ratio, say from a low level around 5 per cent to a high level around 12 per cent in a relatively short period. In order to show how such a rapid rise in the savings ratio occurred, Lewis divides the economy into two sectors – a traditional sector and a modern sector, in contrast to the division between the consumer goods and capital goods sector of the neo-classical model. The dualistic model then traces the process of transition from a traditional economy largely based on agriculture to a modern economy with a large industrial sector.

Lewis assumed the traditional sector to consist mainly of self-employed people, typically peasants cultivating a family farm with their family labour. In this sector, there is surplus labour in the sense that withdrawing labour will not reduce the output of the sector. This does not mean that the marginal product of labour is zero; instead, it implies that the remaining workers will increase their labour effort to produce the same output as before. The essential feature of the modern sector is that it is capitalistic, i.e. it is run by capitalists who hire labour at a wage to make a profit. Thus, the modern sector is not necessarily the same as the industrial or the urban sectors, though the capitalistic feature is more prominent in these sectors.

Because it is assumed that the traditional sector consists typically of family agricultural enterprises, the standard of living of workers in this sector is determined by the average product of labour. This is sometimes described as the subsistence level, but the concept is different from that of the classical economists. Under these conditions, workers in the traditional sector move to the modern sector only if the wage offered there is at least equal to the average product of labour in the traditional sector. At that wage, there is an 'unlimited' supply of labour, i.e. a perfectly elastic supply.

The modern sector uses labour and capital in a neo-classical way. In this sector, the stock of capital determines the marginal product of labour, and employment is determined at the point where the marginal product of labour equals the wage rate. Thus, it is the wage which determines employment rather than employment determining wages. The model is set in historical motion by the accumulation of capital. The accumulation of capital is determined by the propensity of capitalists to save out of their profit incomes. However, profits grow rapidly, as labour is available to the modern sector at a constant wage so long as there is surplus labour in the traditional sector. Therefore, capital accumulates at a rapid rate in the modern sector. The effect of capital accumulation is to absorb the surplus labour of the traditional sector into the modern sector. The process goes on until a turning point is reached when all surplus labour is absorbed, the marginal product of labour becomes equal in both sectors, and the economy enters into its neo-classical phase. When the process is completed, the centre of gravity of the economy will have shifted from the traditional or agricultural sector to the modern or industrial sector. The model has also been developed in a number of versions taking account of both the movement of labour and the trade in commodities between the two sectors and with the rest of the world.

(b) Critique

The model was constructed out of, and designed to explain, European and especially British experience of economic development. Hence, it is fairly consistent with that history. But it is not so satisfactory in explaining other histories, especially that of LDCs either in the historical period or in the more recent post-war period.

It is especially with regard to its application to LDCs that the model has been subject to severe criticism (see e.g. Singh, 1975).

The model depends on two basic assumptions, namely surplus labour in the traditional sector and a high propensity to save out of profit incomes in the modern sector. The surplus labour assumption has been most severely criticised on the ground that the marginal product of labour in the traditional sector of LDCs is not zero but, as Lewis (1972) himself has stressed, the concept of surplus labour does not depend only on this interpretation. In fact, it cannot be denied that a large fraction of the rural labour force is seriously under-employed, especially in the more densely populated LDCs. The more serious problem is that, even if there is surplus labour, the supply of labour to the modern sector is not necessarily perfectly elastic. This has been recognised by Lewis (1972) himself when he says, 'When we turn to the less developed countries of our own time and ask what is happening to the industrial wage, the answer, from a very large number, if not from all, is that the wage is rising, even in situations where there is open mass urban unemployment, not to speak of under-employment'.

A more serious problem relates to the assumption of a high propensity to save in the modern sector. The data from many countries suggests that savings have not risen with the growth of incomes as rapidly as assumed in the model. Hence Singh, (1975, p. 236) has concluded that: 'When we come to testing, we find the dualistic models as a whole falsified. This is so most clearly with respect to saving and investment behaviour, which Lewis justly thought to be the central feature of the phenomenon of development.'

The main reason is that savings do not depend only on incomes but, as Lewis himself has argued, on the opportunities for profitable investment. Without such opportunities, rising incomes are mostly spent on unproductive and conspicuous consumption both at home and abroad. But when such opportunities arise, the required savings will be forthcoming from various sources. Hence, the central problem of economic development is not just a rise in the savings ratio, but rather the growth in the opportunities for profitable investment. This is true as much in LDCs at present as it was in the historical experience of the DCs, about which Landes (1969, pp. 77–8) says:

it was in large measure the pressure of demand on the mode of production that called forth the new techniques in Britain, and the abundant, responsive supply of the factors that made possible their rapid exploitation and diffusion. The point will bear stressing, the more so as economists, particularly theorists, are inclined to concentrate exclusively on the supply side. The student of economic development, impressed on the one hand by the high cost of industrialisation, on the other by the low level of savings in underdeveloped countries, has devoted most of his attention to the problem of capital formation: on ways to raise the rate of net investment from, say, 5 per cent to 12 or more; and on devices to prevent increased income from dissipating itself on increased consumption.

4.5 THE MECHANISATION PROCESS OF BUTT

(a) Summary

One of the main weaknesses of the classical theory of growth is its reliance on capital in its circulating form rather than in the form of fixed capital. This weakness is remedied to some extent in the neo-classical theory, but a serious weakness of that theory is its failure to distinguish between different types of consumer goods and the differences in the way they are produced in different sectors. As we have argued, these differences play an important role in the structural transformation that generally accompanies the growth process. Therefore, it is useful to consider another theory of growth which takes more account both of fixed capital and of differences between commodities, and the sectors in which they are produced. Such a theory has been advanced by Butt (1960). As this theory also relies heavily on supply factors, especially the role of capital accumulation in economic growth, we summarise it briefly in this section.

In order to bring out the role of capital as clearly as possible, Butt distinguishes sharply between two types of techniques. One type consists of 'handicraft' techniques, which use labour alone to produce different commodities. Units are defined so that one unit of labour produces one unit of output of each commodity. Taking the wage rate as the numeraire, this means that the price of commodities produced by the handicraft techniques is 1. The other type consists of 'mechanised' techniques, which produce commodities using both labour and capital. Capital is measured in units, described as machines, each unit being the quantity that can be produced by one worker using the handicraft technique. The mechanised technique in the i-th sector is described by the quantity of labour, A_i and the quantity of capital, C_i used to produce one unit of output. The productivity of capital S_i is measured by the saving in labour cost as a ratio of the amount of capital used, i.e. as $(1 - A) / C$, and varies from sector to sector. Sectors may therefore be arranged according to their capital productivity, and named in alphabetical order so that

$$S_a > S_b > \ ..... \ S_n > 0 > S_p > \ ..... > S_z$$

In some sectors the productivity of capital is less than zero; therefore, mechanised techniques will never be used in these sectors, which remain ineluctably handicraft sectors.

As capital accumulates, it is first used to mechanise the A-sector. The mechanisation of the A-sector has two phases. In the first phase, both handicraft and mechanised techniques are used, so that the price of the product remains 1. In this phase, the saving in wage cost accrues as profit on capital; the rate of profit in this phase is equal to the productivity of capital in the A-sector. As the stock of machines rises, the mechanisation of the A-sector enters its second phase, when the output of A produced by the mechanised technique alone is sufficient to meet the whole demand, and the sector is completely mechanised. With further accumulation of capital, the supply of A output from the mechanised technique grows faster than demand at the initial price, and the price of A, p_a falls below unity. The rate of profit then becomes

$$r_t = (p_a - A_a) / C_a \qquad (4.3)$$

With further accumulation of capital, the price of A falls, and with it, the rate of profit until it becomes equal to the productivity of capital in the B-sector. Then, the margin of mechanisation moves to the B-sector. The mechanisation of the B-sector also passes through two phases, with the rate of profit falling further in the second phase. The margin of mechanisation then moves to the C-sector, and so on down the alphabet. Alongside, there is a steady fall in the rate of profit as in the classical theory, but this time it is due to the steady shift of the margin of mechanisation through the various sectors, as illustrated in Figure 4.2.

In this figure, the productivity of capital in the various sectors is shown by the flat lines, reflecting the assumption of fixed coefficients between labour, capital and output. The horizontal sections of the r_t

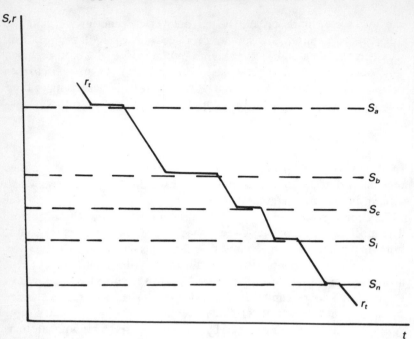

Figure 4.2

curve represent the first phase of the mechanisation of each sector, and the downward sloping sections represent the second phase.

There are a number of possible outcomes. The progress of mechanisation depends on the rate of capital accumulation, and the rate of population growth. Population growth is assumed to follow the demographic transition theory. So long as the capital stock grows faster than population, the process of mechanisation moves forward. If in the process, incomes rise to the point where its marginal utility becomes zero, further growth will cease and the economy will have reached the state of Bliss identified by Ramsey (1928). Alternatively, further accumulation of capital may cease because the rate of profit declines to zero – the stage of the 'euthanasia of the rentier'; this is the state of Exhaustion corresponding to the classical Stationary State, when the 'full possibilities of capitalism are realized'. Yet another possibility is that further accumulation ceases because the rate of profit has become too low, even though it is still positive; this is the state of Premature Stagnation. Finally, there is the case when the rate of capital accumulation is equal to the rate of population growth at an earlier stage; then the economy will be stuck in a 'spreading stationary state', referred to by Marshall (1961, p. 368; see also Pigou, 1935, pp. 5, 267).

A particularly interesting application of the model is to the mechanisation of the agricultural sector, which is discussed in the next chapter.

(b) Critique

The model is based on very simple assumptions about production conditions (fixed factor proportions) and about market performance (equilibrium and full employment at all times). It does not take account of technological progress. To some extent, these assumptions can be relaxed, but such severe simplifications have been introduced in order to construct a model which shows the growth process in much greater structural detail than most others. The main theme of the theory is to bring out the importance of distinguishing different sectors of the economy, especially the sequence in which they are mechanised. This sequence is one of the main reasons for differences in the growth rate of labour productivity in different sectors, which were identified as one of the major structural determinants of growth in Chapter 3. Thus, an important reason for the slow growth of labour productivity in agriculture and services is the fact that the possibilities of mechanisation of these sectors are limited, in the sense that the productivity of capital in these sectors is low, while the growth of labour productivity is much higher in the industrial sector because it has much greater possibilities of being mechanised in the sense of this model.

To sum up, the present chapter has been concerned with the role of supply factors – land, labour, capital and technology – in the growth process. Most of the current literature on growth theory has concentrated on these factors, and we have illustrated the main thrust of the argument by considering some of the leading theories on the subject, namely: the classical theory set in the context of the agricultural sector and dealing with the effects of population growth on limited land; the neo-classical theory set in the context of the industrial sector and dealing with the interaction between population growth and capital accumulation; the dualistic theory of Lewis mainly concerned with capital accumulation in the modern sector in the special case of an unlimited supply of labour from the traditional sector; and the mechanisation model of Butt dealing with a wider variety of sectors and dealing with all three factors of production.

While these supply factors are certainly important, these theories on the whole do not provide a satisfactory explanation of growth as it has occurred in practice. Thus, the classical theory with its prediction of a declining rate of growth, and the neo-classical theory with its prediction of a steady rate of growth, are both inconsistent with the logistic pattern of growth as actually observed. One reason is the neglect of demand factors, to be considered in Part III of the book. Another reason is that, these theories have not taken full account of the dominance of different sectors at different stages of the growth process. In Chapter 3, we have already considered the crucial importance of this consideration in explaining the logistic pattern. We consider this relationship in more detail in the next three chapters.

5 Growth in The Agricultural Sector

5.1 PATTERNS OF AGRICULTURAL GROWTH

As discussed in the last chapter, prevailing theories have sought to explain growth by taking the economy as a whole, though the assumptions about the economy have been derived from the characteristics of particular sectors. Thus, the classical theory was based on the agricultural economy, and the neo-classical theory on the industrial economy. The Lewis model distinguishes two sectors, but the main concern is with the growth of the modern or industrial sector, with the traditional sector only playing the role of supplying labour to the modern sector at a constant wage rate. It is only in the Butt model that all sectors of the economy are considered, and the growth process explained in terms of the sequence in which different sectors are mechanised by the introduction of fixed capital.

In fact, a significant feature of the growth process is that it has been associated with a systematic structural transformation of the economy, in terms of the changing sectoral composition of GDP and the changing sectoral allocation of labour. Therefore, any theory of growth must take full account of this association. This is the special feature of the model developed in Chapter 3. In that model, the structural transformation of the economy played a central role in explaining the logistic pattern of growth, in which the growth process follows an S-curve, whereas the classical theory developed in the context of the agricultural sector led to a declining rate of growth, and the neo-classical theory developed in the context of an industrial economy led to steady rates of growth. However, the prototype model of Chapter 3 was based on particular assumptions about the key parameters, such as the income elasticities of demand and the rates of growth of labour productivity in the various sectors. These parameters, however, vary between countries and over time in individual counties, leading to differences in their S-curves. Economists have, of course, discussed these parameters in their microeconomic theories, though this discussion is not fully integrated with their growth theories. The general tendency, however, has been to explain these parameters in terms of relative factor and commodity prices. In fact, however, they are also much influenced by other factors, especially institutional factors. We therefore proceed to consider how all these factors have influenced growth in each of the three major sectors into which the economy is usually divided. In particular, we shall consider these influences in an historical perspective covering long periods of time.

We begin with the agricultural sector, which is the dominant sector in the earliest phase of the growth process. In this phase, agriculture accounts for a large share of GDP because, at the prevailing low level of income, consumers spend the bulk of their incomes on food produced in the agricultural sector. Agriculture also employs a high proportion of the labour force, because the productivity of labour in the agricultural sector is low. Because of the dominance of agriculture in this phase, the overall growth rate is heavily influenced by the growth rate of agriculture. In this sector, land is a very important factor of production, and the area of cultivable land cannot be easily expanded, especially in long-settled countries. Therefore, the growth of agricultural production is subject to the powerful force of diminishing returns in the course of population growth, except to the extent to which it is offset by technological progress. Further, the extent to which fixed capital can be invested to substitute for the growing scarcity of land and thus to stave off the full force of diminishing returns is limited at the low levels of income prevailing in the early phases of the growth process.

However, the rate of agricultural growth has varied greatly between different countries. Long-term historical data on agricultural growth and the factors influencing that process are not available on a comparable basis for a large number of countries. Therefore, to begin with, we rely primarily on data for two or three decades of the post-war period, which are now available for a much larger number of countries. These data will then be supplemented as far as possible by information covering longer periods for particular countries to illustrate special points of the argument.

The most comprehensive data for the post-war period are those compiled by Hayami and Ruttan (2nd ed, 1985). A serious problem in the study of agricultural growth is that the agricultural sector produces a wide variety of products. In order to deal with this problem, Hayami and Ruttan combined the data on agricultural output into wheat units on the basis of their relative prices. They have also presented data on agricultural land and the agricultural labour force. Because of considerable confusion and great differences

Table 5.1   Changes in output per agricultural worker, yields, and
land–man ratios: 1960–80

Country Groups	Output (tons, wheat units) per worker 1960	1980	Yields per ha. 1960	1980	Ha. per male worker 1960	1980
DCs						
(a) Land abundant	83.1	197.3	0.43	0.62	171.9	265.8
(b) Medium	34.1	102.4	2.33	3.68	14.9	27.9
(c) Land scarce	22.6	69.6	2.27	3.61	6.4	12.4
(c) Japan	10.3	27.8	8.64	12.23	1.2	2.3
LDCs						
(a) Land abundant	11.3	20.8	0.28	0.42	60.0	62.1
(b) Medium	7.2	12.7	0.48	0.76	15.2	15.5
(c) Land scarce	5.5	10.5	1.26	1.91	1.9	1.7

Country Classification:
DCs:
(a) Land abundant: Australia, Canada, New Zealand, South Africa, USA
(b) Medium: Austria, Denmark, Finland, France, Ireland, Israel,
                     Norway, Sweden, UK
(c) Land scarce: Belgium, W. Germany, Greece, Italy, Netherlands,
                     Portugal, Spain, Switzerland, Yugoslavia.
(c) Extreme:
    Land scarcity: Japan
LDCs:
(a) Land abundant: Argentina, Chile, Libya, Paraguay, Peru, Syria,
                     Venezuela.
(b) Medium: Brazil, Colombia, Mexico, Turkey.
(c) Land scarce: Bangladesh, Egypt, India, Mauritius, Pakistan,
                     Philippines, Sri Lanka, Surinam, Taiwan.

Source: Hayami and Ruttan (1985), table 5.1, p. 120.

between countries in defining how far female workers, who work on
their family farms only for some periods and only in some operations,
should be included in the agricultural labour force, Hayami and
Ruttan have only taken male workers in agriculture into account.
They have presented these data for 44 countries for two years, 1960
and 1980. Based on these data, Table 5.1 shows the changes in output
per male worker, the yield per hectare, and the land–man ratio
(hectares per male worker). In this table, countries have been
grouped according to their relative land abundance, separately for
developed and less-developed countries.

Table 5.2   Components of increases in agricultural output: 1960–80

Group	Annual average growth rate of Output	Area	Due to increases in: Labour intensity	Due to increases in: Labour productivity	Yields
DCs:					
Land Abundant	2.35	0.15	–2.15	4.35	2.20
Medium	1.96	–0.42	–3.85	6.23	2.38
Land Scarce	2.01	–0.40	–3.81	6.22	2.41
Japan	1.23	–0.59	–3.70	5.52	1.82
LDCs:					
Land Abundant	3.03	0.36	–0.45	3.12	2.67
Medium	3.18	0.51	–0.13	2.80	2.67
Land Scarce	2.73	0.59	0.24	1.90	2.14

Source: Derived from Table 5.1.

The principal conclusion that emerges from this table is that the productivity of labour (the output per worker) is lower in the land scarce countries than in the land abundant countries, both among DCs and among LDCs. This is because, while the yield of land per hectare is greater in the land scarce countries, the higher yield is not sufficient to offset the much smaller area of land per agricultural worker in these countries.

The second point to note in the table is that, in all groups, there was an increase in the output per worker during the two decades of the period. In the DCs, this was due both to a rise in yields and a significant increase in the area cultivated by each worker, mainly because of an absolute decline in the size of the agricultural labour force. In the LDCs, the rise in output per worker was mostly due to a rise in the yield of land; the area cultivated by each worker actually declined in the most land scarce countries, and increased only slightly in other LDCs.

An alternative way of analysing the data is shown in Table 5.2, which divides the annual growth rates of agricultural output for the various groups of countries into three components, namely the growth due to area extension, changes in labour intensity, and to changes in the productivity of labour. Such a decomposition can be done in different ways, and will give different estimates of the various components depending on the sequence in which they are estimated. In order to avoid the effects due to any arbitrariness in this procedure, we consider all possible sequences in which these components may be estimated and take the average. This leads to a decomposition based on the following identity:

$$Y_1 - Y_0 = [(b_0 + b_1)(c_0 + c_1) + (b_0 c_0 + b_1 c_1)] (a_1 - a_0)/6$$
due to area extension

$$+ [(a_0 + a_1)(c_0 + c_1) + (a_0 c_0 + a_1 c_1)] (b_1 - b_0)/6$$
due to increase of labour intensity

$$+ [(a_0 + a_1)(b_0 + b_1) + (a_0 b_0 + a_1 b_1)] (c_1 - c_0)/6$$
due to increase of labour productivity

where Y is output; a = area; b = labour intensity, i.e. amount of labour per hectare; and c = labour productivity, i.e. output per worker; with suffix 0 for the initial year and suffix 1 for the final year. The sum of the last two components, therefore, indicates the growth due to increases in yields, i.e. output per hectare.

LDCs increased their agricultural output faster than the DCs, enabling them to cope with a faster growth of population and also to increase their levels of nutrition from its previous low levels. One reason was that area under cultivation expanded in the LDCs, while it contracted in the DCs. Further, yields also rose faster in the LDCs, though they were still lower than in the DCs. The faster growth of yields in the LDCs was due mainly to the development of a new agricultural technology in a number of international agricultural research centres. This technology was based on new varieties of seed which were more responsive to the use of fertilisers, and which was spread by greater investments in irrigation. In the DCs and in the more land abundant LDCs, there was a decline in labour intensity, so that most of the growth of yields was accompanied by a rise in labour productivity. By contrast, labour intensity increased in the land scarce LDCs.

This analysis shows the part played by area extension, labour intensity of cultivation, and increases in labour productivity in the recent growth of agricultural output in DCs and LDCs. The historical growth of agricultural output in these countries can also be explained in terms of these components. Some theoretical explanations relating to these elements are discussed below.

(a) Area Extension

The classical economists set the fashion of assuming the supply of land to be fixed over time. This is, of course, true in the sense of the

Table 5.3   Per capita adjusted geographical area and the proportion of arable land; selected Asian countries around 1980

	Per capita geographical area (Ha)	Per capita adjusted area (Ha)	Arable land as % of adjusted area
Bangladesh	.16	.11	91
India	.48	.28	87
China	.96	.31	32
Sri Lanka	.44	.18	72
Pakistan	.93	.33	72
Indonesia	1.28	.36	37
Thailand	1.09	.50	78
Philippines	.61	.31	77
South Korea	.26	.09	6
Malaysia	2.33	.67	46
Taiwan	.20	–	–
LDCs (Average)	2.38	.75	32
Japan	.32	.09	45
DMEs (Average)	4.17	1.41	36

Source: FAO Production Yearbooks.

total geographical area of countries, which can change only by gains or losses through conquest. But within a given geographical area, the area available for cultivation may vary from time to time. To estimate this area, we must allow for that part of the total geographical area which is not usable because it consists of mountainous territory and deserts or is too heavily forested. A rough estimate of the usable area may be obtained by converting the total area into arable land equivalents, for example, by giving a weight of 1 to arable land, 0.5 to permanent pasture land, 0.2 to forest and woodland, and 0.1 to other land, as classified in the FAO Production Yearbooks. The results for Asian countries are shown in Table 5.3.

The area actually cultivated is generally less than the adjusted geographical area shown in this table, and varies over time. Ricardo explained this variation in terms of the differences in fertility of the soil in different regions, arguing that labour was allocated to different regions so as to make the marginal product of labour the same in all farms. This meant that labour was first allocated to the most fertile areas, and the margin of cultivation was gradually extended to the less and less fertile areas as the marginal product of labour declined on the intra-marginal farms.

In fact, however, the extension of area involved a considerable amount of effort in clearing forests, filling swamps, and irrigating dry lands. Such area extension takes place when land becomes scarce relative to demand. For example, more area is brought under cultivation when there is a new demand for crops which can be grown on such land. One of the most dramatic examples of such area extension was the reclamation of the Irrawaddy Delta in Lower Burma, by which about 4 million hectares were brought under cultivation from the mid-nineteenth to the mid-twentieth century, especially after the opening up of the Suez Canal made the production of rice for export highly profitable. The process has been described by Furnivall (1931, p. 45) as follows: 'In Lower Burma we have had a vast area of thick jungle with a secure rainfall rapidly brought under cultivation by peasant cultivators with seasonal labour and a ready supply of capital producing a single crop for the export market. It is doubtful whether the same combination of circumstances has ever existed anywhere else.' (See also Aye Hlaing, 1965.)

In most cases, the area under cultivation has been extended in response to increasing demand for food due to population growth. This suggests that long settled countries, with a high density of population, would generally have a high proportion of their adjusted geographical area under cultivation. The interesting thing, however, is that, even among such long settled countries, there is much variation in the proportion of the adjusted geographical area which is cultivated, as shown in the third column of Table 5.3. This is because countries can respond to increasing population pressure in two ways, either by extending the area under cultivation or by intensifying cultivation on a more limited area. These two routes are illustrated most clearly by India and China. India, where cultivated area is a high proportion of the adjusted geographical area, seems to have followed the extensification route, and extended the area under cultivation. The process continued even after independence until the mid-1960s, when area extension contributed nearly as much to growth of food output as the growth of yields due to the Green Revolution (Sundrum, 1987, table 5.11, p. 117). By contrast, China, with a relatively low proportion of adjusted geographical area under cultivation, has relied more heavily on the route of intensive cultivation on a more limited area of land. Following this route, 'The nation had perfected the labour-intensive economy, and the world marvelled at the ingenuity with which this had been achieved' (Lewis, 1978, p. 207). The reason why some countries have been able to feed their growing populations by more intensive use of labour on a limited area of land, while others have done so more by extending the area under cultivation, lies in the nature of their economic institutions; some of the relevant aspects of these institutions are discussed in the next section.

A third mechanism by which countries have coped with population pressure and the growing demand for agricultural output is illustrated by the experience of the advanced countries. These countries have increased the productivity of their land mainly by more intensive use of capital. There has therefore been less pressure for extending the area under cultivation. Instead, the progress of urbanisation has been so rapid that there has even been a decline in land under cultivation in these countries, mainly to provide for the expansion of urban areas.

(b) Labour Intensity of Cultivation

Given the area of cultivable land, the agricultural productivity of labour depends on the labour intensity with which that land is cultivated. In the Ricardian theory summarised in section 4.2, it was assumed that the labour intensity at any time was determined by the relationship between land area and population size at that time, with population growth being determined by the expansion of the Wage Fund. We also saw how some of its assumptions failed to materialise in subsequent history, particularly the Malthusian assumption regarding demographic behaviour. Instead, population growth followed a different course, slowing down significantly in the DCs as their per capita income rose beyond a certain level, but accelerating in the LDCs beyond the rate indicated by the subsistence level, mainly due to exogenous factors. The classical theory also assumed full employment of labour at all times. By contrast, the dualistic theory of Lewis, summarised in section 4.4, was based on the assumption of surplus labour in the agricultural sector, taken as the traditional sector, but that theory assumed that production in the traditional sector was carried out by peasants employing their family labour on their own farms.

In fact, however, the labour intensity of cultivation and the growth of labour productivity vary greatly between countries. These differences are due to a number of factors. One is clearly the growth of population. But there are also a number of other factors, such as the following:

Growth of the Non-agricultural Sector

For any given rate of growth of total labour force, the growth of the agricultural labour force depends on the rate at which the growing labour force is absorbed in the non-agricultural sectors. The growth of the non-agricultural sectors was rapid in the DCs, but much slower in the LDCs, leading to a faster growth of the agricultural labour force in these countries.

Extension of Land Frontier

For a given rate of growth of the agricultural labour force, the way the labour intensity of cultivation varies depends on the extent to which cultivated area is extended. Differences in the rate at which the land frontier was extended in different countries were discussed above.

Institutions of Land Tenure

Then, we have to consider the role of different institutions of land tenure. At least two major types may be distinguished, with innumerable variations around them. One is the system of peasant family production assumed in the Lewis model. The other is the case of land divided into large estates, owned by landlords, and cultivated with hired labour, as assumed in the classical model. The difference between these forms is clearly very important in determining the productivity of labour in the agricultural sector. In the case of peasant production, with the growth of population and increasing amounts of family labour relative to the size of the family farm, the family farm will be cultivated more and more intensively until the marginal product of labour declines to near zero. But in the case of the capitalist farm, the employment of labour will be limited to the point where its marginal product equals the wage rate at which labour can get alternative employment. In both cases, the available stock of land may be insufficient to provide employment for the available labour force, so that there may be considerable under-employment among the landless labourers.

Inequality of Land Ownership

In addition, the labour intensity of cultivation will also depend on how the distribution of land varies in the course of population growth. One leading theory on this question is that of Marx, who assumed that the tendency for increasing concentration which he observed in the case of industrial capital also applied to the case of agricultural land. But an alternative theory was advanced by the Russian economist, Chayanov (1966), who argued that the ability of small farmers to cultivate their family farms more intensively may provide a check to the tendency towards increasing concentration.

In practice, the position has varied in different countries. Some countries, such as Pakistan, seem to have followed the Marxist hypothesis, so that in fact there has been a rise in the average holding size together with an increase in landlessness. On the other hand, the trends in land distribution in some densely populated countries, such as India and Indonesia, seem to have been more consistent with the Chayanov than the Marxian hypothesis, so that there has been a steady decline in average holding size, and hence an increase in labour intensity of cultivation. However, the process is also influenced by institutions of property rights in land. For example, in India, the British colonial administration vested such property rights on some large farmers, leading to a more unequal distribution of land than in other countries such as Indonesia. In some other countries, such as Thailand and Philippines, there has been a rise in the proportion of total area consisting of relatively large holdings.

Leasing of Land

When the ownership of land is very unequally distributed, one way of cultivating large estates is by hired labour; in this case, the land may not be very intensively cultivated, and labour productivity may not grow rapidly. But it is also possible that parcels of land are leased out to tenant farmers. If tenant farmers also use their family labour to maximise output, land will be cultivated more intensively than in the case of hired labour. The prevalence of the leasing of land also varies from country to country, being greater in countries such as China and Japan than in other countries of Asia.

(c) Land and Labour Productivity

So far we have been considering the ways in which the labour intensity of cultivation rises in the course of population growth. Now, we consider the factors influencing the yield of land in the process. As land is more and more intensively cultivated, there is a steady rise in the yield of land, but the application of more and more labour to a

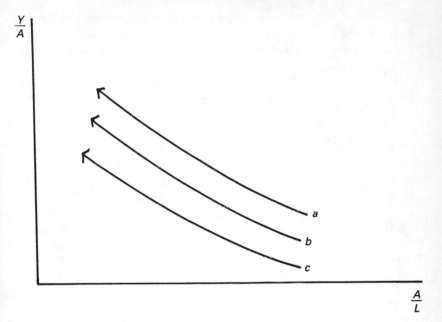

Figure 5.1

given plot of land will be subject to diminishing returns. Therefore, yields will rise less than proportionately with the amount of labour applied to each hectare of land, and output per worker will fall. A convenient way to represent these tendencies is illustrated in Figure 5.1.

In this figure, the area cultivated by each worker is measured on the horizontal axis, so that increasing labour intensity is shown by a movement from right to left. The output per hectare, i.e. the yield of land, is measured on the vertical axis. The relationship between yield and labour intensity is then shown by a curve which rises as we move from right to left. If this curve is a rectangular hyperbola, the output per worker will be constant at all points. But because of diminishing returns, this curve will be flatter than the rectangular hyperbola, and will not rise as steeply towards the left, as labour intensity of cultivation increases.

One point to note is that the relationship between yield and labour intensity will not be the same in all countries, and cannot therefore be represented by a single curve. This is because, as Vaidyanathan (1978) has stressed, countries vary considerably in their bio-physical

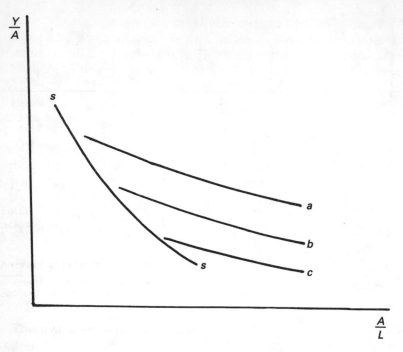

Figure 5.2

conditions, such as the nature of their soil and the amount and seasonal distribution of their rainfall. This means that the yield of land will vary between countries even for the same labour intensity. Therefore, we have drawn a number of curves in the diagram to illustrate conditions in different countries.

The movement in the direction of the arrows along the curves such as (a) in Figure 5.1 is propelled by population growth. In the course of this movement, the output per worker declines steadily, as mentioned above. Eventually, the output per capita will decline to the subsistence level. Then, according to the classical theory, profits will be zero, there will be no further increase in the Wage Fund, population growth will cease, and the economy will reach the classical Stationary State.

The ultimate position will be shown by a set of points, one on each of the curves drawn in Figure 5.1. Such points will lie on a curve, such as SS shown in Figure 5.2. If the subsistence level at which population growth reaches a limit is the same on countries moving along the different curves, then a curve drawn through these final points will be a rectangular hyperbola, i.e. the yield per hectare multiplied by the area cultivated by each worker will be the same at all points of the curve. In fact, this is the pattern observed by Ishikawa (1967, pp. 78–9) for a number of long-settled Asian countries. He has therefore argued that 'every point along this curve represents a constant magnitude ($XY = A$) and it seems that this magnitude (A) is in the neighbourhood of the subsistence level'.

This result provides some support for the classical theory of the trend towards the Stationary State, based on the Malthusian hypothesis that demographic behaviour is determined by economic conditions, especially the supply of food. This hypothesis may well have operated in LDCs in historical times. But, as we have argued earlier, this relationship may not be operating to the same extent under modern conditions. Instead, population growth is determined much more by non-economic conditions such as improvements in public health and advances in medical science. It is still true that the population of a country cannot continue to grow for a long period if the nutrition level of large sections of the people falls below the subsistence level, taken as the minimum requirements for maintaining life. But the concept of a minimum standard of living is an elastic one, and at least for the short to medium period, population may continue to grow with many people subsisting at a low level of nutrition. This is the explanation for the emergence of mass poverty, i.e. people living in conditions of absolute poverty, especially in densely populated countries such as India. This phenomenon is closely related to intense population pressure on land under conditions of traditional agricultural technology, leading to a low productivity of labour. Consequently, the incidence of absolute poverty is particularly great among landless agricultural labourers unable to get secure employment. The problem is aggravated when the conditions of land tenure are such that a considerable part of the land is held in relatively large farms, which are generally cultivated at a lower labour intensity than family farms.

5.2 TECHNICAL PROGRESS IN AGRICULTURE

The above discussion was mainly concerned with the effects of diminishing returns on land and labour productivity, under conditions of a constant technology. But agricultural technology has not remained constant, and there has been considerable technological progress both in DCs and LDCs.

One important theory of how such technological progress occurred is that of Boserup (1965). According to her theory, technological progress in traditional agriculture occurs by the invention of productive ways of using labour more intensively as land becomes more and more scarce. It is through this mechanism that she explains the great transformation of agriculture from the hunting and gathering stage, through the slash and burn stage of swidden agriculture, to settled agriculture and multiple cropping. In order to produce these innovations, labour intensive methods were also used to improve the land by land terracing, irrigation, and the use of green manure. The intense use of these methods in Indonesia has been described by Geertz (1963) as 'agricultural involution'.

Further, according to Boserup, these innovations were induced by population growth. This is a useful explanation up to a point but is not complete since the process has clearly varied considerably from country to country. Generally speaking, it occurred faster in countries imbued with what Ishikawa (1978) has called the 'community principle', like the countries of East Asia, and slower in countries where this principle operated more weakly. The main reason is that these innovations require the cooperation of all farmers in any given area and will only be undertaken when the benefits accrue to all these farmers. Hence, the community principle is more active in countries where land ownership and control are more equally distributed, as they were in the countries of East Asia.

We must, however, distinguish two types of innovations. One type of innovations is that which is induced by population growth within the traditional system of agriculture, i.e. the case where agricultural production depends mainly on inputs produced within that sector. The other type consists of innovations involved in modern agriculture, based on the use of modern inputs. When both types of innovations are taken into account, we get a different relationship between labour intensity and land yields. This relationship has been described by Ishikawa (1978) by the curve shown in Figure 5.3 on the basis of data from Japan and Taiwan.

Ishikawa (1978, p. 32) has distinguished the two types of innovations involved in the process as follows:

1. Labour-using technological factors – e.g. irrigation and drainage,

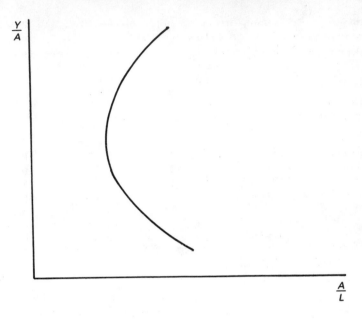

Figure 5.3

higher yielding varieties, and application of larger amounts of
fertiliser, and improved cultivation practices, all of which have
yield-increasing properties at the same time.

2. Labour-saving technological factors – mainly improvement of
   traditional farm implements and agricultural mechanisation in
   irrigation, weeding, threshing, ploughing, harrowing and even
   harvesting. These two types of innovations then explain the two
   phases of the curve drawn in Figure 5.3, with factors of type (1)
   dominating in the forward-rising part, and those of type (2) in the
   backward-rising part of the curve.

The importance of the Ishikawa curve lies in the fact that it shows
both phases from the experience of the East Asian countries. Most
studies of the historical experience of DCs, especially western countries,
have concentrated only on the second phase in which a rising yield of
land was associated with a falling labour intensity of cultivation. But
there may also have been an earlier phase in which rising yields were
associated with increasing labour intensity of cultivation. The historical evidence from countries such as Japan and Taiwan makes clear

Table 5.4   Relationship between land per worker and relative factor
prices in six countries

Country	Time period	Coefficient of the price ratio of: Land and labour (P_A/P_L)	Machinery and labour (P_M/P_L)	R^2
Japan	1880–1960	0.159	−0.219	0.75
West	1880–1913	−0.264*	0.066*	0.39
Germany	1950–1968	−0.177	−0.476*	0.98
Denmark	1910–1965	0.148	−0.357*	0.91
France	1870–1965	0.398*	−0.088	0.32
	1920–1965	0.050	−0.498*	0.46
UK	1870–1925	−0.129*	−0.139*	0.61
	1925–1965	0.279	−0.065	0.44
USA	1880–1960	−0.451*	−0.486*	0.83

Note: *Statistically significant at 5%.
Source: Binswanger and Ruttan (1978), p. 63.

that this second stage only occurs after a certain threshold of economic development has been reached.

With regard to these innovations, a theory of 'induced innovation'
has been advanced recently by Hayami and Ruttan (1985). They
argue that these modern innovations have been induced by changes
in the relative prices of the factors of production, i.e. a rise in the
price of one factor relative to that of other factors induces a sequence
of technical changes that reduces the use of that factor relative to the
use of other factors. This is an application of Hicks's (1932) theory of
induced innovation; some theoretical issues about this hypothesis are
discussed in the next chapter. But here we discuss the application to
the agricultural sector, particularly the empirical tests carried out by
Hayami and Ruttan, and their colleagues. A simple version holds
that the ratio in which factors are used in production varies inversely
with the ratio of their prices. This theory is then tested by regressing
time series of the factor–use ratios on time series of the factor–price
ratios for a number of countries, mostly among the developed countries.
Their results for the case of the land-labour ratios are summarised in
Table 5.4.

The best statistical result is obtained in the case of the United
States. This is because of the abundance of capital and scientific
manpower in that country, so that the rate and direction of technological progress were largely determined by the demand for it.
However, the theory does not fare so well in many of the other

countries. For example, 5 of the 9 coefficients of the land–labour price ratio are positive, and hence inconsistent with this simple version of the induced innovation hypothesis. By contrast, 8 of the 9 coefficients of the price ratio of machinery and labour are negative. This suggests that to the extent that changes in the land–labour ratio were induced by changes in relative factor prices, it was the price ratio of machinery and labour which was most important. Further, it is possible that changes in the land–labour ratio in many countries were due to innovations borrowed from countries such as the United States, rather than induced by the relative factor–price ratio of the countries themselves. On the contrary, it is more likely that changes in the price of land, and with it, the price ratio of land and labour, were the consequence of the changes in the land-labour ratio, rather than their cause (see also Binswanger and Ruttan, 1978, pp. 63–4, 68).

However, these regression equations are not entirely adequate to test the hypothesis of induced innovation. This simple test does not distinguish between differences in factor ratios due to the choice between different techniques from a given technology at different price ratios, and those due to changes in the technology itself. Therefore, Binswanger and Ruttan (1978) devised a more stringent test of the hypothesis, but even this provides only a rough measure of the two components described above. When the more refined method is applied to the US data, there is again some support for the induced innovation hypothesis. However, when it was applied to Japanese data by Yeung and Roe (1978), the results were again inconsistent with the induced innovation hypothesis. These authors have concluded that 'This unforeseen bias in the direction of technical change may reflect some fundamental bias in innovation possibilities or it may imply that transfer of technology took place only from countries or regions that were endowed with land and other agricultural resources of greater quantity and quality than was Japan'. They also recognised that part of the problem may have been due to the treatment of the price of land as exogenous, whereas in fact it may have been almost totally endogenous to agriculture, at least in some of the early stages of development.

5.3 THE MECHANISATION PROCESS IN AGRICULTURE

In the last section, we considered the extent to which changes in the productivity of land and labour in agriculture could be explained in terms of technological progress. But these changes may also be explained as the result of investment of fixed capital in agriculture. A convenient model of this explanation is that of Butt (1960) in terms of the mechanisation process in agriculture.

In section 4.5, the role of capital in the non-agricultural sectors was highlighted by distinguishing between handicraft techniques which produce output using only labour, and mechanised techniques which use both labour and capital. But in the agricultural sector, land is an essential factor of production. Therefore, Butt makes a distinction between 'peasant techniques' which use land and labour to produce output in this sector, and 'mechanised farming techniques' which use all three factors of production – land, labour and capital.

Because peasant techniques depend on two factors of production – land and labour, there is a whole spectrum of such techniques differing in the amounts of land and labour required to produce a unit of food output. Let a_i be the amount of labour and b_i the amount of land required to produce one unit of output by the i-th peasant technique. These techniques can then be arranged in a sequence according to increasing labour intensity. In the earliest stage of growth, when population is small in relation to land, each farmer cultivates as much land as will maximise his output; the technique of cultivation used under these conditions is known as the 'standard peasant technique'. So long as there is abundant land, the price of food consists only of its labour cost, and is therefore equal to 1. As population grows, all the available land is used up for cultivation by the standard peasant technique. With further growth of population, the price of food u rises above its wage cost, and the difference $z = u-1$ emerges as rent. As the price of food and with it the rent of land rise further, it will become profitable to use the next peasant technique, which is more economical in the use of land and more intensive in the use of labour, compared with the standard peasant technique. The second peasant technique will begin to be substituted for the standard technique when rent reaches the level z given by

$$u = a_1+b_1z = a_2+b_2z \qquad (5.1)$$

Hence, at the point of transition,

$$z = (a_2-a_1) / (b_1-b_2) \qquad (5.2)$$

i.e., z is the marginal rate of substitution between land and labour. So long as only peasant techniques are used, there will be a continuous rise in the rent of land, and a corresponding succession of peasant techniques as shown below:

where x_i refers to the i-th peasant technique in the sequence according to labour intensity of cultivation. This succession of peasant techniques represents the calendar of the peasant technology. (For further discussion, see Booth and Sundrum, 1984, section 3.4.)

The mechanisation of agriculture can be analysed against this background of the peasant technology. Suppose that, at the time when a mechanised farming technique is introduced, the k-th peasant technique is in vogue, i.e. the technique in which a_k amount of labour cultivating an area b_k of land produces one unit of output. As the mechanised farming uses all three factors of production, it has to be described by three parameters, namely the amount of labour A, the amount of land B, and the amount of capital C, required to produce one unit of food output. As in the case of the non-agricultural sectors, the productivity of capital is measured by the extent to which costs of production are reduced by the mechanised technique per unit of capital employed. The reduction in labour costs is $(a_k - A)$ and the reduction in rent cost is $(b_k - B)z$. Therefore, the productivity of the mechanised farming technique *vis-à-vis* the k-th peasant technique is:

$$S(k) = \frac{1}{C}\left[(a_k - A) + (b_k - B)z\right] \tag{5.3}$$

The productivity of capital depends on the rent of land, and therefore on the peasant technique in vogue at the time of the mechanisation of agriculture. It is related to the saving in labour cost plus the saving in land cost. For this mechanised farming technique to be profitable, these two types of cost saving must together be positive, and therefore at least one of them must be positive. The mechanised farming technique may be described as 'labour saving' relative to the k-th peasant technique if the saving in labour cost is positive, and as 'land saving' if the saving in land cost is positive.

According to equation (5.3), the productivity of the mechanised technique is a linear function of the rent of land z. A particular case is illustrated in Figure 5.4.

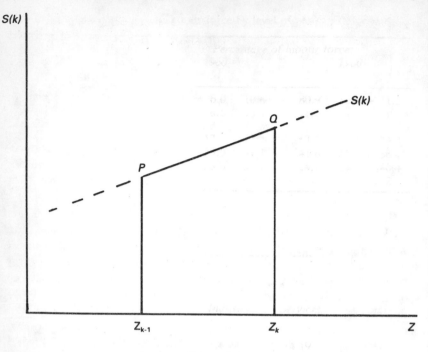

Figure 5.4

where the rent of land is measured on the horizontal axis. Then, the intercept of $S(k)$ on the vertical axis represents the labour-saving component, while the slope of the line $S(k)$ represents the land-saving component. The particular case described in this figure represents one in which the mechanised technique is both labour and land saving.

But the k-th peasant technique will be in vogue only between two critical values z_{k-1} and z_k of the rent of land. Therefore, the comparison of the mechanised technique with the k-th peasant technique is valid only between these values of z, i.e. the $S(k)$ line applies only in the segment PQ. As the rent of land rises steadily as we advance in the calendar of peasant technology, the prevailing peasant technology becomes steadily more and more labour intensive. The comparison of the mechanised technique with these peasant techniques is then shown by segments of a series of S curves, as shown in Figure 5.5.

It is obvious that the vertical intercept of the S lines rises, and the slope of these lines falls steadily in the course of the peasant

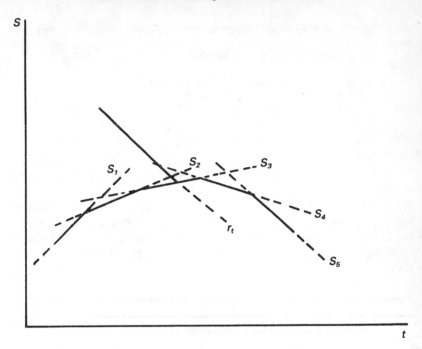

Figure 5.5

calendar. Agriculture becomes mechanised when the rate of profit equals the productivity of capital shown by the segmented S curve.

In Sen's (1959) analysis of the problem, the use of capital in agriculture was classified as 'landesque' if capital substitutes for land, and as 'labouresque' if it substitutes for labour. This classification was based only on the technical characteristics of various uses of capital, and so were assumed to be constant over time. But the above analysis shows that whether capital substitutes for land or for labour in the agricultural sector depends on the peasant technique in vogue, and hence on the stage of the peasant calendar at which agriculture is mechanised. In particular, agricultural mechanisation will be land-saving if it occurs early in the peasant calendar; then the mechanisation of agriculture serves to overcome the scarcity of land and to slow down the rise in the rent of land. This is what happened in the developed countries. But if agricultural mechanisation occurs late in the peasant calendar, when the prevailing peasant techniques are highly labour-intensive, the mechanised technique may be labour-saving and even land-using. To some extent, this may explain the position in less-developed countries which are only now beginning to mechanise their agricultural sector. (For further discussion, see Booth and Sundrum, 1984, ch. 7.)

5.4 THE HISTORICAL MISSION OF AGRICULTURE

Finally, we consider the effect of agricultural development on growth in the rest of the economy. First we consider the early stages of development. At those stages, per capita income is low. Food being at the bottom of the hierarchy of commodities, it has a high income elasticity of demand at those income levels. Also, the productivity of labour in agriculture is low, so that the bulk of the labour force will be engaged in that sector. At the same time, the price of food is also high, so that the non-agricultural sectors have to pay a high wage for their labour. During this phase, there is also a rapid growth of population. Therefore, agricultural production and the supply of food cannot rise much faster than the growth of population. Hence, the agricultural sector will be a constraint on the growth of other sectors, both on the demand side and on the supply side.

But as development proceeds, there comes a time when population growth slows down, the income elasticity of demand for food falls, the productivity of labour in agriculture rises, and more labour becomes available to other sectors at lower wages. Then the agricultural sector is no longer a constraint on overall growth. To reach this stage is the historical mission of agriculture (a concept gratefully borrowed from Fei and Ranis, 1971). The concept is designed to stress the finiteness of the period required for creating the conditions for moving the centre of gravity of the economy from agriculture to industry. But countries vary in the time their agricultural sectors take to fulfil this historical mission.

It was no accident that the first group of countries which started their modern economic growth were the countries of western Europe, because these were the countries which experienced an agricultural revolution first. To a great extent, this was due to the invention of new techniques of cultivation. But these technical developments were in turn due to important institutional changes occurring over a longer period. For example, it has been argued that they began with the effect of the Black Plague in the fourteenth century, which depleted the stock of labour. The feudal lords of the time tried to cope with the problem of labour scarcity by exacting more labour from the reduced number of serfs but this provoked a series of peasant revolts. These revolts were suppressed in the East European countries leading to what has been called the second serfdom of the fifteenth and sixteenth centuries; the result was agricultural stagnation in these countries. But in western Europe, the revolt of the peasants broke the power of the feudal lords and brought about the end of feudalism. However, in countries like France, the result was an economy based on small peasant units, with some land held in common. But it is argued that in England, there was a capitalist transformation in which land became concentrated in relatively few hands during the enclosure movement. Hence, the peasants in England were not squeezed as hard, and this less forceful treatment enabled peasants to innovate. Their innovation provided the grain surplus that could be used to feed the industrial proletariat in towns and was a pre-condition for successful industrialisation (see e.g. Brenner, 1986).

The historical mission of agriculture was also fulfilled in Japan in quite early times, but there is some controversy over the date at which this occurred. One view is that agricultural and industrial expansion took place together, after the Meiji Restoration of 1868. Another view is that great progress in agricultural production had already been achieved during the long period of Tokugawa rule, and that this prior agricultural development was an important reason for the dramatic industrial career of Japan since that time. (For a review of the statistical evidence and a balanced judgment, see Minami, 1986.)

European settlements overseas started off with the great advantage of an abundance of land. The problem there was a scarcity of labour, leading to high wages. This was a spur to rapid capital accumulation, and the innovation of capital-intensive methods of cultivation. The rapid growth of agricultural output relaxed the agricultural constraint on overall growth, so that these countries could make an early start with industrialisation.

Barring a few exceptions, such as Taiwan which experienced a major agricultural development under Japanese colonial rule, agricultural development was generally slow in other LDCs. Such development as occurred historically was soon overtaken by population growth along Malthusian lines. Therefore, the agricultural sector has long been a constraint on growth in the rest of the economy. It was only in recent times that there was a spurt of agricultural growth as a result of the Green Revolution, but the progress of this new technology has been sporadic, confined to particular crops and particular regions.

To sum up, this chapter has been concerned with agricultural growth in a long-term historical perspective. The sources of agricultural growth were defined as the extension of area, and the increase of labour intensity and of labour productivity. These sources were estimated for different groups of countries in the post-war period in section 5.1, which also pointed out how these factors varied in different countries in their historical experience. Section 5.2 then discussed the extent to which technological progress was induced by various factors, and section 5.3 discussed the role of capital accumulation in promoting agricultural development. Finally, in section 5.4, it was argued that there is a stage at which agriculture is no longer a constraint on overall growth, and agricultural will have fulfilled its historical mission.

6 Growth in the Industrial Sector

6.1 THE BEGINNINGS OF INDUSTRIALISATION

Industrialisation is the process in which there is a sharp increase in the industrial share of GDP and of the labour force. It is thus the process by which the centre of gravity of the economy shifts from agriculture to industry. The process is also marked by a significant change in the techniques by which these goods are produced. In particular, these goods come to be produced by techniques which make greater use of fixed capital in the form of machinery of various kinds. As Hicks (1969, p. 142) says: 'It is at the point when fixed capital moves, or begins to move, into the central position that the "revolution" occurs.'

In Chapter 4, we considered theories about the mechanism of the industrialisation process, such as the dualistic theory of Lewis and the mechanisation theory of Butt. But here we have to consider why this process occurred at different times in different countries, thereby influencing the timing of different phases of their economic growth. Although all countries are currently engaged in various aspects of their industrialisation, it is a process which became a significant phase of economic growth in comparatively recent times when considered against the time scale of human history. Therefore, we must also consider why the beginnings of industrialisation occurred in a few countries only since the late eighteenth century.

(a) Industry in Traditional Societies

A certain quantity of industrial goods was produced even in traditional societies. But they were produced almost entirely by what Butt has described as handicraft techniques, i.e. mainly by labour with a minimum of capital equipment. Therefore, the quantity of such goods that could be produced depended on the amount of labour that could be released from the production of food, the prime necessity. So long as the agricultural productivity of labour was low, i.e. so long as each agricultural worker could produce only little more than what was needed to feed his family, the amount of labour

101

available for producing industrial goods was extremely limited. Hence, such goods were produced mostly to meet the demand from the nobility.

As agricultural productivity grew with improvements in the techniques of cultivation, such as the clearing and levelling of land, and the construction of irrigation works, more labour became available for other than agricultural activities. However, there was only a limited range of industrial goods, and the demand for them from a small ruling class was quickly satiated. The increasing supply of labour, which was surplus to agricultural requirements, was then devoted to the construction of large buildings, such as temples, pyramids and other monuments. The use of the surplus labour extending industrial production further had to wait for technological innovations which expanded the range of industrial goods that could be produced.

(b) Failure of Industrialisation in Traditional Societies

However, the scientific basis of such technological advances was already present in traditional societies, especially in the ancient civilisations of the Middle East, India and China. One of the great puzzles of economic history is why these traditional societies failed to use this scientific basis to begin their industrialisation. This is one of the principal themes of the voluminous research into the history of science and civilisation in China carried out by Needham and his associates (see e.g. Needham, 1970). It is also the question that Rostovtzeff (1957) raises regarding Roman history: 'The problem remains. Why was the victorious advance of capitalism stopped? Why was machinery not invented? Why were the business systems not perfected? Why were the primal forces of primitive economy not overcome?'

But given the lack of sufficient data about these early historical times, it is not possible to reach any definitive solution of the puzzle, and we can only speculate about some of the factors which may have played a part. Some of these speculations have been reviewed by Rostow (1975, especially ch. 1).

One line of explanation is the argument that, in traditional countries, significant advances in agricultural technology were overtaken by rapid population growth. This meant that there was such an abundance of labour supply that there was little inducement for the development of capital-using technology. The most notable version of this explanation is Elvin's (1973, p. 312) theory of a 'high-level equilibrium trap' in the Chinese economy even by the fourteenth century:

> through a number of interlocking causes, the input-output relationships of the late traditional economy had assumed a pattern that was almost incapable of change through internally-generated forces. Both in technological and investment terms, agricultural productivity per acre had nearly reached the limits of what was possible without industrial-scientific inputs, and the increase of population had therefore steadily reduced the surplus product above what was needed for subsistence.

This raises the question why new technology with wider application to industrial production was not developed. An influential view on this question focuses on the role of the merchant (see e.g. Hicks, 1969). Applying this view to explain the failure of technological innovation in China, Needham (1970, pp. 31–2) has argued:

> the merchants were always kept down and unable to rise to a position of power in the State. They had guilds, it is true, but these were never as important as in Europe. Here we might be putting our finger on the main cause of the failure of Chinese civilisation to develop modern technology, because in Europe (as is universally admitted) the development of technology was closely bound up with the rise of the merchant class to power.

But this view is challenged by Rostow (1975, pp. 19–20) on the ground that the view of merchants as a despised profession in China and India is greatly exaggerated, that in any case merchants were not a particularly good vehicle for generating and rapidly spreading new technology, and that the rise of technological innovation in Europe since the eighteenth century was 'set in motion primarily from the top – by bureaucrats, soldiers and modernising politicians – rather than by merchants'.

The most important explanation, however, lies in the application of science to technology. It was not as if there was no scientific progress in the traditional societies. After all, the progress of science in Europe since the Renaissance had its roots in the ancient civilisations. As Elvin (1973, p. 297) points out, 'Almost every element usually regarded by historians as a major contributory cause to the industrial revolution in northwestern Europe was also present in China'. Therefore, Rostow (1975, p. 28) concludes that 'the decisive formal weakness in traditional societies was on the demand side: in the lack of innovators, of men moved by economic or other incentives or perceptions to seek changes in technology'.

(c) The Industrial Revolution in Europe

Industrialisation finally got under way in western Europe in the late eighteenth century. It was ultimately based on a scientific revolution that had been simmering since Renaissance times. Rostow (1975, p. 132) therefore offers as the central thesis of his book that 'the scientific revolution, in all its consequences, is the element in the equation of history that distinguishes early modern Europe from all previous periods of economic expansion'. There had been scientific advance in earlier societies, but what distinguished the European experience was the sheer scale of the effort, so that progress in one field led to progress in others, and hence to a cumulative advance along a wide front. As Kuznets (1966, p. 2) puts it, 'there was an addition to the stock of human knowledge so major that its exploitation and utilisation absorbed the energies of human societies and their growth for a period long enough to constitute an epoch in human history'.

But scientific advance by itself was not sufficient. What was needed was its application to industrial production. It is on this front that Europe of the late eighteenth century excelled over earlier civilisations. To begin with, the major discoveries of the Industrial Revolution in Europe were made by practical men of affairs. They were able to do this because of the more massive progress of science and its wider spread among the population. It was only later that scientific research came to be applied systematically to industrial production. As Lewis (1978, p. 129) explains it,

> Whereas any intelligent and observant person with a stroke of genius could invent the steam engine or the flying shuttle or the hot blast, innovation after 1880 for the most part needed something more than genius. It required scientific knowledge to develop electrical machinery, organic chemicals or workable internal combustion engines. To put the matter differently, academic science contributed next to nothing to the industrial revolution, and did not become entwined with industrial progress until after 1880.

As mentioned earlier, the application of the new techniques was closely associated with the use of capital, and the emergence of a class of capitalists who accumulated such capital and directed its use. That is why the growth of industry is so often associated with, and even referred to as, the development of capitalism. Capitalism as a form of economic organisation was developed in Europe in the course of the industrial revolution, characterised by private owner-ship of capital and its increasing concentration in a few hands. There were a number of features associated with this capitalist develop-ment. One was the development of new institutions, such as joint stock and limited liability corporations. This required 'much social invention' (Kuznets, 1966, p. 5). Another feature was the develop-ment of the factory system, in which large groups of workers were brought to the location of capital goods in the form of machinery, rather than the cottage industry system in which small quantities of capital were used by workers in their own homes. On the one hand, the concentration of labour in a single place of production led to great economies of scale, the phenomenon of Increasing Returns to Scale, which is a distinguishing feature of industrial production. On the other, it led to the emergence of a disciplined labour force.

In modern growth theory, much store is set on the use of capital as a substitute for labour. But as Rostow (1975, p. 21) points out, 'the critical inventions of eighteenth-century Europe were not primarily addressed to labour saving'. Instead, their main role was to substitute for labour skills. Thus, the explosive expansion in British cotton textile production was based on 'machines largely created as substi-tutes for the skill of Indian hands that Europeans could not match' (Rostow, 1975, p. viii). Thus, by reducing the cost of production on a large scale, the use of machines actually gave industrial employment to unskilled labour on a larger scale than ever before.

The sharp transition to industrialisation occurred first in Britain, and then spread to other countries in Europe, to European settle-ments overseas, largely by a process of diffusion, then to Japan by a more deliberate policy of the government in close collaboration with big business, and finally to Russia largely under a command economy controlled by State planning. Why the process commenced first in Britain, rather than in other European countries such as, say, France, is still the subject of continuing research and controversy. One theory on the demand side is that of Deane and Cole (1967), who argued that it was mainly due to faster agricultural growth in Britain, and hence that 'the growth of the home market for industrial goods was closely bound up with the fortunes of the agricultural community'. Another theory also on the demand side has been advanced by Landes (1969, pp. 47–8) as follows:

> Within the market of Britain, purchasing power per head and standard of living were significantly higher than on the continent. The English labourer not only ate better; he spent less of his income on food than his continental counterpart, and in most areas this portion was shrinking, whereas across the Channel it may well have risen during much of the eighteenth century. As a result, he had more to spare for other things, including manufactures . . . Defoe's reference to the Englishman's 'expensive, generous, free way of living' calls to mind a final aspect of the British domestic market: a consumption pattern favourable to the growth of manufactures. More than any other in Europe, probably, British society was open. Not only was income more evenly distributed than across the Channel, but the barriers to mobility were lower, the definitions of status looser.

Against this, there are those who stress factors on the supply side as the main explanation for the earlier industrialisation of Britain. For example, Nef (1940) and Harris (1972) have referred to Britain's advantage in coal resources and coal-based technology. Rostow (1975, pp. 174–5) himself leans to the view that 'it is somewhere in the interlocked network (of science, invention and innovation) that British superiority over the French is mainly to be found, but it certainly does not lie in the superiority of British science', and refers to a contemporary proverb that 'for a thing to be perfect it must be invented in France and worked out in England'. He also notes the important role played by British Nonconformists who 'contributed a scale and thrust to the generation and application of new technology that larger France could not match' (p. 188).

(d) The Industrial Revolution as a Take-off

From the point of view of growth theory, the importance of the industrialisation episode is that it led to a significant acceleration in the growth process. That is why the aftermath of the Industrial Revolution has been identified with modern economic growth. Economic historians studying this experience have explained the growth process as a succession of different stages, with industrialisation as the stage associated with growth acceleration. But what is needed is to explain the process, not just in terms of the passage of historical time, but rather in terms of more fundamental factors which affect different countries in different ways.

The simple explanation of this relationship lies in the structural determinants of growth analysed in Chapter 3. On the one hand, the intense use of capital in the new techniques of production raised the productivity of labour in the industrial sector significantly above that in other sectors. Further, the continuous accumulation of capital enabled the productivity of labour to grow faster in the industrial sector than in other sectors. At the same time, due to a variety of causes on the demand side, there was a shift of labour from the other sectors to the industrial sector. The result was a growth of overall labour productivity.

This analysis may be compared with the 'take-off' theory of Rostow (1960). According to this theory, the beginnings of industrialisation occur in a sharply discontinuous step, dramatised by the analogy with aircraft achieving enough speed to become airborne, and that for such a dramatic take-off to occur, certain pre-conditions must be fulfilled, especially a high rate of investment. Subsequent research has, however, cast serious doubt on this explanation. On the one hand, Bicanic (1962, pp. 19–20) has challenged the sharpness of the discontinuity involved in this process: 'The second stage can be described more realistically as a painful process of creeping over the threshold of economic growth rather than an elegant "take-off" which does not adequately convey the difficulty and intensity of the problem of this stage of economic growth'. On the other hand, Gerschenkron (1962, 1963) has challenged the concept of pre-conditions, insisting instead that these so-called pre-conditions were in fact created by the process of development itself. In particular, he has argued that the state has often played a major role in promoting these pre-conditions more rapidly in countries which start from a more backward situation. Finally, the take-off theory assigns an excessive role to the attainment of a high rate of investment in initiating a take-off; in fact, there have been many countries, especially LDCs, which had high investment ratios but nevertheless failed to achieve a sustained take-off, a notable example being Burma, one of the countries referred to by Rostow. Instead, a more decisive factor has been the progress of industrial technology and of the institutional framework needed to mobilise capital, and thus to raise the level and growth of labour productivity in the industrial sector.

6.2 SOURCES OF INDUSTRIAL GROWTH

Among the minimum set of assumptions used in Chapter 3 to generate a logistic pattern of growth, one was the assumption that the rate of growth of labour productivity in the M-sector was constant over time, and higher than the rates of growth of labour productivity in other sectors. It is generally true that labour productivity grows more rapidly in the M-sector than in others. This is essentially because the stock of capital per worker is higher in this sector, and further that it grows more rapidly. However, the level and growth of labour productivity in the M-sector varies greatly over time and between countries. One of the main problems in the study of industrial growth is to explain this variation.

Ultimately, this variation is due to both demand and supply factors and to the interaction between them. One of the factors on the demand side is that related to the growth of per capita income; this is the relationship which operates through the income elasticity of demand, which was taken as one of the structural determinants of growth in Chapter 3. But there are also other important demand factors; these are discussed in Part III of the book. In this section, we consider in more detail the supply factors, i.e. the factors affecting the level and growth of labour productivity at different times and in different countries. We discuss these supply factors separately here mainly for convenience of exposition. In fact, there is a considerable interaction between these supply and demand factors, as discussed in later chapters.

(a) Sources of Growth: Theory

The two main factors of production in the industrial sector are labour and capital. Therefore, the growth of industrial production depends on the growth of labour, the growth of capital, and improvements in the efficiency with which they are used. The last factor is generally known as technological progress. Regarding the first two factors, there are profound problems of measuring the quantities of labour and capital at any point of time, and their growth over time, because units of labour and capital vary greatly in quality. Statisticians have made heroic efforts to produce rough estimates for some countries, which may be used for our analysis. There are, however, much more serious problems even in defining the concept of technological progress.

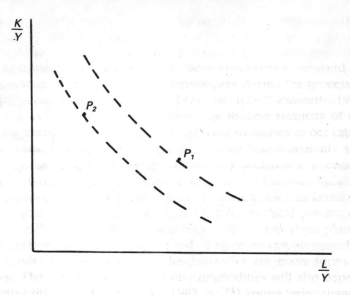

Figure 6.1

The method most frequently used in the literature may be illustrated by Figure 6.1. In this diagram, the conditions of production are described by the quantities of labour and capital used to produce one unit of output. Measuring these quantities along the two axes of the diagram, the conditions of production in two years are shown by the points P_1 and P_2.

First, it must be noted that this way of representing the conditions of production abstracts from the scale of production. Therefore, it is strictly valid only on the assumption of constant returns to scale. This is a very serious limitation of the analysis, because increasing returns is an important characteristic of industrial production, and a significant source of industrial growth (section 6.2 (d) below). Most theoretical studies have, however, assumed constant returns to scale, not only because of its mathematical convenience, but also because it is only on this assumption that the neo-classical marginal productivity theory of factor prices can be consistently applied to all factors of production.

Assuming constant returns to scale, the above diagram has been used to analyse industrial growth. In this diagram, if P_2 lies to the south-west of P_1 then clearly there has been technological progress between the two years, because each unit of output is produced with less labour and less capital in the second period than in the first. But it is rarely that changes occur in this way. The more typical situation as analysed, for example, in Butt's theory of the mechanisation process, is one in which the point P_2 lies to the north-west of the point P_1, i.e. a unit of output in the later period is usually produced with more capital and less labour.

The standard method used to explain the shift from P_1 to P_2 is to draw isoquants through each of these points, to represent the technology of production at each date. The results depend on the assumptions about the shape of these isoquants and how they change from time to time. Generally, a particular, convenient, form of the production function is assumed, such as a Cobb-Douglas or a constant elasticity of substitution (CES) function.

The change from P_1 to P_2 is then the result of both a movement along a given isoquant, i.e. technology being constant, and a shift of the isoquant, representing technological progress. Thus, if the same isoquant passes through the two points, then the growth of production is explained by the growth of the two factors of production, and the changes in the capital and labour coefficients due to changes in their relative prices, on the further assumption that the growing stocks of the two factors are fully utilised. But if the isoquant through P_2 lies within that through P_1 the inward shift is defined as technological progress, and part of the growth of production is attributed to this improvement in technology. Clearly, the magnitudes of the two components of growth of production depend crucially on the assumptions made to draw the two isoquants.

Much of the theoretical literature has been devoted to classify different types of technological progress, i.e. different ways in which the isoquant shifts from time to time. The case where the isoquant shrinks at a uniform rate is known as neutral technological progress. Neutral technological change itself is further classified into different categories. For example, technological progress is said to be Harrod-neutral if the isoquant shifts at a uniform rate in the downward direction, i.e. towards the labour axis; such progress is also described as labour-augmenting, for the results are the same as if there was an increase in the efficiency of labour. Technological progress is known as Solow-neutral if the isoquant shrinks at a uniform rate in the leftward direction, i.e. towards the capital axis; such technological progress is also described as capital-augmenting. Finally, technological progress is said to be Hicks-neutral if the isoquant shrinks at a uniform rate towards the origin. Based on these definitions of neutrality, technological progress has also been classified as labour-saving or capital-saving, depending on differences in the rate at which the isoquant shrinks in different directions.

Combined with their usual assumptions about the determination of factor prices according to marginal productivity, neo-classical economists have then studied the effects of different types of technological progress on the distribution of income. For example, it has been shown that, if technological progress is Harrod-neutral, factor shares will be constant along paths on which the capital-output ratio is constant; in the case of Solow-neutral technological progress, factor shares will be constant along paths on which the labour–output ratio is constant; and in the case of Hicks-neutral technological progress, factor shares will be constant along paths on which the capital–labour ratio is constant. Much of the theoretical work along these lines has been motivated by an interest in working out the conditions under which it is possible to get steady growth paths. Thus, for example, it has been argued that the constancy of factor shares and constancy of the capital–output ratio, two features believed to characterise the economic growth of advanced industrial countries, may be explained by technological progress which is Harrod-neutral. However, in the present context we are more interested in explaining how rates of industrial growth have varied over time and among a larger group of countries. Therefore, we turn to some problems of the measurement of the sources of growth.

(b) Sources of Growth: Measurement

A considerable amount of work has been done to measure the sources of growth based on the above approach. The method most commonly used is to assume a production function:

$$Y = F(K, L, t); F_K, F_L, F_t > 0 \qquad (6.1)$$

where output Y is taken as a function of capital K, labour L, and of time t, and F_i is the partial derivative of the function F with respect to the argument i. In particular, F_t/F represents the rate of technological progress, interpreted as the proportionate increase in output that would occur over time when the quantities of capital and labour remain constant. Differentiating (6.1) logarithmically with respect to time, we get:

$$G_Y = G_A + \in_K G_K + \in_L G_L \tag{6.2}$$

where G_i is the rate of growth of the variable i (with A referring to technology) and $\in_j$ is the elasticity of output with respect to the factor j. This equation is then used to decompose overall growth into components corresponding to the factor contributions, namely:

1. effect of growth of labour;
2. effect of growth of capital; and
3. effect of technological progress.

The main problem in using (6.2) to decompose growth of output into these components is to estimate the elasticities of output with respect to the two factors. One approach that has been followed is to fit a production function of a simple mathematical form to time series data of Y, K, and L, and derive these elasticities from the estimated function. A function often used for this purpose is the Cobb–Douglas function; as is well known, this is a function in which factor shares in output are constant, and equal to the respective output elasticities. In an alternative approach, no assumption is made about the production function, except that it is linear homogeneous, but it is assumed that the factor markets are perfectly competitive and speedily reach their equilibrium, so that the factors are paid according to their marginal productivities. On this assumption, the observed factor shares are used as estimates of the corresponding elasticities.

This method was first applied to the historical experience of some developed countries. For example, applying the method to US data for the period 1909–49, Solow (1957) found that most (seven-eighths) of the increase in gross output per worker was attributable to technological change, with only a small part (one-eighth) attributable to the growth of capital per worker. However, because of the very stringent assumptions of the model, and the neglect of many factors such as changes in the quality of capital and labour, the role of increasing returns and the effect of changing composition of output, such large estimates of the role of technological progress, derived as a residual after allowing for the growth of factor inputs, came to be interpreted as 'some sort of measure of our ignorance about the causes of economic growth' (Abramovitz, 1956, p. 328). As a result, there has been further refinement of the method in order to reduce the size of this residual factor. For example, by taking account of

Table 6.1   Factor contributions by stage of growth

Period	% of GDP growth due to			% of Sector-M growth due to:		
	Labour	Capital	Technical progress	Labour	Capital	Technical progress
0	36	53	11	31	59	10
1	34	51	15	29	54	16
2	27	48	25	25	51	24
3	21	43	36	25	47	28
4	17	39	44	25	43	32
5	15	35	50	17	40	43
6	18	32	50	9	35	56

Source: Chenery *et al.* (1986), table 8–6, pp. 246–7.

changes in education, work hours, types of capital, etc., Denison (1962) reduced the contribution of technological progress in the growth of per capita output in the United States in the period 1909–57 to 46 per cent. Making further corrections for other errors in the measurement of various factors, Jorgensen and Griliches (1967) reduced the contribution of technological progress in the growth of GDP in the United States from 1945 to 1965 to only 3 per cent.

The basic method has now been applied to a number of countries, for which some estimates of the growth of labour and capital were available. Chenery *et al.* (1986, pp. 20–2) have brought together 57 estimates of the sources of growth for 39 countries (12 DCs, 20 LDCs at the semi-industrial stage; and seven centrally planned countries). One problem with these estimates is that they refer mostly to growth of total GDP, rather than of the industrial sector. However, because the methodology is the same, we use the available estimates to discuss the weaknesses of the approach. Based on their econometric analysis of post-war data, Chenery *et al.* (1986) have estimated the relative factor contributions to total GDP growth and to growth of the industrial sector, at different stages of the growth process (Table 6.1).

These estimates show the extent to which the relative factor contributions in industrial growth are similar to those in overall growth. They also suggest that the contribution of technological progress increases steadily, while that of factor growth falls steadily, during the growth process.

The estimates of the various sources of growth are shown in Table 6.2 for DCs and in Table 6.3 for LDCs.

Table 6.2   Growth (% p.a) of GDP per worker and of TFP: DCs

Countries (period)	G_Y-G_L	G_A
(A) Slow Growth (G_Y-G_L) < 4%		
Belgium (49–59)	2.70	2.05
Canada (60–73)	3.10	1.80
Denmark (50–62)	2.30	1.64
Ireland (53–65)	3.00	2.00
Netherlands (51–60)	3.60	2.30
Sweden (49–59)	2.90	2.50
UK (49–59)	1.90	1.20
UK (60–73)	3.80	2.10
USA (47–60)	2.30	1.40
USA (60–73)	2.10	1.30
Average	2.77	1.84
(B) Rapid Growth (G_Y-G_L) > 4%		
Canada (47–60)	4.10	3.50
France (50–60)	4.60	2.90
France (60–73)	5.50	3.00
West Germany (50–60)	6.60	3.60
West Germany (60–73)	6.10	3.00
Greece (51–65)	4.10	2.39
Israel (52–58)	6.60	3.90
Israel (60–65)	6.00	3.40
Italy (52–60)	4.40	3.80
Italy (60–73)	5.50	3.10
Japan (60–73)	8.20	4.50
Netherlands (60–73)	5.30	2.60
Norway (53–65)	4.60	2.88
Spain (59–65)	5.70	5.02
Average	5.52	3.40

Source: Chenery *et al*. (1986), table 2–2 pp. 20–4.

These estimates are very rough, beset with serious doubts especially about the measurement of the growth of capital stock. The principal conclusion suggested by these estimates as they stand is that the greater part of the variation in the growth of output per worker is due to the growth of total factor productivity. The correlation between ($G_Y - G_L$) and G_A is 0.85 for the DCs and 0.68 for the LDCs. In the case of the DCs, the rate of growth of *TFP* is with only one exception (Greece) greater than 2.5 per cent for the fast growing countries, and is less than or equal to 2.5 per cent per annum for all slow growing countries. The relationship is only slightly weaker in the

Table 6.3   Growth (% p.a) of GDP per worker and of TFP: LDCs

Country (period)	G_Y-G_L	G_A
(A) Slow Growth $(G_Y-G_L) \leq 2.5\%$		
Argentina (50–60)	2.20	1.05
Argentina (60–74)	1.90	0.70
Chile (50–60)	1.00	0.85
Chile (60–74)	2.50	1.20
Colombia (50–60)	1.85	0.95
Ecuador (50–62)	1.31	2.18
Honduras (30–62)	1.59	1.40
Hong Kong (55–60)	1.62	2.40
S. Korea (55–60)	1.97	2.00
Peru (50–60)	1.80	–0.70
Singapore (72–80)	2.48	0
Venezuela (60–74)	1.80	0.60
Average	1.84	1.05
(B) Rapid Growth $(G_Y-G_L) > 2.5\%$		
Brazil (50–60)	4.00	3.65
Brazil (60–74)	4.00	1.60
Colombia (60–74)	2.80	2.10
Hong Kong (60–70)	6.13	4.28
S. Korea (60–73)	4.70	4.10
Mexico (50–60)	3.00	1.60
Mexico (60–74)	2.80	2.10
Peru (60–70)	2.60	1.50
Taiwan (55–60)	3.49	3.12
Turkey (63–75)	5.38	2.23
Venezuela (50–60)	4.15	2.15
Average	3.91	2.58

Source: Chenery *et al.* (1986), table 2.2, pp. 21–2.

LDCs, where the industrial sector is a much smaller part of the whole economy.

(c) Interaction between Factoral Contributions to Growth

Technological progress is certainly an important source of growth, especially in the industrial sector. But the conclusion, suggested by the above estimates, that variations in growth rates of production are mainly due to differences in rates of technological progress, is rather misleading. One reason is the way the sources of growth are classified, as if they operated independently of each other. Another reason is the production function approach to the analysis, especially the assumption that technological progress is essentially disembodied, i.e. it occurs mainly as a function of time, independently of the factors of production. It is only on this assumption that growth of production can be decomposed into the components distinguished above.

In fact, it is rarely that technological progress occurs in this disembodied way in practice, especially in the industrial sector. Instead, it is typically embodied in labour and capital. For technological progress to influence growth of production, innovations must be embodied in new capital equipment. One consequence is that it is not possible to disentangle the effects of technological progress from that of capital accumulation. Another consequence, stressed by Usher (1980, ch. 12), is that technological change alters the nature of commodities, especially capital goods, so that the very attempt to measure the rate of change in the stock of capital becomes a very dubious exercise. Usher has therefore rejected the whole concept of technological change as the change in the output per unit of input. Instead, he prefers to take the rate of technical change as equal to the rate of growth of consumption per head; i.e. he attributes the growth of consumption per head entirely to technological change: 'No Technical Change, No Growth'.

A different way of dealing with the interaction between technological change and capital accumulation has been studied in various 'vintage' models, which distinguish capital goods according to the date of their manufacture. Because the proportion of capital goods embodying the latest technology is higher, the faster the growth of the capital stock, the higher the rate of technological progress. (For a detailed summary and review of the vintage models of growth, see Allen, 1967, ch. 15.)

In view of this intimate connection between the rate of technological progress and the rate of capital accumulation, Kaldor (1957, 1961) has suggested that we must abandon the whole production function concept, and instead takes the relationship between the rate of growth of per capita output and the rate of growth of capital per worker as the basic unit of analysis, defined as the Technical Progress Function. He has developed alternative theories of growth based on this concept. But as in the other approach, much of the theoretical discussion of embodied technological progress has been concerned with the question of explaining the possibility of steady growth patterns. There has been little work on measuring the sources of growth based on this new approach.

The main problem is that, if the various factoral contributions to growth are so tightly linked together, it is not possible to measure the various sources of growth as distinguished above. Therefore, we consider an alternative classification of the sources of growth, and a way of measuring them which involves the minimum of assumptions about an underlying production function. The first step in this alternative approach is to decompose the growth of output into two components according to the following identity:

$$Y_1 - Y_0 = 1/2[(Y_0/L_0) + (Y_1/L_1)] (L_1 - L_0)$$
$$+ 1/2(L_0 + L_1)[(Y_1/L_1) - (Y_0/L_0)] \qquad (6.3)$$

where Y = output and L is employment, with suffix 0 for the initial year and 1 for the final year. The first term on the right-hand side measures the component associated with the growth of employment, and the second that associated with the growth of labour productivity. However, the first term does not refer to the growth of output *due* only to the growth of employment; instead, it measures that part of output growth which would have occurred together with the growth of employment, if the extra workers are equipped with the same amount of capital per worker as in the initial year. Therefore, the first term refers to the contribution of the growth of employment together with the corresponding amount of 'capital widening'.

The growth of labour productivity in the second term may be related to the growth of capital per worker, i.e. to capital deepening. A convenient measure of the relationship is then given by the ratio β defined as:

$$\beta = [(Y_1/L_1) - (Y_0/L_0)]/[(K_1/L_1) - (K_0/L_0)] \qquad (6.4)$$

where Y, K and L represent output, capital and labour respectively, and the suffices 0 and 1 refer to the initial and final years of the period considered. This coefficient may be interpreted as the incremental output-capital ratio in per capita terms. Although this ratio is defined in terms of capital deepening, the growth of labour productivity is not only due to the deepening of capital. It is also due to the technological progress, which is linked with the process of capital deepening.

Without making more detailed assumptions about the production

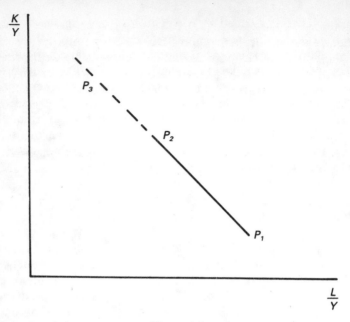

Figure 6.2

function, it is not possible to separate out the effects of capital deepening from that of technological progress. However, what can be done without such assumptions is to estimate the effect on growth of changes in the rate of technological progress associated with capital deepening in different periods. Thus, we can estimate what would have been the growth rate in any period, if the rate of technological progress associated with capital deepening was the same as in a base period, i.e. assuming the same value of the coefficient. Then, we can decompose the growth rate of total output into the following three components:

1. effect of growth of employment and capital widening
2. effect of capital deepening and base period technological progress, and
3. effect of change in rate of technological progress.

The third component in this classification may be illustrated simply as in Figure 6.2. In this figure, as in Figure 6.1, the horizontal axis measures labour per unit of output and the vertical axis the capital per unit of output. These ratios observed at three points of time are represented by the points P_1, P_2 and P_3. In this figure, the point P_2 is plotted to the left of the ray going from the origin to the point P_1 to indicate that there has been capital deepening between the first two years, which may be taken as the base period, with a certain amount of technological progress associated with it. In view of the difficulties mentioned above, we do not attempt to separate the effect of capital deepening from that of technological progress. Instead, the slope of the line joining P_1 and P_2 will be used as a composite measure of technological progress associated with capital deepening. We then ask whether the composite rate of technological progress associated with capital deepening between the second and third points, as measured in this way, has been faster or slower than that in the base period between the first and second points. It is easy to show that the three points must lie on the same line, if the technological progress associated with capital deepening has been at the same rate in both periods. Then, we have the simple answer that technological progress between $t = 2$ and $t = 3$ has been faster than that between $t = 1$ and $t = 2$ if P_3 lies below the line joining P_1 and P_2, and slower otherwise.

The difference between the two approaches may be illustrated using some data of employment, capital and output that have been assembled for six developed countries by Maddison (1987) as shown in Table 6.4. (For comparison with LDCs, see Sundrum, 1986, for some estimates for Indonesia in the period 1968–81.)

Using these data, but refining it further to take account of some additional factors such as changes in the quality of capital and labour, and the effects of changes in trade, economies of scale, and allocation of resources, Maddison obtained the decomposition of growth rates as shown in Table 6.5. In this analysis, the residual contribution is identified with the contribution of technological progress.

Applying the alternative method to the same data, we first get estimates of the coefficient, β, shown in Table 6.6. The table shows that there were some significant variations in the effects of capital deepening. Using these estimates, we then estimate the sources of growth according to the alternative classification, as shown in Table 6.7. In this table, the change in the rate of technological progress in each period is obtained by comparing with the previous period.

According to this analysis, the main contribution to economic growth of these countries in each period is the capital deepening that occurred in that period, associated with technological progress at the rate observed in the previous period. Regarding the effect of changing technology, as defined here, it was positive in the period 1950–69

Table 6.4   Growth of labour, capital and GDP: DCs

Country (year)		Employment (millions)	Index of capital stock	GDP (billions of 1984 US$)
France	1950	19.218	100.00	173.49
	1960	19.662	126.62	271.03
	1973	21.455	226.56	547.98
	1984	21.509	348.67	694.70
West Germany	1950	21.164	100.00	179.92
	1960	26.080	163.09	387.21
	1973	26.849	331.78	675.49
	1984	25.111	478.99	811.60
Japan	1913	26.046	56.66	54.76
	1950	35.683	100.00	124.34
	1960	44.670	156.06	295.17
	1973	52.590	584.77	976.50
	1984	57.660	1255.23	1468.40
Netherlands	1913	2.330	45.99	20.33
	1950	3.625	100.00	49.40
	1960	4.101	138.46	76.99
	1973	4.646	238.25	142.20
	1984	4.971	344.53	168.90
UK	1913	18.566	65.17	174.78
	1950	22.400	100.00	281.04
	1960	24.225	128.51	372.80
	1973	24.993	210.12	556.60
	1984	23.984	276.06	625.20
USA	1913	38.821	51.34	454.53
	1950	61.651	100.00	1257.86
	1960	69.195	137.18	1735.92
	1973	88.868	214.74	2911.78
	1984	107.734	290.66	3746.50

Source: Maddison (1987), tables A–1, A–7 and A–15.

in three of the four countries for which the comparison could be made, indicating faster technological progress, the exception being the United States. This was probably because these countries were going through a period of rehabilitation of war damage, so that even modest rates of capital accumulation gave rise to substantial improvements in growth performance. Again with the exception of the United States, technological progress in the sense defined here was slower in the period 1960–73 compared with 1950–60 in all other

Table 6.5   Sources of growth I: six DCs

Country (period)		Labour	Capital	GDP Growth Rate due to: Other factors	Residual	Total
France	1913–50	–0.31	0.76	0.13	0.48	1.06
	1980–73	0.36	1.66	1.30	1.81	5.13
	1973–84	–0.38	1.63	0.34	0.59	2.18
West Germany	1913–50	0.20	0.58	0.20	0.32	1.30
	1950–73	0.47	2.41	1.41	1.63	5.92
	1973–84	–0.83	1.38	0.44	0.89	1.68
Japan	1913–50	0.41	0.99	0.71	0.13	2.24
	1950–73	2.51	3.46	2.76	0.64	9.37
	1973–84	0.59	2.55	0.60	0.04	3.78
Netherlands	1913–50	0.80	1.10	0.12	0.41	2.43
	1950–73	0.58	1.74	1.32	1.06	4.70
	1973–84	0.08	1.36	–0.32	0.46	1.58
UK	1913–50	0.12	0.79	0	0.38	1.29
	1950–73	–0.02	1.51	0.47	1.06	3.02
	1973–84	–0.73	1.15	0.15	0.49	1.06
USA	1913–50	0.60	0.99	0.38	0.81	2.78
	1950–73	1.14	1.53	0.24	0.81	3.72
	1973–84	1.31	1.28	–0.26	–0.01	2.32

Source: Maddison (1987), table 20, p. 679.

countries. During this period, most of the growth was associated with a high rate of capital deepening.

The period 1973–84 is particularly interesting, because this was the period of slower growth in all the six countries. To some extent, the slower growth was due to slower growth of capital stock. But apart from this factor, there was also a significant negative effect due to slower technological progress. The same conclusions also appear in Maddison's estimates of the sources of growth shown in Table 6.5. It is difficult to explain the slowing down of the rate of technological progress associated with capital accumulation only in terms of supply conditions. The above analysis has not taken account of some other factors affecting growth, such as the effect of foreign trade and the re-allocation effect. But even allowing for these, the large negative effect due to the technological factor remains a puzzle. It suggests that it may have been due to a significant effect from the demand side as will be discussed in later chapters.

Table 6.6   Per worker incremental output–capital ratio: 6 DCs

Country (period)		Per Worker ICOR (β)
France	(1950–60)	3.85
	(1960–73)	2.85
	(1973–80)	1.20
West Germany	(1950–60)	4.15
	(1960–73)	1.69
	(1973–84)	1.07
Japan	(1913–50)	2.20
	(1950–60)	4.52
	(1960–73)	1.57
	(1973–82)	0.65
Netherlands	(1913–50)	0.62
	(1950–60)	0.83
	(1960–73)	0.68
	(1973–82)	0.19
UK	(1913–50)	3.28
	(1950–60)	3.38
	(1960–73)	2.22
	(1973–84)	1.22
USA	(1913–50)	29.03
	(1950–60)	13.00
	(1960–73)	17.70
	(1973–84)	7.14

Source: Table 6.4.

(d) Increasing Returns to Scale

Most studies of the sources of growth have been based on production functions subject to constant returns to scale, thus ruling out the role of increasing returns. There have been some attempts to estimate the effect of increasing returns, but these estimates have generally been quite low. For example, Maddison (1987, p. 671) assumes that 'the scale bonus at the national level for these six countries is only 3 per cent of GDP growth'.

In fact, increasing returns have played a much greater role in economic growth, especially in the industrial sector. This has been recognised ever since Adam Smith. There have been many studies of actual production processes showing the significance of increasing returns (see e.g. E.A.G. Robinson, 1953; Marshall, 1961, ch.

Table 6.7 Alternative sources of growth: 6 DCs

Country (period)		Growth of employment and capital widening	Capital deepening and previous period technical progress	Change in rate of technical progress since previous period	Total
France	1950–60	0.24	4.32	0	4.56
	1960–73	0.71	6.54	–1.69	5.56
	1973–84	0.02	5.15	–2.99	2.18
West Germany	1950–60	2.21	5.76	0	7.97
	1960–73	0.23	10.17	–6.03	4.37
	1973–84	–0.62	3.64	–1.34	1.68
Japan	1913–50	0.87	1.37	0	2.24
	1950–60	2.40	3.23	3.40	9.03
	1960–73	1.41	23.71	–15.48	9.64
	1973–84	0.86	7.07	–4.15	3.78
Netherlands	1913–50	1.21	1.22	0	2.43
	1950–60	1.27	2.45	0.82	4.54
	1960–73	1.00	4.73	–0.90	4.83
	1973–84	0.62	3.47	–2.51	1.58
UK	1913–50	1.51	0.78	0	1.29
	1950–60	0.80	2.01	0.06	2.87
	1960–73	0.24	4.40	–1.51	3.13
	1973–84	–0.38	2.60	–1.16	1.06
USA	1913–50	1.27	1.51	0	2.78
	1950–80	1.17	4.68	–2.58	3.27
	1960–73	1.96	1.54	0.56	4.06
	1973–80	1.77	1.36	–0.81	2.32

Source: Derived from Table 6.5.

X–XIII; United Nations, 1964; Pratten, 1971). In spite of a widespread recognition of its importance in practice, the role of increasing returns has not been fully taken into account in theoretical studies of its contribution to economic growth.

This is because the theoretical study of the phenomenon of increasing returns raises some major problems, which were first noted in the celebrated article of Young (1928). One problem is that the realisation of increasing returns in practice is tightly interlinked with the processes of technological change and of capital accumulation. As Young (1928, pp. 530–1) says:

It is generally assumed that Adam Smith, when he suggested that the division of labour leads to inventions because workmen engaged in specialized routine operations come to see better ways of accomplishing the same results, missed the main point. The important thing, of course, is that with division of labour, a group of complex processes is transformed into a succession of simpler processes, some of which, at least, lend themselves to the use of machinery . . . The principal economies of scale which manifest themselves are the economies of capitalistic or roundabout methods of production . . . The economies of roundabout methods, even more than the economies of other forms of the division of labour, depend upon the extent of the market.

From this, it follows that increasing returns are an essentially dynamic phenomenon. They cannot be studied just by relating them to the scale of production of individual firms or industries, nor just to the mere passage of time. In particular, they cannot be studied by the highly static models of neo-classical economics. As Young (1928, pp. 528, 533) says further:

Change becomes progressive and propagates itself in a cumulative way. No analysis of the forces making for economic equilibrium, forces which we might say are tangential at any moment of time, will serve to illumine this field for movements away from equilibrium, departures from previous trends, are characteristic of it . . . the counter forces which are continually defeating the forces which make for equilibrium are more pervasive and more deeply rooted in the constitution of the modern economic system than we commonly realise.

Further, the occurrence of increasing returns depends on the interaction between supply and demand factors. Again, to cite Young (1928, p. 534):

An increase in the supply of one commodity *is* an increase in the demand for other commodities, and it must be supposed that every increase in demand will evoke an increase in supply . . . Even in a stationary population and in the absence of new discoveries in pure or applied science, there are no limits to the process of expansion except the limits beyond which demand is not elastic and returns do not increase.

It is in this sense that Rostow (1975, p. 16) described the historical experience of developed countries as 'an explosive interaction between cost-reducing innovation and elastic demand embraced by the case of increasing returns'.

While there are difficulties in applying the static equlibrium theories of mainstream economics to the study of increasing returns, the practical importance of the phenomenon cannot be ignored in any study of the process of industrial growth. One of the most useful ways of studying the process is the generalisation known as Verdoorn's Law (for a survey of statistical estimates of this relationship, see Cornwall, 1977, pp. 126–8; 148–9). In this generalisation, the role of increasing returns is shown by a relationship between the rate of growth of productivity and the rate of growth of output, rather than the relationship between the level of output and the level of average productivity. A more significant point is that, the relationship between the growth of output and the growth of productivity may be interpreted as showing the influence of the growth of output on the growth of productivity, rather than only the influence of the growth of productivity on the growth of output. Hence, for example, part of the explanation for the slow-down of technological progress in the developed countries since 1973, noted above, may be the slow-down of economic growth, rather than the other way about. Then, we have to look elsewhere to explain the slow-down of output growth, such as the demand factors to be considered in Part III.

6.3 CAUSES OF TECHNOLOGICAL PROGRESS

As discussed in the previous section, the process of technological change is tightly intertwined with that of capital accumulation and the phenomenon of increasing returns. This interaction is the source of much of the difficulty of estimating the contribution of technological progress to the growth of output. But it is obvious that technological progress has been a significant factor in the long-term growth process. Therefore, we now turn to consider the causes of technological progress as it has occurred in various countries at various times.

The process of technological progress consists of various phases. A convenient classification of these phases is that suggested by Nabseth and Ray (1974; see also Cornwall, 1977, p. 105, and Hacche, 1979, ch. 9) as follows:

1. the discovery of new products or processes, i.e. 'inventions';
2. the development of inventions into commercially feasible and profitable techniques, i.e. 'innovations':

3. the modification of innovations in the course of actual use, i.e. 'the learning process'; and
4. the spread of profitable innovations among firms in an industry or between countries i.e. 'diffusion'.

The scientific breakthroughs leading to new inventions (the first phase) may be a random process. If technological progress consisted only of these strokes of luck, it may largely be an exogenous process. This is in fact how it was viewed in many of the earliest studies. But this is only one phase of the whole process. Later phases deal with the application of a given stock of inventions to actual production activities. Therefore, at least in these later phases, the rate of technological progress will be subject to economic influences, i.e. to be endogenous to some extent. Some of the economic influences that have been discussed in the literature are discussed in this section.

Technological progress itself can be analysed in terms of supply and demand factors. Because technological progress, especially in the industrial sector, depends so much on the application of modern science, it depends on such supply factors as the stock of scientific and technical manpower, and the state of the scientific establishment. On the demand side, technological progress depends on the profitability of applying the new inventions that may be available, and the demand for the products which can be produced with them.

Some theories of technological progress have stressed the demand side exclusively, following the principle that 'necessity is the mother of invention'. We have already discussed Boserup's theory that agricultural innovations were induced by population growth on limited land (section 5.2). An application to the industrial sector is that advanced by Schmookler (1966). On the basis of the number of patents taken out by inventors in the United States, he concluded that technological change was largely induced by the rate at which the demand for various products grew over time: 'the amount of invention is governed by the size of the market . . . A million dollars spent on one kind of good is likely to induce as much invention as the same sum spent on any other good' (Schmookler, 1966, p. 172). For demand to have played such a dominant role implies that the supply of inventions was infinitely elastic. This may indeed have been the case in the United States and other developed countries, in which most of such studies had been carried out. To the extent that this is not true in other countries, we have to allow for both supply and demand factors in the process of technological change.

Another major theme in the literature, also based on the primacy of demand factors, is the theory that the direction of technological change is influenced by the relative prices of factors of production. This theory was originally advanced by Hicks (1932, ch. 6) to explain the predominance of labour-saving inventions in the history of the developed countries. According to him, some inventions are 'autonomous' while others are 'induced'. Autonomous inventions are just as likely to be labour saving as capital saving. Induced innovations on the other hand, are more likely to be influenced by changes in the relative prices of the factors of production.

> A change in the relative prices of the factors of production is itself a spur to invention, and to invention of a particular kind – directed to economising the use of a factor of production which has become relatively expensive. The general tendency to a more rapid increase of capital than labour which has marked European history during the last few centuries has naturally provided a stimulus to labour-saving invention (Hicks, 1932, pp. 124–5).

(For the application of this theory by Hayami and Ruttan to the agricultural sector, see section 5.2).

However, the approach has been challenged by Salter (1960, pp. 43–4) on the ground that:

> If (Hicks's) theory implies that dearer labour stimulates the search for new knowledge aimed specifically at saving labour, then it is open to serious objection. The entrepreneur is interested in reducing costs in total, not particular costs such as labour costs or capital costs. When labour costs rise any advance that reduces total cost is welcome, and whether this is achieved by saving labour or capital is irrelevant. There is no reason to assume that attention should be concentrated on labour-saving techniques, unless, because of some inherent characteristic of technology, labour-saving knowledge is easier to acquire than capital-saving knowledge.

In order to deal with such criticisms, Hicks's theory was then elaborated by Ahmad (1966) by introducing the concept of an 'innovation possibility curve'. It is then assumed that the choice of innovations from this curve of possibilities is itself responsive to the prevailing relative factor prices. But even this development does not quite distinguish between substitution of factors along a given production function and the bias of technological change as we move from one production function to another. As Hicks (1973, p. 2) himself admitted, 'whether "induced innovations" were to be regarded as shifts in the production function, or as substitutions within an unchanged production function, was left rather obscure'.

The question of how factor prices influence the nature of technological change was also discussed by Kennedy (1964) and Samuelson (1965), but these studies have been primarily concerned with how far induced technological progress occurs in the Harrod-neutral form, which was assumed necessary to explain the stylised facts of growth in the developed countries (for a summary of these discussions, see Hacche, 1979, ch. 8). But these stylised facts do not represent the actual experience of even the developed countries, and much less that of other countries.

In contrast to these studies which stress the demand side, there have been others which stress the supply side, especially in relation to the diffusion phase of technological progress. According to this approach, countries can borrow new technology from more advanced countries, and the rate at which innovations actually occur in a country depends on the technology gap between that country and the most advanced country from which it can borrow. However, if a country is too backward, it may not be able to absorb as much technology as countries higher up the scale of development. Thus, for example, Gomulka (1971, p. 67) suggested that maximum benefits from borrowing technologies occur when per capita incomes in the imitating countries vary from one-tenth to one-half that of the industrial leader. In fact, however, the most successful example of technology borrowing in the post-war period was Japan, whose per capita income in the early 1950s was approximately 12 per cent of the United States.

A remarkable feature of the long-term growth of the developed countries is that the rates of growth of individual countries during any period have been highly negatively correlated with their initial income levels. The rank correlations between initial levels and subsequent growth rates of labour productivity for various periods calculated by Abramovitz (1986), based on estimates compiled by Maddison (1982), are shown in Table 6.8.

The consequence of this negative relationship has been that the dispersion of average incomes among these countries has declined steadily, as shown by the coefficients of variation in the last column of the table. But this relationship holds only for the developed countries

Table 6.8   The catching-up process of DCs: 1870–1979

Year	Rank correlation of growth rates and initial incomes		Coefficient of variation of income levels
	Since last date	Since 1870	
1870	–	–	.58
1890	–.32	–.32	.48
1913	–.56	–.59	.33
1929	–.35	–.72	.29
1938	–.57	–.83	.22
1950	+.48	–.16	.36
1960	–.81	–.66	.29
1973	–.90	–.95	.14
1978	–.13	–.97	.15

Source: Abramovitz (1986), table 2, p. 391.

studied by Maddison. There is no such relationship when we include less-developed countries (see Baumol, 1986, p. 1088).

In commenting on this result, Baumol (1986, p. 1077) has remarked as follows:

The strong inverse correlation between the 1870 productivity levels of the 16 nations and their subsequent productivity growth record seems to have a startling implication. Of course, hindsight always permits "forecasts" of great accuracy – that itself is not surprising. Rather, what is striking is the apparent implication that *only one variable*, a country's 1870 GDP per work-hour, or its relation to that of the productivity leader, matters to any substantial degree, and that other variables have only a peripheral influence. It seems not to have mattered much whether or not a particular country had free markets, a high propensity to invest, or used policy to stimulate growth. Whatever its behaviour, that nation was apparently fated to land close to its predestined position . . . Industrialized countries, whose product lines overlap substantially and which sell a good deal in markets where foreign producers of similar products are also present, will find themselves constantly running in this Schumpeterian race, while those less developed countries which supply few products competing with those of the industrialized economies will not participate to the same degree.

The convergence of income levels has been explained as the result of a 'catching-up' process. It has been expressed by Abramovitz (1986) as follows:

> the larger the technological and, therefore, the productivity gap between leader and follower, the stronger the follower's potential for growth in productivity, and other things being equal, the faster one expects the follower's growth rate to be . . . Countries that are technologically backward have a potentiality for generating growth more rapid than that of more advanced countries provided their social capabilities are sufficiently developed to permit successful exploitation of technology already employed by the technological leaders . . . One should say therefore that a country's potential for rapid growth is strong not when it is backward without qualification, but rather when it is technologically backward but socially advanced . . . The pace at which the potential for catch-up is actually realised in a particular period depends on factors limiting the diffusion of knowledge, the rate of structural changes, the accumulation of capital, and the expansion of demand.

The post-World War II decades then proved to be the period when – exceptionally – the three elements required for rapid growth by catching up came together. The three elements were a large technological gap; enlarged social competence; reflecting higher levels of education and greater experience with large scale production, distribution and finance; and conditions favouring rapid realization of potential.

On this argument, the mere fact that a country has a larger technological gap is not sufficient for it to have faster growth. Whether it does or not depends first on whether it is able to absorb the new technology. The importance of this consideration has been highlighted in the study of Japanese economic growth since the Meiji Restoration. As Kuznets (1973) pointed out, this cannot be explained only by Japan's low initial income, her late arrival, and the greater backlog of technology available for absorption. These conditions were also present in other LDCs which nevertheless failed to achieve rapid growth. For the backlog of technology to promote growth, the superior technology of the more advanced countries must also be relevant to the economy of the borrowing country, and the borrowing country must also have the skills and institutions needed to acquire and adapt the new technology successfully. It was only because Japan had a political and social structure, the education and skills of its labour force, that it was able to grow rapidly by exploiting the backlog of technology from which it had previously been debarred by its historical and geographical isolation. It is to describe these conditions that Okhawa and Rosovsky (1973, esp. ch. 9) coined the phrase 'social capability' to refer to all those factors which determine a country's ability to utilise the international backlog of technological progress.

Further, as pointed out by Abramovitz, even the social capability to absorb new technology is not sufficient to take full advantage of a backlog of technology. It depends also on a rapid expansion of demand both for the goods to be produced with the new technology and for the growth of capital to embody the new technology. This role of demand in promoting the rapid absorption of technology is discussed in Part III.

6.4 DE-INDUSTRIALISATION

As pointed out in Chapter 2, the experience of many countries shows that, once the agricultural sector has fulfilled its historical mission or come near to doing so, there is a long period marked by industrialisation, i.e. a continuous rise in the industrial sector's share of employment and GDP. The process is the result of a complex interaction between supply and demand factors. On the one hand, rapid capital accumulation and technological progress in the industrial sector lead to a high rate of growth of labour productivity. On the other hand, a high income elasticity of demand for manufactures combined with rising income levels leads to a shift of resources to the industrial sector, in particular, it absorbs a large part of the shift of labour out of the agricultural sector. In this process, the industrial sector is the engine of growth for the economy as a whole. The faster growth of labour productivity in the industrial sector and its increasing dominance in the economy leads to an acceleration of growth for the economy as a whole. The rate at which the process occurs varies both across countries and over time, because of differences in the underlying supply and demand factors.

This raises the question whether the process will go on indefinitely. The answer to this question lies in the experience of the most developed countries, which have had the longest experience of industrialisation and which have attained the highest levels of income. We first consider some data which indicate that the process of industrialisation is slowing down in these countries, tendencies which have come to be described as 'de-industrialisation'. One such indication is the cross-section data on the share of the industrial sector in employment and GDP. The data presented in Table 3.6 shows that, while the industrial share of the labour force increases with per capita income most of the way, it is lower in countries at the highest level of income. This is supported by the data presented in Table 3.7, which shows a tendency for the rate of growth of industrial employment to fall as per capita income rises beyond a certain level. Turning next to the industrial share of GDP, Table 3.1 shows that this share also fell as per capita income rose above a certain level, especially in the 1960s and 1970s. This is also supported by the data of Table 3.2 which shows that the growth rate of output in the industrial sector declines with increases in per capita income beyond a certain point, and is lower than the growth rate of GDP.

These results are based on cross-section data for groups of countries. If there is any trend towards de-industrialisation, it must be a tendency which particularly affects the countries at the highest level of income. Therefore, we consider the experience of individual DCs in the post-war period. The data on changes in the industrial share of employment during 1965–80 are summarised in Table 6.9.

The industrial share of employment has declined in 15 of the 19 countries covered. The corresponding data on changes in the industrial share of GDP are summarised in Table 6.10. This shows a decline in 12 of the 15 countries.

These results establish a strong case for a presumption that the highest stages of economic growth are marked by a process of de-industrialisation. However, this presumption is subject to some limitations, which must be examined. For example, it might be thought that the decline in the growth rate of industrial production and in the industrial share of GDP over the period 1965–86 might have been due to the special conditions prevailing in the period after 1973. The slackening of industrial growth in the developed market economies (DMEs) after 1973 coincided with certain other developments, notably the oil shocks, the breakdown of the Bretton Woods arrangements of international payments, and the slowing down in the growth of world trade. A consequence of these developments, and especially their consequences for inflation, unemployment and balance of payments problems was that economic activity became much more sensitive to the role of government policies, especially fiscal and monetary policies designed to influence aggregate demand and the

Table 6.9   Industrial share of employment in DCs: 1965–80

| Country | Industrial Share (%) of Labour Force | |
	1965	1980
Spain	35	37
Ireland	28	34
New Zealand	36	33
Italy	42	41
UK	47	38
Belgium	46	36
Austria	45	41
Netherlands	41	32
France	39	35
Australia	38	32
West Germany	48	44
Finland	35	35
Denmark	37	32
Japan	32	34
Sweden	43	33
Canada	33	29
Norway	37	29
USA	35	31
Switzerland	49	39
Average	38	35

Source: World Bank (1988) table 31, p. 283.

growing inflationary bias. The slackening of industrial growth in this period may have been specially affected by these policy stances of governments. Therefore, it is useful to test the trend towards de-industrialisation against growth rates of industrial production in these countries over shorter periods before 1973. Such data have been compiled by Cornwall (1977, table 11.1, p. 201); they show that 'With the exception of Austria and the United States the trends were downward, certainly since the 1960s'. Therefore, the de-industrialisation process seems to have set in these countries even before 1973, during the years of their most rapid growth.

The de-industrialisation tendency is sometimes thought to be a problem of particular developed countries. Thus, it was for long thought to be a specially British problem in the post-war period (see e.g. Blackaby, 1979). In fact, the rate of growth of industrial production declined continually from 1873 onwards in Britain, the country which led the world in the Industrial Revolution. However, as Lewis

Table 6.10   Industry share of GDP in DCs: 1965–86

Country	Industrial share (%) of GDP	
	1965	*1986*
Spain	36	37
Italy	41	39
UK	46	43
Belgium	41	33
Austria	46	38
France	39	34
Australia	39	34
West Germany	53	40
Finland	37	37
Denmark	36	28
Japan	43	41
Sweden	40	35
Canada	40	36
Norway	33	41
USA	38	31
Average	40	35

Source: World Bank (1988) table 3, p. 227.

(1978, ch. 5) has pointed out in his study of the British climacteric, the early onset of de-industrialisation in Britain was due to special circumstances applying to that country, especially the decline in its competitive power in the international trade in manufactures, the slowing down of technological progress, and the continued adherence to a free trade ideology: 'The British relied on the market economy to bring them into equilibrium; but the market pays no heed to external economies; instead it brought them to relative stagnation'. But the data now available on the more recent experience shows that the tendency towards de-industrialisation is not a problem of particular countries, but one which has begun to affect all the developed market economies. 'If this is, as some say, the "English sickness", it is a sickness which other countries appear to be catching' (Hicks, 1977, p. 38).

Therefore, we have to search for a more general explanation of the process of de-industrialisation. As far as the decline in the industrial share of employment in the DCs is concerned, the main influence is the rapid growth of labour productivity, due to the particularly rapid rate of technological progress in the post-war period and the associated high levels of investment, at least until 1973. But there has also been a tendency for the industrial share of GDP to decline. This must ultimately be due to a shift of demand away from manufactures at these levels of income. Manufactures had been high in the hierarchy of commodities, but eventually the basic human wants satisfied by manufactures must approach satiation, and the invention of new consumption goods to satisfy these wants must slacken off. Then demand will shift to the satisfaction of other wants, especially services which lie higher in the hierarchy of commodities. The role of the service sector, especially at the higher income levels, is considered in the next chapter.

To sum up, this chapter has been concerned with the growth of the industrial sector in a long-term historical perspective. Industrialisation as a major feature of economic growth occurred first in a few countries in western Europe in the late eighteenth century and spread to Japan and European settlements overseas in the nineteenth century. The reasons why industrialisation began in these countries and not in other parts of the world in spite of considerable scientific attainments were discussed in section 6.1. The sources of industrial growth were then discussed in section 6.2. In the standard method based on neo-classical production functions, these sources are defined as the contributions of labour, capital and technological progress. There are, however, serious problems in separately quantifying sources of growth defined in this way, because of the difficulty of estimating the underlying production function. Therefore, an alternative method was proposed which makes fewer assumptions about the production function but takes greater account of the interaction between different factors. The most important source of industrial growth is technological progress, especially embodied in capital accumulation. In section 6.3, it was argued that technological progress, particularly the catching up process by which advanced technology spread to DCs in the post-war period, was determined both by demand and supply factors, especially the growth of industrial exports. Finally, section 6.4 discussed some indications of the process of de-industrialisation in the most advanced countries, especially a tendency for a decline in the industrial share of the labour force.

7 Growth in the Service Sector

7.1 CHARACTERISTICS OF SERVICES

As Solow (1977) put it, 'There is an awful lot of GDP that is neither manufacturing nor primary production'. In fact, in the classification of sectors generally adopted in national accounts, all production other than those which clearly belong to the agricultural (or primary) and industrial sectors is put into the service sector. When goods are put into the service sector on the negative criterion that they do not belong to the commodity producing sectors, one of the main characteristics distinguishing them from other goods is that of intangibility. Another related characteristic is that they are generally not storable, for example, they cannot be embodied in investment or durable consumer goods which can serve for a long period; it is for this reason that the classical economists considered the hiring of labour by the landlord class as 'unproductive consumption'. Another consequence is that they are not generally the subject of trade between countries, and are treated as non-tradables; in fact, however, they enter into international trade in some forms.

(a) Structure of Service Sector

The category of goods defined in this way are a rather mixed bag, consisting of a number of categories differing in many respects other than their intangibility, which are even more important for analysing their role in the growth of the sector. These categories and their relative importance within the service sector are shown in Table 7.1.

One basic distinction between these items is that some of them, such as trade, transport and communications, roads, and non-residential buildings, relate to services involved in production, while others relate to services provided directly to consumers. Kahn (1979) considered this distinction so significant that he suggested that consumer services should be called 'quaternary services', in contradistinction with 'tertiary services' which should be reserved for producer services and personal business services.

136

Table 7.1   Relative importance of categories of services, 1975

Service categories	% of GDP	
	LDCs	DCs
Housing	20.2	22.5
Medical care	6.1	11.2
Transport & communications	11.0	8.0
Recreation & education	15.9	15.2
Other consumption services	13.7	16.5
Government	33.1	26.6
Total Services	100.0	100.0

Sources: Summers (1985), table 1.1, pp. 32–3.

Table 7.2   Capital–labour ratios of commodities and services

Income group	Capital ($000) per man year:	
	Commodities	Services
I	(8)	4.39	2.48
II	(6)	9.24	5.16
III	(6)	5.64	6.21
IV	(4)	6.91	6.32
V	(9)	16.27	9.44
VI	(1)	21.94	10.96

Source: Kravis *et al.* (1983), table 12, p. 206.

Services are generally more labour-intensive than commodities. The difference is shown in Table 7.2 in terms of the capital–labour ratios of commodities and services at different income levels.

The capital–labour ratio rises both for commodities and for services as income level rises, but at most income levels, the capital–labour ratio is lower in services than in commodities. While most services are highly labour intensive, there are also some service activities, especially transport and communication services generally included in infrastructure and provided by the public sector, which are highly capital intensive. These distinctions are particularly important for the analysis of the changes that occur in the service sector in the process of economic growth.

(b) Service Sector Share in GDP

The role of the service sector in the economy as a whole was considered in Chapter 3 in terms of the service sector share in GDP and in employment. The service sector has become particularly important in the developed countries. As Inman (1985, p.1) says:

> In the last three decades we have witnessed a quiet revolution in the composition of economic activity in most major developed countries. The provision of services has replaced the manufacturing of goods as the predominant production activity of advanced economies . . . As we watch the daily affairs of workers and consumers in developed economies we would no longer observe nations of factories, but rather societies predominantly involved in the provision and consumption of services – an economy of doctor's visits, of data collection and processing, of psychological and financial consultations, of teaching, of dining and of travelling.

The dominance of the service sector is sometimes considered a 'post-industrial' phenomenon (e.g. Bell, 1974), but in fact the service sector is quite important even in the less-developed countries. But as shown in Chapter 3, the service sector share of GDP shows a steady increase with the per capita income of countries. That result was based on data at current prices prevailing in the different countries. But the relative prices of commodities vary considerably between countries. That is why a major effort was undertaken by the United Nations in the International Comparison Project (ICP) to estimate national income and its various components at uniform international prices.

The results of the project show that, even in the case of agricultural and industrial products, there is considerable variation in the relative prices between countries. However, in the case of such commodities, the variation of relative prices between countries is smaller than in the case of the relative prices between services and commodities, mainly because commodities enter into international trade much more than services. In fact, it is found from the ICP results that the relative price between services and commodities varies quite systematically with the per capita income of countries, the relative price of services being generally higher in the more developed countries. Because of this tendency, part of the growing share of the service sector at current prices prevailing in different countries may in fact be

Table 7.3   Service sector share of GDP and relative price of services by
income level of countries: 1975

Income group (no. of countries)	Mean index of real GDP per capita (US = 100)	Service sector share of GDP at national prices	Relative price of services in terms of commodities	Service sector shares of GDP at PPP ratio
I (8)	9.0	22.2	36.2	33.8
II (6)	23.1	28.4	51.7	31.7
III (6)	37.3	27.4	49.6	31.8
IV (4)	52.4	25.6	49.3	30.3
V (9)	76.0	36.8	79.5	31.2
VI (1)	100.0	43.9	100.0	32.3

Source: Kravis *et al.* (1983), table 2, p. 191.

due to differences in these prices. This is clearly shown by the
comparison of the ratios of the national prices of services and commodities with the ratios at uniform international prices.

The results for a sample of 30 countries (excluding four centrally
planned economies) divided equally into five classes according to per
capita income are presented in Table 7.3. The third column shows the
steady increase in the service sector share of GDP at current prices,
already noted. The fourth column shows the steady rise in the
relative price of services in terms of commodities with income level.
Hence, we find in the last column that the service sector share in
constant ICP prices does not rise with per capita income, but in fact
shows a slight decline. This adjustment, however, does not affect the
finding in Chapter 3 of a steady rise in the service sector share of
employment with per capita income. In order to explain the variations in the service sector share of GDP and of employment, we now
consider some aspects of the demand for, and supply of, services.

7.2 THE DEMAND FOR SERVICES

(a) The Income Elasticity of Demand for Services

Because of the close relationship between the service sector share of
GDP and per capita income, the first approach that suggests itself is
to consider an explanation in terms of the income elasticity of

demand for services. But we have seen that there is a systematic variation in the relative price of services as per capita income rises. Therefore, we have to allow for the price elasticity of demand also. On the basis of the cross-section data of ICP adjusted values, Summers (1985, p. 41) has estimated that the income elasticity of demand at 0.977 was not significantly different from unity, while the price elasticity of demand at -0.063 was not significantly different from zero.

One weakness of this estimate is that it assumes that the income elasticity of demand is constant at all income levels. It is more likely, however, that the income elasticity of demand varies with the income level, but data are not sufficient to estimate such varying income elasticities. The rapid rise in the role of the service sector in the more advanced countries suggests, however, that the income elasticity of demand for services has also increased with income level, as assumed in the simulation exercises of Chapter 3.

(b) Trade and Transport

In studying the influence of income on demand, we must distinguish among the categories of the service sector. First, we consider trade, transport and communications as illustrating the case of services related to the production process. The demand for these services are likely to be closely related to the volume of production in other sectors. In fact, Summers (1985, p. 41) obtains an income elasticity of demand for transport and communications services at 1.076 which is not significantly different from unity. Further, he also obtains a price elasticity of demand at -0.605 which is significantly different from zero.

(c) Other Services

By contrast, the demand for other services is much more elastic with respect to income. Thus, Summers (1985, p. 41) finds income elasticities of demand significantly different from unity (1.219 for housing; 1.458 for medical care; 0.794 for recreation and education, and 1.301 for other consumption services). The low income elasticity for education may be due to the fact that the proportion of young persons in the population declines as the per capita income of countries rises, and therefore offsets to some extent the higher quantity of education per child demanded at higher income levels.

Summers has also estimated price elasticities of demand and found them to be significantly different from zero (−0.474 for housing, −0.586 for medical care; −0.365 for recreation and education; and −0.682 for other consumption services).

In some cases, there may be an increase in the quantity of services that is consumed at higher income levels. For example, there may be more demand for higher quality of such services as education and health care provided by highly skilled workers. A particularly important factor leading to such a growth of demand is the growth in tourism; tourists are a significant group of consumers of services. Apart from such cases of an increase in the quantity of services consumed at higher income levels, part of the rise in the market demand for services in the course of development is the growing commercialisation of domestic services formerly provided outside the market, especially the demand for domestic service. The commercialisation of domestic services may occur either through the employment of domestic servants or through the provision of domestic services in some other forms.

The employment of domestic servants is quite extensive in low-income LDCs, but this is often due, not so much to the average level of income in these countries, but rather to the unequal distribution of income. This is partly because there is a higher proportion of rich people in unequal societies who can afford to employ such workers. It is also partly because domestic service is a form of disguised unemployment for workers who would otherwise be completely unemployed. In the course of development, employment of domestic servants for this reason tends to decline. In fact, Lewis once remarked that when middle-class families in any country complain about the difficulty of getting domestic servants, it is a sign of development of the country.

Against this, however, there are other forces leading to greater commercialisation of domestic services. In the early stages of development, such services are performed in middle income households by female members of the household. Such services are then not even included in the national income as usually estimated. But in the course of economic development, there is a rise in the labour force participation of these household members. One way in which households adjust to their female members working outside the home may be to employ domestic servants to perform various forms of domestic service, such as babysitting, housekeeping, cooking, etc. But a more common way in the more developed countries is to buy goods in which various forms of service are already packaged with commodities, such as semi-prepared foods and household goods ready to be assembled by the consumers themselves.

(d) Non-market Services

As shown in Table 7.1, a considerable part of the output of the service sector consists of the services provided in the public sector. This is a very special category of services, because the demand for such services comes from public authorities, and is largely independent of market considerations. Attempts have, however, been made to estimate income and price elasticities of demand for such services. For example, Summers (1985, p. 41) has estimated the income elasticity of demand for government services at 0.912 not significantly different from unity, and the price elasticity of demand at −0.448 not significantly different from zero.

A high proportion of government expenditures is spent on services. Therefore, one reason for the growth of government services in the course of economic growth is the well-known tendency for government expenditures to increase with income level, a tendency generally known as Wagner's Law. But the level of government expenditures in a country does not depend only on the level of income. It also depends on special factors such as war expenditures; it has been argued that such expenditures are subject to a ratchet effect, such that once they rise due to special circumstances, they do not fall back entirely after the special circumstances disappear. Another reason for the growth of government expenditures with economic growth is the greater role that governments take on in many countries at high income levels, especially in more intensive regulation of economic affairs. This tendency also operates in LDCs, where governments tend to spend a high proportion of their increasing revenues in expanding the public administration.

7.3 LABOUR PRODUCTIVITY IN THE SERVICE SECTOR

(a) Variations within Service Sector

Next, we turn to the supply factors in the service sector, in particular the level and growth of labour productivity. In some low income countries, the data show that the output per worker in the service sector is quite high, compared with that in other sectors. But this is often due to the fact that a large proportion of service sector workers in these countries are employed in the public sector at high wages determined by government authorities rather than as a result of market forces. Then, the output of these service sector workers tend to be valued at the cost to the government, and hence leads to the impression of high labour productivity.

Apart from such cases, labour productivity in the service sector is lower than in the industrial sector at high levels of income, mainly because labour productivity grows more slowly in the service sector than in the industrial sector. The extreme case of this tendency, cited by Baumol, is the fact that the productivity of labour is practically stagnant in many aspects of the performing arts, where the same work has to be performed almost by the same number of performers. The slower growth of productivity in the service sector is also shown by the fact that differences in labour productivity in services between countries at different income levels are much smaller than that in other sectors.

But as in the discussion of demand factors, we must distinguish between different categories of the service sector. Among services related to production activities, one category is that of transport and communications. Such activities are generally highly capital-intensive, where the average quantity of capital per worker is very high. Hence, the productivity of labour is generally very high. Another category of such services is trade. Such activities are generally highly labour-intensive in the LDCs, so that the productivity of labour is quite low, often not much higher than the productivity of labour in agriculture. In the more developed countries, even trade activities become more capital-intensive, and the productivity of labour is much higher.

In the case of the consumption-related services, the typical situation is that they are highly labour-intensive. In the case of sophisticated services, a great deal of human capital is invested in the workers, so that the productivity of labour is high. In the case of other services provided by unskilled workers, the productivity of labour is much lower. In both cases, however, the growth of productivity is quite low, lower than in the case of the industrial sector and not much higher than in the agricultural sector.

In discussing the growth of labour productivity with special reference to the developed countries, Baumol *et al.* (1985) point out that the service sector contains some of the economy's most progressive as well as its most stagnant activities, but that the growth of employment in the service sector occurs mostly in the stagnant sub-sector of services; therefore, the growth of labour productivity in the service sector as a whole tends to be low. The lag in productivity growth of the sector has a number of important effects on the economy, which are considered below.

(b) Effects of Lagging Productivity in Service Sector

In one of the earliest studies of the subject, Fuchs (1968) offered three explanations for the widespread drift to a service economy in the developed countries, namely (a) an income elasticity of demand for services greater than, or approximately equal to, unity; (b) an increasing commercialisation of service sector activities; and (c) the slower growth of labour productivity in the service sector. Baumol (1967) also considered another factor, the rising relative price of services, itself a consequence of the slower growth of labour productivity in the service sector compared to other sectors.

Baumol (1967) has proposed a mathematical model based on these explanations. The model, as extended by Inman (1985, pp. 17–19) may be summarised as follows, in terms of two sectors – M (industry) and S (services). Let Q_m, Q_s be the outputs, L_m, L_s be the employment of labour, μ and σ be the rates of growth of labour productivity, and p_m, p_s the product prices, in the two sectors respectively. Then, we have

$$Q_m = aL_m e^{\mu t} \tag{7.1}$$

$$Q_s = bL_s e^{\sigma t} \tag{7.2}$$

Taking the price of manufactures as the *numeraire*,

$$p_m = 1 \tag{7.3}$$

Then, wages are given by

$$W = \left(\frac{dQ_m}{dL_m}\right)p_m = ae^{\mu t} \tag{7.4}$$

and the price of services by

$$p_s = \frac{1}{b} W e^{-\sigma t} = \frac{a}{b} e^{(\mu-\sigma)t} \tag{7.5}$$

i.e. p_s rises at the rate equal to the difference between the rates of growth of labour productivity in the two sectors.

Next, we assume that the per capita demand for services is given by

$$\frac{Q_s}{L} = c \left(\frac{p_s}{p_m}\right)^{\beta} W^{\alpha} e^{\Delta t} \tag{7.6}$$

where α is the income elasticity, β the price elasticity, and Δ the rate at which services are commercialised. Then, the labour share of the service sector is given by

$$\lambda_s = \frac{L_s}{L} = \frac{1}{b}\left(\frac{Q_s}{L}\right) e^{-\sigma t}$$

$$= \frac{c}{b} W^{\alpha} e^{\Delta t} \left(\frac{p_s}{p_m}\right)^{\beta} e^{-\sigma t}$$

$$= \frac{c}{b} a^{\alpha} \left(\frac{p_s}{p_m}\right)^{\beta} e^{\alpha\mu t - \sigma t + \Delta t}$$

$$= \frac{c}{b} a^{\alpha} \left(\frac{a}{b}\right)^{\beta} \exp\left[(\alpha\mu-\sigma) + \Delta + \beta(\mu-\sigma)\right]t \tag{7.7}$$

Hence, the growth rate of λ_s is given by

$$\frac{1}{\lambda_s} \frac{d\lambda_s}{dt} = (\alpha-1)\mu + \Delta + (\mu-\sigma)(1+\beta) \tag{7.8}$$

The first term of this expression refers to Fuchs's explanation of the growth of service employment in terms of an income elasticity of demand greater than unity. The second term refers to his explanation in terms of the growing commercialisation of services. The third term refers to the effect of the lagging productivity of the service sector operating through relative prices; this effect is positive if the price elasticity of demand is numerically less than one, as seems to be the case.

Some differences between this model and the analysis of Chapter 3 may be noted. Unlike the previous analysis, the present model takes account of changes in relative prices. However, the present model deals with only two sectors instead of three. Therefore, it is applicable mainly to countries at a high level of development, where the agricultural sector is very small. Because only two sectors are considered, the income elasticity of demand for manufactures can be expressed in terms of the income elasticity of demand for services. In fact, from the above equations we can derive:

Income elasticity of demand for manufactures:

$$\in_m = (1 - \alpha K\lambda_s) / (1 - K\lambda_s) \tag{7.9}$$

where K is a constant. The equation implies first that, if the income elasticity of demand for services is greater than one, that for manufactures must be less than one. Further, the equation shows that, if the service sector share of employment keeps rising, the income elasticity of demand for manufactures must decline continuously. According to the analysis of Chapter 3, the service sector's rising share of employment was explained in terms of both the income elasticity of demand reflecting the demand factor, and slower growth of labour productivity reflecting the supply factor. In estimating the relative importance of the two factors, Kravis *et al.* (1983, pp. 210–11) conclude:

> the driving force behind the expansion of service employment associated with higher per capita incomes in both cross-national and intertemporal data is the evolution of technology rather than the change in wants associated with rising income. This inference rests on the absence of any clear evidence that the income elasticity of demand is consistently (or even on the average) higher for final-product services than for final-product commodities, and the tendency for service prices to rise relative to commodity prices as incomes rise (a tendency observed in both cross-national and intertemporal data)

The implications of these changes in the service sector for economic growth are considered in the following section.

7.4 SERVICES AND OVERALL GROWTH

One aspect of the logistic pattern of growth noted in Chapter 2 was a slackening of economic growth at high levels of income. In Chapter

3, it was argued that this tendency was linked with the service sector for two reasons, one being the increase in the employment share of the service sector with its slower growth of labour productivity, and the other because of the re-allocation of labour from the industrial sector with its higher level of labour productivity to the service sector with its lower level of labour productivity. This process has been going on for a considerable time, perhaps having started in Britain even in the last century (section 6.4).

It is against this background that we have to consider the recent experience of DCs. In the first 25 years of the post-war period, these countries experienced economic growth at an unprecedented rate. This was mainly due to the rapid growth of their industrial sectors, brought about by the liberalisation of trade mainly among the industrial countries themselves. But since 1973, there was a sharp fall in the growth of their industrial sectors, mainly because of the decline in world trade. The decline of world trade among these countries was in turn due to the breakdown of the Bretton Woods system of international payments and the lack of any alternative system based on flexible exchange rates.

Within this broad pattern, however, there were considerable differences between countries. Some countries, notably Japan, were able to maintain or expand their share of declining world exports of industrial products. This was ultimately due to the way their labour markets were organised, so that wage claims could be met without leading to inflationary forces which could not be offset by exchange rate adjustments. On the other hand, there were other countries whose labour markets were organised in such a way that wage claims led to an inflationary trend which could not be offset by policies such as those relating to exchange rates. There may still be considerable scope for continued expansion of the industrial sector to be achieved by improvements in labour market institutions and macroeconomic policies relating to aggregate demand, inflation and the balance of payments.

But apart from these problems of the industrial sector, there is also a trend for labour to shift from the industrial to the service sector for the reasons considered in Chapter 3. Even if this process occurs with full employment of labour, i.e. if all the labour which is surplus to the requirements of the agricultural and industrial sectors is fully absorbed into the service sector, there will be some slackening of economic growth. But in fact, the surplus labour is not being fully absorbed by the service sector, as shown by the high and rising average levels of unemployment in the DCs. Here again there is considerable variation between countries, because of differences in the parameters influencing labour allocation among sectors.

Underlying these differences, a particularly important influence is the role of government policies. This is mainly because a large proportion of services are produced in the public sector, and a large part of government expenditures consists of the purchase of services. For example, Bacon and Eltis (1976) have argued that the rapid growth of the non-market sector in the United Kingdom was one of the main causes of its slower growth, higher inflation and more severe balance of payments problems. Gemmell (1986) has analysed the international experience of a large sample of DCs and LDCs to show that the expansion of the non-market sector has tended to limit the expansion of market output.

The importance of government policy for the service sector is not confined to employment in the public sector alone. It is also important for the effect on some categories of private sector service employment. This may be illustrated by considering the case of the performing arts, particularly in the developed countries. In these countries, the rising price of services means that the performing arts cannot be financed only from box office sales, and require a subsidy from the government (Peacock, 1976). The policies of governments regarding such subsidies therefore has a significant influence on the expansion of this category of services, and its consequences for employment and growth. The case of the performing arts illustrates a problem common to all service sector activities. This is the problem that the developed countries face in absorbing the labour that shifts out of the industrial sector, as labour productivity rises rapidly in that sector. This problem has ultimately to be solved by government policies for expanding aggregate demand. But because the shift of labour has ultimately to be absorbed in the service sector, the growth of aggregate demand has to be directed particularly to that sector.

To sum up, in this chapter, we discussed the growth of the service sector in long-term historical perspective. Section 7.1 dealt with the many different activities which comprise the service sector, and their characteristics. The demand for the various components of the service sector was discussed in section 7.2, especially the extent to which it was determined by non-market forces in the public sector. Section 7.3 then noted the tendency for labour productivity in the service sector to lag behind that in other sectors, and its implications for the price of services relative to the price of commodities. Finally, in section 7.4, we discussed the influence of the service sector on overall growth, especially its role in explaining the slackening of growth in countries at the highest level of development, an aspect of the logistic pattern of growth.

Part III
Demand Factors: The Keynesian Determinants

conditions, such as the nature of their ... as
seasonal distribution of their rainfall ... and
land will vary between areas, however by the ... land
therefore, as to the character which to ... to
illustrate conditions in which ...

The movement in the direction of the ...
as (a) in Figure ... is brought about by ...
of the movement ...

Stationary State

The ultimate position will be ... as one of
of the curves shown in Figure ...
as SS shown in Figure 5.2. It the season level of which
growth reaches a limit is the same as ...

8 Investment

8.1 ROLE OF DEMAND

The supply factors discussed in Part II, i.e. the stocks of the various factors of production and the state of technology, determine an economy's productive capacity. For economic growth to be sustained over any length of time, there must be an expansion of productive capacity. But as pointed out in section 1.3, the level of production in a country does not depend only on its productive capacity. It depends also on the extent to which that productive capacity is actually utilised. Further, to explain growth fully we must also consider how the productive capacity expands from time to time. Both the degree of utilisation of productive capacity at a point of time, and the growth of productive capacity over time, depend on the level and growth of demand. The nature of these relationships is briefly summarised in this section, and the relationships themselves are discussed more fully in the rest of Part III.

(a) Utilisation of Productive Capacity

For productive capacity to be fully utilised, there must be sufficient effective demand for the goods and services that can be produced in the country. This was fully recognised by the classical economists, but they assumed that there would generally be this level of demand, because of their belief in Say's Law that supply creates its own demand. Hence, they concluded that the level of production would correspond to productive capacity. The belief in Say's Law was, in turn, based ultimately on the assumption of the efficient working of markets, especially factor markets, and the speedy adjustment of prices to their equilibrium levels at which demand equals supply. This view of markets was greatly refined by neo-classical economists and reached its most elaborate and sophisticated version in modern general equilibrium theory.

Keynes (1936, p. 32) attributed the dominance of this view to a 'complex of suitabilities in the doctrine to the environment into which it was projected', such as its logical elegance, its intellectual prestige, its apparent justification of various social ills, and the support of the dominant social classes in the capitalist system. But it may also have been due to the fact that, throughout the period of modern economic growth in the western countries, aggregate demand was, on the whole, quite buoyant and sufficient to utilise the expanding productive capacity fairly fully.

The classical economists were, of course, aware that resources were not always fully utilised, and that some part of the labour force may be unemployed from time to time. They explained such unemployment as due to either frictional unemployment or voluntary idleness, or to wages failing to adjust to their equilibrium level due, perhaps, to trade union pressures. Unemployment due to such rigidity of wages has therefore come to be known as classical unemployment.

But this explanation is not sufficient to account for the extent to which resources may not be fully utilised. This became most obvious in the early 1930s, when the western industrial countries were plunged into deep depression. By about 1932, the GDP of these countries was, on average, 10 per cent lower than in 1929, after having grown at an average annual rate of over 4 per cent in the previous decade; the GDP of the United States is estimated to have fallen nearly 30 per cent below the 1929 level (Maddison, 1982, p. 175). Unemployment rates of labour in 1932 reached such high levels as 22 per cent in the United States, 19 per cent in Australia, 18 per cent in Canada, 16 per cent in Denmark, and 15 per cent in U.K. That this occurred even in the developed countries where markets have generally been assumed to work more efficiently than in the less-developed countries showed that markets could not always be relied on to ensure the full utilisation of productive capacity.

Keynes (1936) offered an explanation why markets may fail to bring about full employment, but there has been continuing controversy over what Keynes really meant, and whether his theory is valid. Therefore, the theory is briefly summarised below, in the light of some recent interpretations. According to these interpretations of Keynes's theory, (see e.g. Clower, 1965; Leijonhufvud, 1968), we must distinguish between 'notional' supply and demand in a particular market based on the assumption that all other markets are in equilibrium, and 'effective' supply and demand in a particular market when other markets are not in equilibrium. The coordination of economic activities required to attain full utilisation of resources requires the equilibrium of notional supply and demand, which can only be brought about by simultaneous equilibrium in all markets. But in a world of uncertainty and incomplete information, there is no mechanism to bring this about. Hence, actual utilisation of resources is determined by the equilibrium of effective supply and demand.

Hence the usual methods of analysis are not appropriate. Equilibrium of notional supply and demand is usually studied in what may be called *p-q* diagrams, which show quantities as functions of prices. But if all other markets are not necessarily in equilibrium, the effective demand in a particular market depends not only on the price in that market, but also on the prices and quantities in other markets. However, price adjustments are usually slower than quantity adjustments. Therefore, for simplifying the analysis, we may assume prices to be constant. Then, to study the equilibrium of effective supply and demand, we must use *q-q* diagrams, in which quantities transacted in individual markets depend on quantities transacted in other markets.

Keynes advanced his theory of the determination of national income in terms of certain macroeconomic relationships, a model in which demand factors have a more central place than in classical theory. The theory is best understood by distinguishing sources of demand according to whether they are endogenous, i.e. depend on the level of income, in which case they cannot be used to explain that level, or whether they are exogenous of income level. The endogenous sources of demand are usually classified as consumption, imports and taxes. Alternatively, they may be expressed as 'leakages' of demand, namely savings (S), imports (M) and taxes (T). The exogenous sources of demand are usually classified as investment (I), government expenditures (G) and exports (X). At any time, the exogenous sources of demand must be equal to the leakages of demand, i.e.

$$S(Y-T) + M(Y-T) + T(Y) = I + G + X$$

Once the functions S, M and T are specified, this equation can be solved to express income Y in terms of the exogenous sources of demand, I, G and X. This relationship is illustrated in the familiar Keynesian cross diagram. Income will correspond to the full utilisation of resources only in the special case when the exogenous sources of demand are equal to the leakages at that income level. If the exogenous sources of demand are less than that critical level, then there will be an equilibrium situation in which resources are underutilised.

From this, certain comparative statics are derived, showing the relationship between changes in the exogenous sources of demand and the change in income brought about by them:

$$\Delta Y = \frac{1}{t + (1-t)(m+s)} \, \Delta(I + G + X)$$

where s and m are the marginal propensities to save and to import out of disposable income, and *t* is the marginal rate of tax. The coefficient on the right hand side is the multiplier; as $(m+s)$ and *t* are less than 1, the multiplier will be greater than 1. If there is an under-utilisation of resources to begin with, an increase in the exogenous sources of demand will increase the level of production. This corresponds to the case of growth illustrated in Figure 1.1 of Chapter 1. This effect for each of the three exogenous sources of demand, namely investment, government expenditure and exports, is discussed in this and the next two chapters. But if resources are fully utilised to begin with, an increase in the exogenous sources of demand will lead to inflation. This effect is considered further in Chapter 11.

An interesting feature of the model is that the propensity to save enters in the denominator of the multiplier formula. This means that for a given level of exogenous demand, a higher propensity to save will *reduce* the level of income. This is contrary to the usual classical argument that a higher propensity to save will lead to a higher level of income. Hence, the present result is sometimes known as the 'paradox of thrift'. The difference is that here we are dealing with the effect of savings on demand, whereas the classical theory was dealing with the effect of savings on capital accumulation.

The Keynesian theory was widely accepted in the developed market economies and used as the basis of macroeconomic policies, at least in the first two decades of the post-war period. However, there is some controversy over whether the high levels of employment and the unprecedented rates of economic growth of these countries were entirely due to the pursuit of these policies. It has been argued, for example, that the maintenance of full employment in the post war period may have been due more to the good luck of an autonomous rise of demand, than good management (see e.g. Matthews, 1968 for a study of the British experience). But even on this view, the experience of the developed market economies in this period confirmed the aptness of the Keynesian analysis, which rendered deliberate policies for raising demand unnecessary.

More recently, however, there has been a growing criticism of the Keynesian model. Some of these criticisms are only restatements of the classical position, such as the hypotheses of a natural rate of unemployment, and a vertical Phillips curve at that rate. Others are a repetition of the criticisms originally advanced against the Keynesian theory, such as Pigou's argument that downward wage and price flexibility in the face of unemployment would increase the real value of cash balances and thus raise demand sufficiently to eliminate the unemployment. There were also new criticisms based, for example, on the theory that policy interventions to influence the economy would be frustrated by the rational expectations of individuals in the private sector. Most serious, however, were the criticisms that the Keynesian theory does not explain the simultaneous occurrence of unemployment and inflation, i.e. 'stagflation' in the developed countries especially since 1973.

Even those who accepted Keynes's theory, however, felt that it was only applicable to the developed countries but not to the less developed countries (see e.g. Rao, 1952; Dasgupta, 1954). Instead, they argued that the limited stocks of land and capital in these countries were already being fully utilised. As far as labour was concerned, it could only be combined with land and capital in rigid proportions determined by the prevailing technology. Hence, the extensive unemployment of labour in these countries was due to the scarcity of the cooperating factors of land and capital, rather than to any deficiency of demand (see e.g. Eckhaus, 1955). Hence, the pursuit of Keynesian policies would only lead to inflation. For example, Nurkse (1952, p. 17) who believed that the slow growth of LDCs was due to some deficiency of demand declared that this deficiency: 'is not a deficiency of "effective demand" in terms of Keynesian economics. There is, as a rule, no deficiency of monetary demand; there is no deflationary gap. On the contrary, many of these countries suffer from a chronic inflationary pressure'.

Similarly, Lewis (1954, p. 400–1) argued:

When Keynes's *General Theory* appeared, it was thought at first that this was the book which would illuminate the problems of countries with surplus labour, since it assumed an unlimited supply of labour at the current price, and also, in its final pages, made a few remarks on secular economic expansion. Further reflection, however, revealed that Keynes's book assumed not only that labour is unlimited in supply, but also, and more fundamentally, that land and capital are unlimited in supply – more fundamentally both in the short run sense that once the monetary tap is turned, the real limit to expansion is not physical resources but the limited supply of labour, and also in the long run sense that secular expansion is embarrassed not by a shortage but by a superfluity of saving. Given the Keynesian remedies, the neo-classical system comes into its own again. Hence, from the point of view of countries with surplus labour, Keynesianism is only a footnote to neo-classicism – albeit a long, important and fascinating footnote.

However, while also rejecting the Keynesian analysis for LDCs such as India, J.P. Lewis (1962, p. 64) comes much closer to that theory, when he argues:

> The diagnosis is not a deficiency of demand in the Western (Keynesian) sense. There the problem is a shortage of demand relative to existing, overt, capacity. Here, in the special circumstances of the Indian countryside, we have instead a situation where the capacity for producing many goods is so variable and can be expected to be so responsive to increases in demand that it can be thought of as being, within limits, virtually determined by demand. Or, as Arthur Smithies has remarked recently, we have the appearance of an almost total inversion of Say's law that supply creates its own demand.

But there is nothing in the Keynesian analysis which makes it inapplicable to LDCs. It will be inapplicable only if, as Rakshit (1982, p. 3) pointed out, markets which fail to attain their simultaneous equilibrium speedily in the DCs nevertheless do so in the LDCs. But this is most unlikely to be the case in LDCs where markets are much less developed than in the DCs. Hence, even in LDCs, productive capacity may remain under-utilised for lack of demand. For example, these countries may also suffer from periods of industrial recession due to lack of demand (see Sundrum, 1987, pp. 132–3 for the Indian experience). Similarly, as argued in later chapters, part of the growth of income in some LDCs in the past two or three decades may be attributed to a growth of demand.

(b) Growth of Productive Capacity

Even those who accept Keynes's theory, however, consider it applicable only to the short run in which productive capacity is fixed. Economic growth in the long run is therefore mostly explained in terms of the growth of productive capacity. One reason may be an assumption that prices, which may be rigid in the short run, will be more flexible in the long run, and restore full equilibrium of markets and ensure full utilisation of productive capacity. But the continuous changes which occur during the process of growth do not allow markets the time required to attain their equilibrium. Another reason offered by Swan (1956, p. 334) is that 'when Keynes solved the great puzzle of "Effective Demand" he made it possible for economists once more to study the progress of society in the long run classical terms'. But this argument does not apply to the LDCs, where Keynesian policies have rarely been followed, and does not always apply even to the DCs, especially in recent years when Keynesian policies have not been followed, and resources have not been fully utilised.

But whether productive capacity is fully utilised or not, for economic growth to be sustained over a long period, there must be an expansion of productive capacity, the case illustrated in Figure 1.3 of Chapter 1. Therefore, to explain growth of national income fully, the factors which lead to the expansion of productive capacity must also be considered. The explanations given by the various theories of growth were discussed in Chapter 4. Of the two main elements of productive capacity other than labour, these theories mostly explain the accumulation of capital in terms of savings behaviour, and the improvement of technology in terms of such factors as innovations induced by relative factor prices or by the technological gap between advanced and backward countries. As argued in earlier chapters, there are serious theoretical problems involved in such explanations, and further such explanations are not sufficient to account for the growth of productive capacity that has occurred in practice.

The main thrust of the prevailing theories of growth is that there are certain forces in the economy which lead to the expansion of productive capacity, which in turn lead to a corresponding growth of demand in accordance with Say's Law. This approach is clearly unsatisfactory. In fact, there is a considerable interaction between supply and demand factors. In particular, there are many ways in which a growth of demand induces the expansion of productive capacity. This type of interaction represents a case of demand creating its own supply, i.e. a reversal of Say's Law. This is not just a case of supply increasing because of changes in the relative price of factors of production. Rather, it is a case of there being such an elastic supply of the factors of production that it responds speedily to the growth of demand, even without significant changes in relative prices. Some examples of this interaction are discussed below.

(c) Say's Law in Reverse

The influence of demand on the growth of supply factors can be illustrated by many examples from the growth experience of various countries. For example, even in the case of land which is often assumed to be in fixed supply, we have noted how the growth of export demand for rice led to the rapid expansion of cultivated land in Burma (section 5.1(a)). In the case of labour, it has been observed, for example, that fertility levels have been consistently higher in the post-war period in the less-densely populated Outer Islands of Indonesia compared with conditions of Java, and this has been attributed to a considerable extent to the growth of demand for labour.

Even more important are the influence of demand on the accumulation of capital and the progress of technology (for a detailed discussion, see Cornwall, 1972, ch. 4). The influence of demand on investment has been widely noted in the acceleration principle. The response of investment to opportunities for profitable investment, irrespective of savings behaviour, has already been noted in the discussion of Nurkse's concept of the 'weak inducement to invest' in LDCs, in the face of an elastic supply of capital, the case of 'unlimited supplies of capital'. The growth of demand, and expectations about such growth, is one of the main elements of the 'animal spirits' which Keynes argued as the basis of investment levels.

In the case of technological progress, we have already noted Boserup's theory of agricultural innovations occurring in response to the growth of demand for food, induced by population growth. We have also noted Schmookler's theory of industrial innovations induced by the growth of demand, in the face of an elastic supply of such innovations. Another major source of technological progress is through the process of learning by doing i.e. the process in which improvements in production techniques are achieved by their more intensive use with the growth of demand for their products. Above all, the significant role of increasing returns to scale is a case of increasing productivity through larger scale of production, also due to the growth of demand.

In view of these interactions, we have to admit that demand factors do play a significant role in the growth process. We consider this role with reference to the three major exogenous sources of demand, beginning with investment in the rest of this chapter, and dealing with government expenditures and exports in the next two chapters. The role of these demand factors is discussed taking account both of their effects on the supply factors, i.e. the classical determinants of growth, and also of their impact on the various sectors of the economy, and then their effects on the structural determinants of growth.

8.2 THE DUAL ROLE OF INVESTMENT

Investment plays a dual role in the growth process. On the one hand, investment increases the productive capacity of the economy in the long run. On the other hand, investment expenditures are a source of demand in the short period when they are incurred. In view of these two roles of investment, the first question that arises is under what conditions the two roles of investment are consistent with each other. This was the question addressed by Harrod (1939) and Domar (1946) and elaborated in a number of subsequent publications (for a detailed survey, see Asimakopoulos, 1986). Their answer was that the two roles will be consistent only if investment grows over time at a particular rate, which Harrod described as the 'warranted rate of growth'.

(a) The Warranted Rate of Growth

The first point to note is that, if Say's Law holds at all times, the above question will not arise because whatever the changes in aggregate supply brought about by investment, aggregate demand will always be equal to it. But if this assumption is rejected as argued in section 8.1(a) demand will not necessarily keep pace with productive capacity, when investment grows at any arbitrary rate. This can be seen most clearly by considering the case in which investment expenditures remain constant year after year. Then, according to the Keynesian multiplier theory, the level of aggregate demand will also remain constant year after year. But even a constant level of investment will steadily increase the productive capacity of the economy. Therefore, in this case, the growth of demand will fall short of the growth of productive capacity. This shows that, for the growth of demand to keep pace with the growth of productive capacity, there must be some growth in investment expenditures over time.

The rate at which investment must grow for demand and supply to be in equilibrium over time was derived by Harrod and Domar as follows. Suppose in year 1, investment is I_1 and the propensity to save is s. Then, neglecting other leakages and other exogenous sources of demand, aggregate demand will be I_1 / s. Suppose also that productive capacity in that year is P_1 and that it is fully utilised. Then

$$Y_1 = P_1 = I_1 / s. \tag{8.1}$$

The investment in year 1 will increase productive capacity in future years. The increase in productive capacity next year may be expressed in terms of the incremental capital–output ratio, C, as follows:

$$P_2 - P_1 = I_1 / C \tag{8.2}$$

If investment in year 2 is I then aggregate demand in year 2 will be

$$Y_2 = I_2 / s \tag{8.3}$$

Then, for this aggregate demand to be equal to productive capacity in year 2,

$$(I_2 / s) = (I_1 / s) + (I_1 / C) \tag{8.4}$$

This can also be written as:

$$GI = (I_2 - I_1) / I_1 = s / C \tag{8.5}$$

This shows the rate at which investment must grow for demand to keep pace with the growth of productive capacity. If it is further assumed that the ICOR is constant over time, it follows that income will also grow at the same rate as investment, i.e. at the rate given by (8.5). This is Harrod's warranted rate of growth.

Alternatively, we can also write (8.4) as:

$$(I_2 - I_1) / sY_1 = I_1 / CY_1 \tag{8.6}$$

It is convenient to write IR for I / Y occurring on the right-hand side to stand for the investment ratio, and to write KI for $(I_2 - I_1) / Y_1$ occurring on the left-hand side to stand for the growth contribution, or the K-ratio for short, of investment. Then equation (8.6) can be written as:

$$KI / s = IR / C \tag{8.7}$$

In equations (8.6) and (8.7), the right-hand side refers to the supply effects of investment, and the left-hand side to the demand effects. This way of measuring supply effects in terms of investment as a ratio to GDP, and demand effects in terms of the K-ratio of investment, is a particularly convenient result, which will also be applied to other exogenous expenditures in later chapters.

In some expositions, equation (8.5) with GY substituted for GI, is derived as follows:

$$\frac{\Delta Y}{Y} \cdot \frac{I}{\Delta Y} = \frac{I}{Y} \tag{8.8}$$

This relationship is often used in development planning to estimate the investment requirements of a *target* rate of growth of income, for an assumed value of the ICOR. But the target rate of growth of income and investment need not necessarily be the rate at which the growth of demand is just right to utilise productive capacity expanded by the new investment. It will be so only if it also assumed that savings will be just equal to this level of investment. By contrast, equation (8.5) defines the warranted rate of growth for given rates of savings and ICOR, at which demand grows just sufficiently to make full use of the growing productive capacity.

The above discussion follows the version due to Harrod. Domar's theory is basically the same as Harrod's, but there are some differences. For example, Domar makes a distinction between the maximum and the actual rate at which investment adds to productive capacity, but this is not essential for the present argument. In assessing the latter rate, Domar also allows for such technological progress as may be occurring at the same time as investment takes place.

So far, we have assumed that investment is the only source of exogenous demand and the only way to expand productive capacity, and that savings are the only leakages of endogenous demand. The model must, therefore, be modified to take account of other leakages, and the role of all exogenous sources of demand and of technological progress in expanding productive capacity, i.e. including government expenditures and exports, which have been very important especially in the post-war decades. These modifications turn out to be quite simple, for it only needs equation (8.7) to be rewritten as:

$$\frac{KI + KG + KX}{t + (1-t)\,(m+s)} = \frac{IR + GR + XR}{C'} \tag{8.9}$$

where *KG* and *KX* are the *K*-ratios of government expenditure and of exports respectively, *C'* represents the productivity effects of investment, government expenditures and exports, and the denominator on the left-hand side is the generalisation of *s* to take account of other leakages.

(b) The Natural Rate of Growth

Harrod also put forward the concept of a 'natural rate of growth' sharply distinguished from the warranted rate of growth. In his latest statement of the concept, he says (Harrod, 1973, pp. 167–8):

> There is a quite different growth rate, that I have called the 'natural' growth rate, namely the growth rate that fully utilises the increase in working population and also embodies technological progress as regards methods for producing goods and services, as and when it is available to be thus embodied. What is not widely recognized in current writings is that there are two normative growth rates, and that the one that enables investment requirements to absorb the savings that people want to make, and the one that corresponds to the increase of manpower and technological progress, currently available for application, may be *entirely different*. Indeed it would be a mighty coincidence if these two growth rates, namely the one that suffices to embody preferred savings into real capital and the one that suffices to embody reasonably available technological progress were the same. I do not find this all important difference much stressed in current writings. It is clearly very fundamental to a correct theory of economic growth.

If we consider technological progress as the means by which labour becomes more productive, and therefore use the concept of 'efficiency' units of labour, then Harrod's natural rate of growth may be considered as the rate of growth which will lead to full employment of labour in efficiency units. Therefore, the distinction between the natural and the warranted rates of growth becomes the difference between the rates of growth needed for the full employment of labour in efficiency units and the full utilisation of the capital stock. Domar, on the other hand, does not make such a sharp distinction, his fundamental equation being essentially one that maintains the full employment of labour, closer to Harrod's natural rate than to his warranted rate.

8.3 THE STABILITY OF GROWTH EQUILIBRIUM

(a) The Actual Rate of Growth

The warranted and the natural rates of growth are normative concepts. So far, we have not considered any mechanism which operates to make the actual rate of growth equal to either of these normative rates. Keynes (1936) himself assumed that the actual level and growth of investment were largely exogenous. In Chapter 11 of his *General Theory*, he sets forth the standard view that the rate of interest determines the point to which new investment will be pushed given the marginal efficiency of capital, but the next seven chapters are devoted to two themes, one that the rate of interest is determined, not by the equilibrium between savings and investment, but rather by the equilibrium between the supply and demand for money, and the other that the marginal efficiency of capital depends on the expectations that entrepreneurs hold about the future profitability of current investments. Further, he held that changes in the marginal efficiency of capital were much more influential in determining investment than changes in the rate of interest. 'Most, probably, of our decisions to do something positive, the full consequences of which will be drawn out over many days to come, can only be taken as a result of animal spirits – of a spontaneous urge to action rather than inaction' (Keynes, 1936, p. 161).

(b) The Instability Principle

But if actual investment is determined by such exogenous factors, there is no reason why the growth rate of investment should equal its warranted rate. In fact, Harrod argued that, if investment does not grow at the warranted rate, the resulting growth process would be highly unstable. To explain this result, he assumed that investment will be determined by the extent to which existing productive capacity is being utilised. In particular, if the economy is on the warranted rate of growth in any year, it will continue to be on that path in future years also. This is because the warranted rate of growth 'will leave all parties satisfied that they have produced neither more nor less than the right amount' (Harrod, 1939, p. 16) and therefore 'it will put them into a frame of mind which will cause them to give such orders as will maintain the same rate of growth'. But if the current level of investment is below that required for the full utilisation of existing capacity, i.e. the case where the economy is below the warranted rate of growth, then entrepreneurs will be so discouraged that they will reduce the amount of investment they undertake in the future. That is, if income falls below productive capacity in any one year, it will fall further below productive capacity in the next year, and so on, so that the movement of income will diverge further and further away from the movement of productive capacity. This is the 'instability principle'. It is implicit in Domar's analysis, but it is explicitly stated by Harrod, who considered it the centre piece of his analysis. As he once described it, 'the warranted rate of growth is surrounded by centrifugal forces and a chance divergence from the warranted rate will be accentuated' (Harrod, 1959, p. 460). The growth process is poised on a 'knife edge', though Harrod himself only claimed that the cumulative divergences from the warranted rate of growth will occur only for large rather than small disturbances.

One criticism of Harrod's exposition, pointed out, for example, by Alexander (1950, p. 728) was that the rate of investment which is just right for one year need not be right for the next year also. Therefore, the underlying assumptions were spelt out more clearly by later writers. According to the formulation of Ackley (1961, pp. 518–21), suppose sales V_t at time t equals consumption C_t and investment I_t at that time:

$$V_t = C_t + I_t \tag{8.10}$$

where consumption depends on the current income, Y according to

$$C_t = aY_t \tag{8.11}$$

and investment depends on the current growth of income according to

$$I_t = b(Y_t - Y_{t-1}) \tag{8.12}$$

Note that, according to equation (8.12) the level of investment is determined by the *current* growth of income. It is then assumed that the growth of income in the current period will be related to that in the last period, according to the relationship:

$$(Y_t / Y_{t-1}) = (Y_{t-1} / Y_{t-2}) (V_{t-1} / Y_{t-1}) \tag{8.13}$$

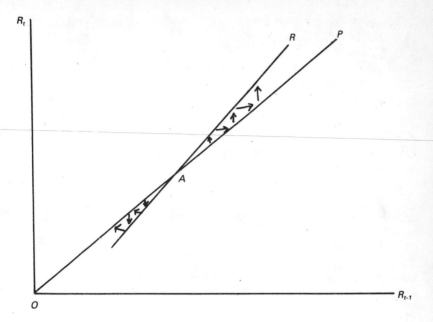

Figure 8.1

i.e. the current growth rate will be equal to, greater or less than, the growth rate in the previous period, according as sales in the last period were equal to, greater or less than, output in that period. This is one way of formalising Harrod's assumption about the behaviour of entrepreneurs. From these equations, writing $R_t = Y_t / Y_{t-1}$ it follows that

$$R_t = (a+b) R_{t-1} - b \qquad (8.14)$$

This relationship is illustrated in Figure 8.1.

In this diagram, the line R represents the relationship between the two growth rates according to equation (8.14), assumed to have a slope greater than 1 because the coefficient b will usually be greater than 1 and OP is the 45° line through the origin. Hence, R will cut the line OP from below, say at the point A. Then, if the initial growth rate is at the point A, it will be reproduced year after year, but if it falls above or below that point, subsequent growth rates will move further and further away from the initial rate, as shown by the arrows in the diagram.

An alternative version of Harrod's model was suggested by Rose (1959) and was followed by other writers (e.g. Ackley, 1961, pp. 526–9; Morishima, 1969, pp. 61–2) based on a capital stock adjustment process. That is, the level of investment in any year depends on the relationship between the actual and the desired stock of capital in the preceding year. The desired capital stock for an income level of Y is given by bY where b stands for the aggregate capital–output ratio. Then, writing K for the actual stock of capital at time t, the investment at that time may be expressed as

$$I_t = bY_{t-1} - K_{t-1} \tag{8.15}$$

Taking first differences, we get

$$(I_t - I_{t-1}) = b(Y_{t-1} - Y_{t-2}) - (K_{t-1} - K_{t-2}) \tag{8.16}$$

But the last term representing the increase in the capital stock equals investment in that year. Therefore, we get

$$(I_t - I_{t-1} + I_{t-2}) = b\,(Y_{t-1} - Y_{t-2}) \tag{8.16a}$$

Then, we have the multiplier relationship which gives income in any year in terms of the investment that year:

$$Y_t = I_t / (1 - a) \tag{8.17}$$

Substituting (8.17) into (8.16), we get

$$(1 - a)\,(Y_t - Y_{t-1} + Y_{t-2}) = b\,(Y_{t-1} - Y_{t-2}) \tag{8.18}$$

This can be written in terms of growth rates R_t as follows:

$$R_t = \left(1 + \frac{b}{1 - a}\right)\left(1 - \frac{1}{R_{t-1}}\right) \tag{8.19}$$

This relationship is illustrated in Figure 8.2, which corresponds to Figure 8.1.

It follows that the rates of growth again show the same cumulative instability, at least in the neighbourhood of the equilibrium point, that was noticed in Figure 8.1.

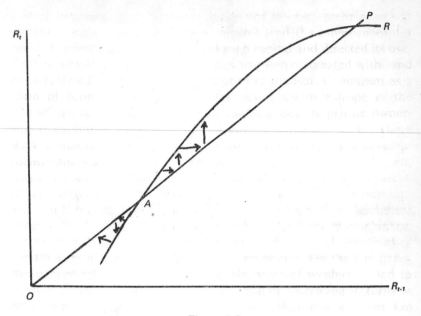

Figure 8.2

The implication of such instability is that 'a capitalist system is perpetually tottering on the brink of disaster' (Cornwall, 1972, p. 36). But in practice capitalist economies have had long periods of growth with only moderate fluctuations. This was the main motivation for developing the neo-classical theory of growth based on the Solow–Swan model as the alternative to the highly unstable Harrod–Domar model. However, it must be noted that the instability of Harrod's model is that between the actual and the warranted rates of growth, while the Solow–Swan model deals with the convergence of the growth rates of capital and labour, which corresponds more closely to the relationship between the warranted and the natural rates of growth in Harrod's analysis. Therefore, the question of stability or instability in the two models refers to different concepts (see Solow, 1988, p. 310). Further, the instability of Harrod's model refers to a fast moving process; he talks about the 'runaways of the actual growth rate from the warranted rate' (Harrod, 1973, p. 178) whereas the stability of the Solow–Swan model is based on a much slower process.

Another confusion in the standard textbook presentation is that the difference in the stability properties of the two models is attributed to the difference in the production functions assumed in them, i.e. the variable factor proportions in the Solow–Swan model and the fixed proportions in the Harrod model. This is not correct, for as Stiglitz and Uzawa (1969, pp. 12–3) clearly point out in their introduction to these theories, 'The reason that the Solow model is stable and the Harrod unstable is not because Solow allows for the possibility of substitution of capital for labour, but because of different assumptions about dynamic adjustments and the determination of aggregate output'. In particular, the Solow–Swan model assumes that investment is determined by savings, while this assumption is rejected by Harrod, following Keynes. It is only by rejecting this assumption that there is any role for demand factors to influence growth.

Ultimately, the reason for the instability of the Harrod model is that there is no mechanism in the model to bring supply and demand into line. One way in which they can be brought into line is by assuming that it is demand which adjusts to supply. This is the adjustment assumed in Say's Law. Attempts have also been made to construct a stable model independently of this assumption by incorporating the interaction between the multiplier and the accelerator principles; these are discussed below.

(c) Multiplier Accelerator Models

One of the earliest of such models is that of Samuelson (1939). The equations of that model are written as follows:

$$Y_t = C_t + I_t + g \tag{8.20}$$

where g represents a constant level of government expenditures. Consumption C and investment I are given by:

$$C_t = \alpha Y_{t-1} \tag{8.21}$$

$$I_t = \beta \left(C_t - C_{t-1} \right) = \alpha\beta \left(Y_{t-1} - Y_{t-2} \right) \tag{8.22}$$

Note that, according to (8.22), investment is determined by the past growth of income. From these equations, we get

$$Y_t = \alpha \, (1 + \beta) \, Y_{t-1} - \alpha\beta \, Y_{t-2} + g \tag{8.23}$$

This is a simple second order difference equation with constant coefficients, which generates various possibilities, such as steady convergence of income to, or divergence away from, an equilibrium value, or damped or explosive cycles, depending on the values of the parameters (for a detailed derivation, see Allen, 1967, pp. 336–9). This model generates cycles, but it does not explain growth, because the equilibrium value of income is a constant given by:

$$\bar{Y} = \frac{1}{1-\alpha} \, g \tag{8.24}$$

Thus, while the Harrod model generates an equilibrium path of steady growth under certain assumptions, the Samuelson model only leads to a constant equilibrium income, although both are based on the accelerator relationship. This is because investment is determined by the *current* growth of income in the Harrod model, while it is determined by the *past* growth of income in the Samuelson model. In other words, in the latter model the growth of investment is explained by the growth of consumption, an endogenous source of demand, and cannot therefore explain growth.

The Samuelson theory was therefore modified by Hicks (1950) to explain both growth and cycles. For the cyclical part, Hicks takes the explosive case of the Samuelson model, but constrains it by a ceiling and a floor. However growth of income in the Hicks model is due to the growth of autonomous investment, which itself is not explained. Similarly, Cornwall (1972, ch. 3) has discussed a version of the multiplier-accelerator interaction based on the capital stock adjustment process, but also assuming autonomous growth in some element of demand.

Another problem with Hicks's model is that it explains growth and cycles by different mechanisms. This does not take full account of the close interconnection between growth and cycles in the historical experience of the DCs. From this point of view, a more satisfactory theory is that of Schumpeter which explains growth and cycles as parts of the same process, i.e. growth was caused by technological progress, and cycles by the bunching of innovations in the same process. According to him, the investment needs for absorbing these new techniques were provided by an elastic banking system.

Finally, we may also mention briefly the treatment of investment in Kaldor's growth models (1957, 1961). The main novelty of his approach is that he takes the desired capital-output ratio as an increasing function of the current profit rate. It then follows that the level of investment in any year is determined both by the growth of income as in the accelerator models and by the profit rate. He combines this investment function with his technical progress function to construct his growth models. Although his model differs from the neo-classical model in many ways, the two models lead to similar results, because both have been concerned to explain the same set of stylised facts, assumed to characterise growth in the developed countries (for a fuller discussion, see Allen, 1967, ch. 16, and Hacche, 1979, ch. 13).

The main problem with these models is that while the interaction between the multiplier and the accelerator solves the problem of the instability of the Harrod model, it does not explain the process of growth itself. This is because the accelerator in these models is based on the past growth of demand, rather than the current growth of demand as in the Harrod model. In their ambition to give a completely self-contained explanation of growth, these models assume that investment behaviour is determined by the growth process itself, in particular, by the growth of such an endogenous source of demand as consumption. Instead, it is more likely that the level and growth of investment are determined much more by the growth of other exogenous variables, such as government expenditures, exports and the rate of technological progress. This is in fact the way in which models such as that of Hicks explain growth. Such influences are studied in more detail in later chapters.

8.4 SUPPLY AND DEMAND EFFECTS OF INVESTMENT

Following the above discussion of the supply and demand effects of investment on the growth of income, some of the empirical evidence about these effects are considered in this section. However, in view of the complex interactions among the variables, the difficulty of disentangling *ex ante* relationships from the *ex post* data which are all that are available, and the paucity of reliable data from many countries, especially in the form of sufficiently long time series, it is a hopeless task to get econometric estimates of the various relationships involved. All that can be done is to use 'descriptive statistics' and sight correlations' to support a few propositions, as suggested by Cornwall

(1972, p. 11) and to apply them to the wealth of comparative data which have now become available from a large number of countries. This section is therefore mainly devoted to an analysis of cross-section data to see what light can be thrown on the role of investment in the growth process.

In dealing with the long-run phenomenon of growth which is our main concern, we cannot rely too heavily on the data for particular years which may be unduly influenced by short run circumstances. Therefore, we shall mostly consider average levels and average rates of growth of variables over periods of a decade at a time. This is the form in which a large body of data has been compiled in various World Bank publications. These data are used to examine a number of relationships, namely (a) the relationship between the level of income and the level of investment; (b) the relationship between the level of investment and the growth of income; and (c) the relationship between the growth of investment and the growth of income.

(a) Level of Investment and Level of Income

Table 8.1 summarises the cross-section data for each decade of the post-war period on the level of income (Y) and the ratio of investment to income (IR).

Table 8.1 Investment ratio (IR) by level of income (Y)

| Per Capita GDP in 1981 US$ (Y) | Investment ratio (IR) (%) in | | | | | |
| | LDCs | | | DCs | | |
	1950s	1960s	1970s	1950s	1960s	1970s
Below 250	13.0	13.6	19.3	–	–	–
250–500	17.5	16.5	20.8	–	–	–
500–750	18.1	17.8	22.7	15.3	–	–
750–1000	18.3	20.7	25.3	27.7	18.9	–
1000–2000	15.6	21.7	24.7	24.9	27.3	28.5
2000–4000	24.8	20.5	27.6	23.5	25.1	26.1
4000–6000	–	–	23.3	23.2	26.6	20.4
6000–8000	–	–	–	19.9	23.1	25.2
8000 and over	–	–	–	–	18.9	21.2
Average IR:	16.3	17.2	22.3	23.9	25.2	24.7
Correlation Between Y and IR:	0.29	0.37	0.27	–0.22	–0.23	–0.45

Source: World Bank (1984).

Table 8.2   Regression of savings and investment on income

Explanatory variables:	Dependent variables:		
	Savings	Investment	Capital inflow
Constant	−.340	−.161	.170
	(5.8)	(4.1)	(3.2)
log Y	.115	.085	−0.27
	(5.8)	(6.3)	(1.5)
$(\log Y)^2$	−.006	−.004	.002
	(3.6)	(3.7)	(1.1)
log N	.051	.013	−0.037
	(9.2)	(3.7)	(7.4)
$(\log N)^2$	−.007	−.002	.005
	(6.9)	(3.3)	(5.2)
R^2	0.32	0.37	.08

Notes: Y = GDP per capita in US\$; N = population in millions.
Source: Chenery and Syrquin (1975), table 4, p. 30.

The first question to consider is what the relationship shown in the table really means. These data are often interpreted as some indication of savings behaviour, as influenced by the level of income. Most theories of savings assume that the marginal rate of savings is higher than the average rate, so that the average rate of savings rises with level of income. There is some indication from the correlation coefficients that this was true in the case of LDCs, but not in the case of the DCs. Even in the case of the LDCs, the correlation is not very high.

However, this hypothesis applies only to *ex ante* savings, whereas the data only show *ex post* savings. The way the data are compiled by national income statisticians, *ex post* savings is necessarily equal to investment adjusted for the net inflow of foreign capital. Hence, the regression of savings on any set of variables is the same as the difference between the regressions of investment and capital inflow on the same variables as may be seen, for example, in the results obtained by Chenery and Syrquin (1975, table, p. 30), reproduced in Table 8.2.

To the extent that it is *ex post* savings which adjusts to investment, it may be more appropriate to interpret the data of Table 8.1 as showing the influence of income on investment. Then, the rise of the investment ratio with income level in the LDCs may be taken as an indication of the acceleration of growth in the intermediate levels of income, brought about by higher investment ratios. In the case of the

Table 8.3   Growth of income (GY) by investment ratio (IR)

Investment ratio (IR) (%)	Average Annual Rate of Growth of Income (GY) in LDCs			DCs		
	1950s	*1960s*	*1970s*	*1950s*	*1960s*	*1970s*
Below 15	3.80	3.47	0.84	–	–	–
15–20	5.38	5.59	3.64	3.23	4.47	2.30
20–25	4.77	6.42	4.84	4.04	5.26	3.11
25 & over	6.36	5.24	5.97	6.10	5.49	3.60
Average *GY*	4.52	4.91	4.44	4.66	5.29	3.23
Average *IR*	16.1	16.8	22.4	23.9	25.2	24.7
R^2	.04	.19	.32	.22	.21	.35
Number of Countries	52	79	83	22	23	23

Source: World Bank (1984).

DCs, the tendency for investment ratios to be higher at the lower income levels fits in with the observation noted in section 6.3 that these countries experienced faster growth, by exploiting the greater technological gap between them and the more advanced countries.

(b) Level of Investment and Growth of Income

Table 8.3 summarises the data on the growth of income (GY) of countries according to the level of investment, as measured by the investment ratio to income (IR)

Any sustained growth of income must be based on an expansion of productive capacity, and investment is one of the ways by which productive capacity may be expanded. This is the supply effect of investment. The first point to note is that this is an effect which can only be shown by the relationship between the *level* of investment and the *growth* of income. For a given ICOR, there is a direct relationship between these variables.

Table 8.3. does show that there is such a relationship in the cross-section data, but it is rather weak. The R^2 values for each group of countries in each decade are quite low, being greater than 0.3 only in the 1970s. Further, there is little relationship between changes of GY over time and changes of IR over time. In the LDCs, the average IR increased steadily but there was little change in the average GY. In the DCs, there was a sharp fall of GY in the 1970s but only a small

Table 8.4   Growth of income (GY) by growth of investment (GI)

| Growth of investment | Average growth of income (GY) (%) in | | | | | |
| | LDCs | | | DCs | | |
GI (%)	1950s	1960s	1970s	1950s	1960s	1970s
Below 1	4.05	3.69	0.51	–	–	2.54
1–3	3.63	2.25	4.08	2.73	–	3.39
3–5	4.74	3.62	3.45	5.16	4.65	4.10
5–8	4.74	5.23	5.06	4.38	5.08	5.70
8–12	5.42	5.24	5.25	5.76	5.80	–
12–15	6.95	9.03	7.13	–	10.40	–
15 & over	4.90	7.57	8.08	–	–	–
Average *GY*	4.89	4.92	4.44	4.77	5.29	3.20
Average *GI*	6.78	7.31	6.85	6.22	6.44	1.25
R^2	.09	.32	.58	.20	.51	.47
Number of Countries	36	80	83	21	23	22

Source: World Bank (1984).

decline in IR. This weak relationship, showing the supply effect of investment, has therefore to be explained by wide variations in ICOR between countries and by the role of many other factors influencing GY. One reason for the weak relationship between GY and the reported values of IR may be that not all investment consists of the acquisition of capital goods which enter into productive activities. About half of the reported figures of investment add to consumption rather than production, and consist of investments in residential construction and public services.

(c) Growth of Investment and Growth of Income

Finally, we consider the relationship between growth of investment (GI) and growth of income (GY). The cross-section data are summarised in Table 8.4. This table shows that there is a positive relationship between GY and GI; in fact, the relationship between GY and GI is even stronger than that between GY and IR. Further, variations of GY over time are also positively correlated with variations in *GI*; this is particularly the case in the DCs, where the sharp fall of *GY* in the 1970s is associated with a fall in *GI*.

This is a rather surprising result because, while there are good

Table 8.5   Growth of income (GY) by investment ratio (IR) and growth of investment (GI): LDCs

Growth of investment GI (%)	Average GY for countries with IR (%)				
	Below 15	15–20	20–25	25 & Over	Total
(a) 1950s					
Below 5	4.40	5.10	4.58	–	4.56
5–10	4.23	5.63	6.10	6.73	5.37
10–15	5.20	5.20	–	–	5.20
15 & Over	3.90	5.90	–	–	4.90
Total	4.41	5.44	5.12	6.73	5.01
(b) 1960s					
Below 5	2.35	3.96	3.93	5.25	3.37
5–10	4.24	5.18	6.72	5.35	5.19
10–15	5.67	7.52	7.80	5.00	6.74
15 & Over	5.20	8.23	8.13	–	7.80
Total	3.47	5.59	6.42	5.24	4.91
(c) 1970s					
Below 5	–0.08	2.81	2.67	3.29	1.98
5–10	3.40	4.57	5.68	5.06	5.14
10–15	3.00	5.20	5.13	6.58	5.80
15 & Over	3.20	–	10.30	8.41	8.08
Total	0.84	3.64	4.84	5.97	4.44

Source: World Bank (1984).

reasons for expecting a positive relationship between *GY* and *IR* as reflecting the supply effect of investment, there are no such reasons for expecting a corresponding relationship between *GY* and *GI*. It is possible that the variations of *GY* are really due to variations in *IR* but these aspects are confounded with the variations in *GI*. To check this possibility, Tables 8.5 and 8.6 show the average *GY* values of LDCs and DCs, classified both by their IR and GI values. From these tables, we see that *GY* varies systematically with *GI*, even when we control for differences in *IR*.

This relationship between *GY* and *GI* has also been noted by some economists, in regressions which have also included the effect of the growth of labour (*GL*). Some of these results are reported below. For example, Tyler (1981) obtained the following regression for a sample of 37 non-OPEC developing countries for the period 1960–77:

Table 8.6   Growth of income (GY) on investment ratio (IR) and growth
of investment (GI): DCs

Growth of investment GI (%)	Average GY for countries with IRT (%)			
	15–20	20–25	25 & over	Total
(a) 1950s				
1–3	2.35	–	3.50	2.73
3–5	2.20	4.10	11.30	4.30
5–8	4.20	3.40	4.83	4.38
8–12	4.10	5.10	6.40	5.70
Total	3.23	4.32	6.10	4.77
(b) 1960s				
3–5	–	4.55	4.70	4.65
5–8	4.47	5.15	5.28	5.07
8 & Over	–	5.80	10.40	6.95
Total	4.47	5.26	5.49	5.29
(c) 1970s				
Below 1	1.70	2.75	2.40	2.54
1–3	2.90	3.40	3.85	3.48
3 & Over	–	3.80	4.73	4.50
Total	2.30	3.11	3.66	3.24

Source: World Bank (1984).

$$GY = 2.035 + 0.289 \ GK + 1.025 \ GL \quad (R^2 = .68)$$
$$\quad\quad\quad (7.05) \quad\quad (2.62) \quad\quad\quad\quad\quad (8.25)$$

It must be noted that the variable described as *GK* in this equation
does not refer to the growth of capital stock, but rather to the growth
of investment which we have represented by *GI*. Similarly, Kavoussi
(1984) obtained the following regressions for the period 1960–78 for a
total sample of 73 developing countries, and for 37 low income LDCs
and 36 middle income LDCs separately:

73 LDCs
$$GY = 2.14 + 0.291 \ GK + 0.440 \ GL \quad (R^2 = .49)$$
$$\quad (3.93) \ (6.87) \quad\quad (1.71) \quad\quad\quad\quad (8.26)$$

37 Low Income LDCs
$$GY = 0.30 + 0.256 \ GK + 1.200 \ GL \quad (R^2 = .49)$$
$$\quad (0.31) \ (4.51) \quad\quad (2.46) \quad\quad\quad\quad (8.27)$$

36 Middle Income LDCs

$$GY = 3.47 + 0.312 \ GK + 0.217 \ GL \quad (R^2 = .56)$$
$$(5.66) \ (5.81) (0.08) \qquad\qquad (8.28)$$

Here again GK stands for the growth of investment.

According to standard theory, investment leads to growth of income through the supply effect. But for this influence to explain the observed relationship between GI and GY, there must be a very prompt response of income to investment. In practice, however, such a supply effect would take a considerable period of time, too long to explain the observed relationship. A more plausible alternative explanation is one which operates through the role of investment as a source of demand, one that is likely to operate faster than the supply effect. In the Keynesian model, investment is an exogeneous source of demand which determines the level of income. Therefore, for a stable value of the investment multiplier, an increase of investment must lead to an increase of income. The observed relationship between *GI* and *GY* may therefore be explained through such a demand effect.

One form of this demand effect is particularly important. This is due to the fact that the growth of investment is itself a part of the growth of income, as usually estimated in the national accounts. This effect is likely to be especially significant where investment constitutes about 20 per cent of GDP in the LDCs and 25 per cent in the DCs. It is therefore useful to separate out this component from the overall growth of GDP. To do this, write C for GDP excluding investment. Then from $Y = I + C$, we get $GY = KI + KC$, where *KI* and *KC* are the *K*-ratios of *I* and *C*, representing their respective contributions to the overall rate. The magnitudes of these components of *GY* are shown in Table 8.7.

Table 8.7   Changes in *K1*, *KC* and *GY* over time average of countries
(coefficients of variation in brackets)

Variable		1950s	1960s	1970s
LDCs	K1	1.20 (0.77)	1.23 (0.97)	1.80 (1.16)
	KC	3.81 (0.37)	3.68 (0.51)	2.64 (0.82)
	GY	5.01 (0.29)	4.91 (0.47)	4.44 (0.72)
DCs	K1	1.53 (0.57)	1.64 (0.55)	0.35 (1.60)
	KC	3.24 (0.58)	3.63 (0.28)	2.89 (0.29)
	GY	4.77 (0.50)	5.29 (0.29)	3.24 (0.35)

Table 8.8   Correlation of *GYs* and *KCs* with *GI*

| Countries/period | Correlation of GI with | |
	GY	KC
LDCs		
1950s	.29	−.40
1960s	.57	.14
1970s	.76	.21
DCs		
1950s	.45	.10
1960s	.72	.27
1970s	.69	.30

The growth contribution of investment, shown by *KI*, is a large part of *GY* both in DCs and in LDCs. This suggests that a considerable part of the variations in *GY* may be due to the variations in *KI*. To check this, Table 8.8 compares the correlation between *GI* and *GY* with that between *GI* and *KC*, i.e. *GY–KI*. The correlations between GI and KC are much lower than that between GI and GY, showing that the latter correlation is mainly due to the fact that *GI* is itself a component of *GY*.

We then have to consider the influence of investment on the other component of *GY*, i.e. *KC*. This influence may operate either through a demand effect or through a supply effect. Table 8.7 shows a positive relationship between changes in *KC* and changes in *KI* over time in each group of countries; this is an indication the growth of investment may have had a demand effect on the growth of other components of GDP. In order to consider the possible supply effects of investment on these components, Table 8.9 shows the relationship between *KC* and *IR*. There is only a weak relationship between KC and IR for each group of countries for each decade.

The above analysis may be summed up as follows. The strong relationship between *GY* and *GI* is mainly due to the fact that *GI* is a part of *GY*. To this extent, it represents the influence of investment as a source of demand. When the growth contribution of investment is excluded from *GY*, we find that variations in *KC* are also positively associated with GI though to a lesser extent. This also may be interpreted as due to the demand effect of investment. By contrast, there is only a weak relationship between *KC* and *IR*, which indicates that while investment is certainly a source of the expansion of

Table 8.9 Variation of *KCs* with *IRs*

IRs (%)	Average values of KC LDCs			DCs		
	1950s	*1960s*	*1970s*	*1950s*	*1960s*	*1970s*
Below 15	3.55	2.62	0.71	–	–	–
15–20	4.04	4.36	2.75	2.45	3.34	2.12
20–25	4.26	4.16	3.24	2.82	3.63	2.94
25 & Over	4.44	4.35	3.02	4.04	3.70	3.06
Total	3.81	3.68	2.64	3.24	3.63	2.91
Rcg. Coeff.	.04	.11	.09	.09	.05	.09
R^2	.04	.10	.10	.06	.05	.17

productive capacity, this supply effect explains only a small part of the variation of *KC* and *GY* between countries.

In view of the important role that *GI* plays in accounting for variations in *GY*, we have to explain the variations in *GI* itself. To some extent, the growth of investment itself may be endogenous to the growth process as discussed, for example, in the accelerator principle. But the growth of investment may also be due to other factors, such as the growth of other sources of demand, namely government expenditures and exports. We discuss these influences in the following chapters.

9 Government Expenditures

9.1 VARIATIONS IN GOVERNMENT EXPENDITURES

Another major source of demand distinguished in Chapter 8 is government expenditures. We consider this source of demand in this chapter, and how it is related to the national income of countries. As in the case of investment, there are at least three forms in which this relationship can be studied; (a) the relationship between the *level* of government expenditures and the *level* of income; (b) the relationship between the *level* of government expenditures and the *growth* of income, and (c) the relationship between the *growth* of government expenditures and the *growth* of income. In the literature, all of these relationships have been used to investigate the effect of government expenditures on the national income. But it is important to distinguish among these three relationships, because they refer to different ways in which government expenditures influence the level and the growth of national income. We therefore consider each of these relationships in turn, beginning with the relationship between the level of government expenditures and the level of national income.

In macroeconomic theory, especially in its policy aspects, it is generally assumed that the level of government expenditures is largely within the control of governments, i.e. that it is an exogenous variable, which can be used to stabilise the economy. But economists studying the empirical data on the subject have been more concerned with the relationship flowing from the level of income to the level of government expenditures, i.e. to assume that the level of government expenditures is an endogenous variable determined by the level of national income.

This view was first advanced by Adolf Wagner over a century ago; hence the generalisation that government expenditures as a proportion of national income tends to increase with the level of per capita income has come to be known as Wagner's Law. Wagner's Law was originally derived from the historical trends observed in a few countries. Since then, there have been many studies of the relationship between government expenditures and income levels. In these studies, it is often assumed that the level of government expenditures is determined by the demand for them at different income levels, and hence the data are used to estimate the income elasticity of demand for government services, and in particular, to test whether this income elasticity of demand is greater than one (as implied by the most commonly accepted version of Wagner's Law) or whether it is less than one.

The cross section data from countries at different levels of per capita income do not show any strong relationship between income level and government expenditures as a proportion of GDP. For example, reviewing such data, Musgrave (1969, p. 124) concluded that 'the evidence remains puzzling and in need of further explanation' (see also Gupta, 1968, and Bird, 1971). In another review, Tait and Heller (1982) examined more recent data from a large number of countries varying greatly in their income levels; these data are summarised in Table 9.1 for the latest year for which they are available.

These data do not show any significant relationship between relative government expenditures and per capita income. In fact, among the DCs, the correlation between the two variables is slightly negative, largely due to the variations in capital expenditures. Therefore, Tait and Heller (1982, p. 1) conclude that 'it is striking how uncertain per capita income is as an explanatory variable'.

More comprehensive data are now available from the *World Tables* (1984) in the form of averages for each of the three post-war decades from a large number of countries. These data, however, refer only to government current expenditures, because government capital expenditures are included in the investment expenditures for the economy as a whole. As we have seen in Table 9.1, capital expenditures are a much smaller part of government expenditures, especially in the DCs. The World Bank data are summarised in Table 9.2.

In contrast to the data of Table 9.1 dealing with both capital and current expenditures, we now find that the relationship between government consumption as a percentage of GDP and per capita income is negative for LDCs and positive for DCs. However, the correlation is very weak; 'the correlation between central government expenditure shares and per capita income explains only about 10 per cent of this variation' (World Bank, 1988, pp. 46–7). This suggests that although the government share varies considerably among countries, the variation does not depend primarily on the level of income. The data for Table 9.2 refer to the ratio of govern-

Table 9.1   Public expenditure share of GDP, circa 1977

Per capita income US$ expenditure	Public expenditure	Current expenditure	Capital expenditure
LDCs			
Below 250	21.5	16.5	5.1
250–500	24.1	16.1	5.8
500–750	28.5	17.7	8.4
750–1000	28.1	17.9	8.2
1000 & over	23.8	20.1	6.3
Average	24.3	17.7	6.4
Correlation with per capita Income	.1588	.1206	.0742
DCs			
Below 4000	38.3	34.6	4.2
4000–8000	35.9	33.1	3.1
8000 & over	34.0	41.1	2.9
Average	37.4	36.4	3.4
Correlation with per capita Income	−.0769	.2763	−.2214

Source: Tait and Heller (1982).

ment expenditures to GDP at current prices. But there are systematic differences in the price levels of government expenditures and other items of GDP. To avoid the bias involved in using the ratio at nominal prices, Ram (1987a) studied the relationship in real terms using the ratio at international prices as estimated by the International Comparison Project. He then found that the cross-section relationship between the government share and per capita income was negative both for LDCs and for DCs, though not significant for DCs.

Table 9.2 shows that there has been a steady rise in the average government expenditure ratios, both in the LDCs and the DCs. In fact, this trend is also found in the time series data for individual countries, which are then taken as evidence in support of Wagner's Law. However, in view of the low correlation found in the cross section data, the rise in government expenditures as a percentage of GDP over time cannot be taken as entirely or even largely due to the growth of incomes. In a study using pooled time series data from a number of countries, Chenery and Syrquin (1975, p. 38) fitted a quadratic

Table 9.2 Government consumption expenditure share of GDP by income level

Per capital in 1981 US$	1950s	1960s	1970s
LDCs			
Below 250	11.7	12.6	14.5
250–500	10.3	12.7	15.6
500–750	8.7	13.9	14.4
750–1000	9.3	9.9	15.3
1000–2000	9.5	10.7	14.2
2000 & over	13.1	14.8	12.8
Average	10.2	13.3	14.7
Correlation coefficient	−.1041	−.0700	−.0064
Number of countries	46	72	74
DCs			
Below 2000	13.4	12.0	15.7
2000–4000	13.3	15.8	15.0
4000–6000	13.0	13.2	18.1
6000–8000	–	16.3	18.2
8000 & over	15.3	18.3	21.4
Average	13.4	14.5	17.9
Correlation coefficient	−.1396	−.3239	−.2673
Number of countries	21	23	23

Source: World Bank (1984).

regression of government consumption expenditure as a percentage of GDP on per capita income and population size. The R^2 was only .083; although they found that the regression coefficients on per capita income were highly significant, they were so small that the estimated equation shows that the government share of GDP for a country with a population of 30 millions would increase from 14.6 per cent at an income level of $100 to only 16.9 at an income level of $1000.

In fact, historical data from the developed countries show that there has been a long term tendency for government expenditures as a share of GDP to grow faster than per capita incomes (see e.g. World Bank, 1988, table 2.1, p. 44). This tendency has therefore been explained by a number of factors other than income growth, such as a growing demand for public goods, the extension of suffrage, the demand for redistribution, the rising power of the bureaucracy and a fiscal illusion on the part of the legislatures (for a comprehensive review of recent studies of these factors, see Mueller, 1987).

Peacock and Wiseman (1961) have also pointed out that there is a ratchet effect in the growth of government, as the expansion due to some external shock such as a war tends to become permanent after that shock has ended.

In an early study of the subject, Lewis and Martin (1956) examined the data from a sample of 16 countries in more detail. They found that, as far as basic government expenditures (i.e. expenditures on administration, economic services and transfers) were concerned, there was very little variation with income; instead, it was government expenditures in the form of social insurance, food or agricultural subsidies, defence and public debt that explained most of the difference between rich and poor countries. They also argue that, as far as these basic expenditures are concerned, 'the main reason why (the rich countries) now spend relatively more on their public services than they did a hundred years ago is not that they are richer, but that they have a different conception of the duties of the state' (Lewis and Martin, 1956, p. 206). They also argue that one reason why a larger share of national income may be spent on the public services as the national income rises is because the productivity of labour in these services has grown more slowly than in the commodity producing sectors, the same explanation that was later advanced by Baumol (1967) and Fuchs (1968) for the growth of employment in the service sector as a whole (section 7.3 above).

While government expenditures as a share of GDP are not highly correlated with income levels, it is likely that government revenues are more highly correlated with income levels. This is because, for a given tax structure, tax revenues will increase with income, and tax structures do not change rapidly over time. Thus, for example, Chenery and Syrquin (1975, p. 30) found that a quadratic regression on income levels and population size explained 62 per cent of the variations in government revenue as a percentage of GDP, using pooled time series data from many countries.

But when only cross-section data are used, the relationship is usually much weaker. One of the most comprehensive studies of this type was that carried out by Chelliah *et al.* (1975) in the IMF, in which the regression coefficient of the income variable was small and not at all significant (see also Bird, 1978; and Bolnick, 1978). As a result, two factors have been distinguished to explain the variation of government revenues between countries, one relating to the 'taxable capacity' of countries based on income levels, and the other on 'tax effort' depending on the structure of the economy and on government policies (see, for example, United Nations, 1970, a study on the measurement of development effort). While tax effort varies greatly between countries for a variety of political and economic reasons, it is generally assumed that taxable capacity depends much more on the per capita incomes of countries. If government expenditures were mainly influenced by taxable capacity, then they would have to be considered an endogenous variable, in the sense of being strongly influenced by income levels. But actual tax ratios in different countries also depend on the extent to which they have convenient 'tax handles' (Musgrave, 1969), such as a large share of foreign trade, or a large endowment of mineral or other physical resources, which can be taxed most easily.

Thus, we have to conclude that, for a given tax effort on the part of individual countries, tax revenues will depend on income levels representing the taxable capacity. If government expenditures were fully financed by tax revenues, then they also will be an endogenous variable depending on income level. But we have seen that this is not the case. The reason is government expenditures are also financed by other sources, such as foreign and domestic borrowing, and money creation. Such deficits amounted to 6.3 per cent of GNP in developing countries in 1985, and to 5.1 per cent in the industrial countries (World Bank, 1988, table 2.2, p. 46). Some details about the financing of such deficits are given in the Government Finance Statistics Yearbook, 1985, and are summarised in Table 9.3.

This table shows that a considerable part of public expenditure is financed by sources other than tax revenues, about one fifth in LDCs and a sixth in DCs. On the average, 8 per cent of public expenditure in LDCs is financed by borrowing or getting aid from abroad, the remainder being financed by domestic borrowing; of this, a considerable part, about 8 per cent on average, is financed by borrowing from the monetary authorities. Public expenditure in the DCs is also financed by borrowing from abroad, but to a smaller extent; most of their budget deficits are financed by domestic borrowing, and to a much smaller extent by borrowing from monetary authorities. However, there is no systematic pattern in the resort to these methods of financing public expenditure, which does not seem to be related to level of income or size of government expenditure relative to GDP.

Thus, we may conclude that, government expenditures are not as strongly determined by income levels, as implied by Wagner's Law. Instead, there are many other factors influencing the level of government revenues and expenditures, and governments have consider-

Table 9.3   Financing of government expenditure, circa 1983

Per capita GDP (US$)	Number of countries	Government expenditure (% of GDP)	Deficit (% of expenditure)	Borrowing % of Expenditure		
				Abroad	Domestic	Monetary authorities
(a) LDCs						
Below 250	10	20.4	18.9	8.4	9.2	5.2
250–500	18	25.2	23.5	10.3	14.6	11.6
500–750	8	30.2	24.8	10.0	9.8	9.2
750–1000	8	27.5	16.6	8.4	8.2	9.4
1000–2000	18	26.1	19.2	7.7	9.6	0.5
2000 & over	8	24.7	10.6	1.3	9.3	1.7
Total	70	25.7	19.6	8.0	10.7	8.0
(b) DCs						
Below 5000	3	20.8	17.7	2.0	15.7	7.5
5000–10,000	6	47.7	22.1	3.7	18.3	6.0
10,000–12,000	6	33.9	16.0	1.9	14.1	−0.1
12,000 & over	7	34.1	9.4	2.6	9.8	1.6
Total	22	36.7	15.8	2.5	14.6	3.2

Source: International Monetary Fund (1985).

able freedom to determine their public expenditures, both regarding the extent to which they are financed by revenues and by other sources of funds. Hence, government expenditures may be taken as an exogenous source of demand, in the Keynesian sense.

9.2 LEVEL OF GOVERNMENT EXPENDITURES AND GROWTH OF INCOME

In the last section, we discussed the extent to which the level of income influences government expenditures. In the present section, we consider how government expenditures have influenced the growth of GDP. A considerable part of government expenditures, such as those on administration, maintenance of law and order, and provision of infrastructure, are in fact undertaken to promote the growth of national income. But, as in the case of investment, to the extent that government expenditures have this effect, it must be shown by a relationship between the level of government expenditures, say as a share of national income, and the growth of income.

Table 9.4 GDP growth rates by government consumption expenditure share of GDP

| Government consumption expenditure (% of GDP) (GR) | Average growth rate of GDP (GY) in | | | | | |
| | LDCs | | | DCs | | |
	1950s	1960s	1970s	1950s	1960s	1970s
Below 5	1.4	–	–	–	–	–
5–10	4.3	4.9	6.2	5.2	8.4	4.5
10–15	4.9	5.6	4.2	4.4	5.1	3.0
15–20	4.9	4.4	4.1	5.4	4.5	3.5
20–25	2.3	4.5	5.0	5.6	–	−1.9
25 & over	–	6.7	2.6	–	8.1	2.9
Average GY	4.4	5.1	4.5	4.7	5.3	3.2
Average GR	10.2	12.6	14.7	13.2	14.5	17.9
Correlation of GY and GR	.119	−.034	−.200	−.241	−.160	−.087
Number of Countries	51	74	75	22	23	23

Source: World Bank (1984).

Even if government expenditures had this effect, it is unlikely that it will occur promptly within a year or two. Therefore, it is more useful to consider the relationship between the average share of government expenditures over longer periods, such as a decade at a time, and the growth rates of GDP over the same periods. The data for each of the post-war decades are summarised in Table 9.4.

At least as far as this cross-section study is concerned, we see that the relationship between government consumption expenditures and GDP growth rates in each of these cases is rather erratic, and in fact, is negative in most cases.

A much more detailed analysis was carried out by Landau (1986), in which he regressed the GDP growth rates on various components of government expenditure and a number of other variables which may also be expected to influence the growth rates. His results for growth rates calculated over a seven-year period are summarised in Table 9.5. These results confirm the negative relationship between government expenditures and growth rates found in Table 9.4. Landau (1986, p. 68) has therefore concluded that:

Table 9.5   Regression of GDP growth rates over 7-year period on government expenditure ratios and other variables

Explanatory variable	Regression Coefficient	t-ratio
1. Current government consumption expenditure (other than education or defence) as % of GDP (OCSA)	−.300	3.10
2. Government education expenditure as % of GDP (AEDS)	−.064	0.38
3. Military expenditure as % of GDP (ADS)	−.270	2.75
4. Transfer and other current non-consumption expenditure as % of GDP (ATRNS)	.052	1.02
5. Government capital expenditure as % of GDP (AKES)	−.028	0.33
6. Official transfers (aid) received as % of GDP (AOFTS)	.216	2.88
7. Current revenue as % of GDP, lagged 3-year average (AREVS)	.087	1.40
8. Budget deficit as % of GDP, lagged 3-year average (BREVS)	−.019	0.41
9. Private investment as % of GDP, lagged 3-year average (AIP)	.086	1.74
10. Real per capita GDP lagged 3-year (LRGDP)	−.334	4.31
11. Population in millions (LPOP)	−.007	2.72
12. Population growth rate (PGR)	−.181	0.85
13. Educational enrollment ratio (EDO)	.021	2.44
14. Extent of land-lockedness (DLP)	−.005	2.64
15. Time trend (T)	.029	0.59
16. Interaction terms (INT)	3.41	2.44
R^2	.728	
D-W	1.95	
Degrees of freedom	82	

Source: Landau (1986), table 4, pp. 46–7.

Government consumption expenditure excluding military and educational expenditures appear to have noticeably reduced economic growth. Military and transfer expenditures do not appear to have had much impact on economic growth. Government educational expenditures seem to be inefficient at generating actual education; that is, actual education (measured by enrollment ratios) is strongly correlated with growth rates, but levels of government educational expenditure are not. Government capital development expenditure appears to do nothing to accelerate economic growth.

Table 9.6 Regression-coefficients of GDP growth rates on government
expenditure ratio, investment and population growth
(t-ratios in brackets)

Explanatory variable	115 DCs & LDCs		94 LDCs	
	1960–70	*1970–80*	*1960–70*	*1970–80*
Investment ratio	0.129	0.143	0.155	0.184
	(4.97)	(4.24)	(5.02)	(5.01)
Population growth rate	0.781	1.275	0.597	0.694
	(3.54)	(4.62)	(2.23)	(1.93)
Government expenditure ratio	−0.030	−0.108	−0.037	−0.195
	(0.62)	(2.13)	(1.02)	(3.36)
R^2	0.20	0.23	0.24	0.30

Source: Ram (1986), table 1, p. 1961.

In itself government investment has a weak positive impact on
growth, but, when we allow for the taxation and borrowing needed
to finance such investment plus the crowding out of private investment, the net impact is zero. This result is very important, since
LDC government capital expenditure is large – averaging 7 per
cent of GDP, is supposed to be a major force for development and
growth, and has an opportunity cost in lower consumption.

Another study was carried out by Ram (1986) using estimates
made by the International Comparison Project. His regressions of
growth rates on the share of government expenditures in GDP, and
two other variables are summarised in Table 9.6. Again, we see that
the level of government expenditures seems to have a negative effect
on the growth of GDP. This suggests that in so far as the supply
effects of government expenditures on the growth of GDP act through
the level of such expenditures, these effects have been small and even
unfavourable.

9.3 GROWTH OF GOVERNMENT EXPENDITURES AND GROWTH OF INCOME

Finally, we consider the relationship between the *growth* of government expenditures and the growth of income. Data on these variables
compiled by the World Bank for the post-war period are summarised
in Table 9.7.

Table 9.7   GDP growth rates by growth rates of government consumption expenditure

Growth rates (%) of government consumption expenditure (GG)	Average growth rates (%) of GDP (GY) in					
	LDCs			DCs		
	1950s	*1960s*	*1970s*	*1950s*	*1960s*	*1970s*
Below 3	3.2	3.9	2.3	3.8	4.4	2.5
3–4	4.4	3.1	2.1	5.0	5.0	2.9
4–5	5.5	3.6	2.8	3.8	4.8	4.0
5–6	4.3	5.4	3.6	5.6	4.5	3.5
6–7	5.8	5.3	6.6	–	6.8	4.4
7–8	3.4	5.4	4.1	–	5.9	–
8 & over	5.4	6.0	6.0	11.3	8.1	4.4
Average GY	4.9	5.0	4.4	4.8	5.3	3.2
Average GG	6.5	6.2	6.2	3.7	5.1	4.0
Correlation of GY and GG	.298	.343	.550	.618	.486	.556
Number of Countries	33	69	72	21	23	23

Source: World Bank (1984).

We now see that the correlation between these variables is positive, and much stronger than the correlation between the level of government expenditures and the growth of GDP (Table 9.2).

To some extent, the strong positive relationship between the growth of government expenditures (*GG*) and the growth of income (*GY*) may be due to the fact that *GG* is itself a part of *GY*. A way of avoiding this accounting effect is to consider the relationship between the government component of growth which may be described as the *K*-ratio of government expenditures (*KG*), i.e. that part of the *growth* of income that consists of the growth of government expenditures, and the *K*-ratio of private expenditures (*KP*) i.e. the component of the growth of GDP excluding government expenditures. The regression of *KP* on *KG* is shown in Table 9.8 together with the regression of *GY* on *KG*.

As may be expected, the R^2 values are much smaller, and the regression coefficients of *KP* on *KG* are exactly one less than the regression coefficients of *GY* on *KG*. If the growth of total income is unaffected by the growth of government sector, then changes in government output would be balanced by opposite changes in private

Table 9.8 Regression of GY and KP on KG
(R^2 values in parenthesis)

Countries/period	Regression coefficient of:	
	GY on KG	KP on KG
LDCs		
1950s	1.75 (.219)	.75 (.049)
1969s	1.15 (.064)	.15 (.001)
1970s	1.45 (.163)	.45 (.019)
DCs		
1950s	4.35 (.434)	3.35 (.313)
1960s	.81 (.111)	−.19 (.007)
1970s	1.81 (.177)	.81 (.041)

sector output, and the regression coefficient of *KP* on *KG* would be *minus* one. But we find that the regression coefficient is greater than one in all cases, and positive with only one exception in the case of *DCs* during the 1960s. This shows that the growth of government expenditure had a considerable positive influence on the growth of total output.

The relationship between growth of government expenditure and growth of income has been analysed in much more detail by Ram (1986). The model underlying his analysis is based on the following equations (adapted from a similar study of exports by Feder, 1983).

$$Y = C + G \tag{9.1}$$

i.e. total output Y is the sum of private sector output C and public sector output G. From this, we have

$$\dot{Y} = (C/Y)\,\dot{C} + (G/Y)\,\dot{G} \tag{9.2}$$

where a dot over a variable indicates its rate of growth (Falvey and Gemmell, 1988). The production functions in the two sectors are assumed to be:

$$C = C(L_C, K_C, G) \tag{9.3}$$

$$G = G(L_G, K_G) \tag{9.4}$$

showing that output in each sector is a function of the labour and capital employed in that sector, but public sector output G has also an externality effect on private sector output C. From these production functions, we get

$$(C/Y)\dot{C} = (C_L/Y)(dL_c/dt) + (C_K/Y)(dK_c/dt)$$
$$+ C_g(G/Y)\dot{G} \tag{9.5}$$

$$(G/Y)\dot{G} = (G_L/Y)(dL_g/dt) + G_K/Y(dK_g/dt) \tag{9.6}$$

We also have

$$(dL_c/dt) + (dL_g/dt) = (dL/dt) \tag{9.7}$$

$$(dK_c/dt) + (dK_g/dt) = (dK/dt) \tag{9.8}$$

It is also assumed that

$$(G_L/C_L) = (G_K/C_K) = (1 + \delta) \tag{9.9}$$

where δ is the productivity differential between the two sectors, assumed to be equal for the two factors. Alternatively, this may also be written

$$\delta' = \delta/(1 + \delta) = (G_L - C_L)/G_L = (G_K - C_K)/G_K \tag{9.10}$$

Substituting (9.5) and (9.6) into (9.2), and using (9.7), (9.8) and (9.10), we finally get

$$\dot{Y} = \alpha(IR) + \beta(GL) + (\delta' - \theta)KG + \theta(GG) \tag{9.11}$$

where
α = C_K, the marginal product of capital in the private sector;
β = $(LC_L)/C$, elasticity of private output C with respect to labour;
θ = $(GC_g)/C$, elasticity of private output C with respect to public output G;
IR = (I/Y), the investment ratio;
GL = $\dot{L}$, the growth rate of labour;
GG = $\dot{G}$, the growth rate of public sector output; and
KG = $(G\dot{G}/Y)$, the public sector component of growth of total output.

Table 9.9 Regression of GY on IR, GL, KG, and GG
(t-ratios in brackets)

| Explanatory variables | Regression Coefficients for: | | | |
| | 115 DCs & LDCs | | 94 LDCs | |
	1960–70	1970–80	1960–70	1970–80
IR	.114	.097	.125	.124
	(4.81)	(3.30)	(4.35)	(3.70)
GL	.504	.453	.431	−.014
	(2.45)	(1.87)	(1.75)	(0.04)
KG	.672	−.554	.622	−.722
	(1.59)	(0.76)	(1.35)	(0.91)
GG	.139	−.485	.138	.503
	(1.92)	(3.41)	(1.78)	(3.24)
R^2	.35	.46	.37	.47

Source: Ram (1986) table 1, p. 196.

Ram estimated equation (9.11) using ICP data from a large number of countries. His results are summarised in Table 9.9. From such results, Ram (1986, p. 202) concluded that:

> government size has a positive effect on economic performance and growth . . . Even more interesting seems to be nearly equally pervasive indication of a positive externality effect of government size on the rest of the economy. It is also possible to infer from the cross section evidence that relative factor productivity was higher in government sector than in the rest of the economy at least during the 1960s.

In Ram's analysis, the explanatory variable KG and GG are part of the dependent variable GY; therefore, his results involve an accounting effect to some extent. Therefore, Falvey and Gemmell (1988) estimated the regression of KC (the private sector component of GY) on the same variables, using the revised Summers and Heston (1988) estimates at international prices. They then conclude that their results confirm Ram's finding of positive externality but not his finding of a positive productivity differential in favour of the government sector.

These results clearly show that the growth of government expenditures has a positive effect on growth in the rest of the economy. This is an important conclusion, in view of a popular opinion that the growth of government expenditures may crowd out private investment, and hence have an adverse effect on the growth of GDP because private investments are usually considered to be more productive than government expenditures. Sometimes the argument is applied only to government investment expenditures which are excluded from the data used in some of the above analyses referring only to government consumption expenditures. But the strong positive relationship between the growth of government expenditures and the growth of GDP found in all the above analyses suggests that the crowding out effect has not been significant.

In interpreting his results, Ram has concentrated only on one possible explanation in his model, namely that government expenditure has a positive production externality on the rest of the economy, as embodied in the production function (9.3). For the regression results to be interpreted in this way, the growth of the government sector must have a prompt supply effect on the private sector. Even if there is such an effect, it is extremely unlikely that it will operate so promptly.

There is, however, another explanation for the positive relationship shown by the regression results. This is the effect of a growth of government expenditure in increasing aggregate demand for total output, as argued in the Keynesian multiplier theory. As shown in the Balanced Budget Multiplier theory, an increase in government expenditure will increase total output by the same amount, even if it is fully financed by an increase in tax revenues. The multiplier will be even higher if the increase in government expenditure is not fully financed by an increase in tax revenue. To the extent that such a demand effect operates, it will operate much faster than the supply effect assumed in Ram's analysis. Therefore, it is more plausible to explain his results in terms of a demand effect than in terms of a supply effect.

An increase in aggregate demand brought about by growth of government expenditures will increase total production if there are under-employed resources, as explained in the Keynesian theory. To some extent, the observed relationship between growth of government expenditures and growth of GDP may be explained by this effect. However, it is unlikely that there will be resources, especially capital resources, that will remain under-utilised over a long period. Instead, it is more likely that there is an interaction between demand and supply, as discussed in the preceding chapter, so that the increase

Table 9.10 Correlation of growth of investment (GI) and growth of government consumption expenditure (GG)

	Correlation of GI and GG in	
	LDCs	DCs
1950s	.117	−.019
1960s	.310	.138
1970s	.554	.328

Source: World Bank (1984).

in aggregate demand brought about by the growth of government expenditures leads to a faster growth of investment. The relationship between growth of government expenditures and growth of investment is shown by the data for the post-war period summarised in Table 9.10. We see that there is indeed a positive relationship between the two growth rates in most cases, with the exception only of the DCs in the 1950s. Hence, we may conclude that the growth of government expenditures influences the growth of GDP, not only by increasing the demand for existing productive capacity, but also by inducing faster growth of productive capacity.

This relationship is part of the explanation for the slackening of economic growth in the DCs since 1973. In that period, there was in fact a rise in government expenditures as a percentage of GDP (see Table 9.4) and only a slight decline in the investment ratio (see Table 8.3). This was also the period in which resources were under-utilised as shown, for example, by rising rates of unemployment of labour. Hence, the slackening of economic growth cannot be explained only by the supply effects of the level of government expenditures and investment ratios. But there was a sharp decline in the *growth* rate of government expenditures (see Table 9.7) and the growth rate of investment (see Table 8.4). As argued above, the decline in these growth rates cannot explain the fall in the growth rates of GDP only through their supply effects. Instead, it is more likely that it was their demand effects which led to the slackening of economic growth. In fact, the governments of these countries pursued contractionary fiscal and monetary policies precisely to have this demand effect in order to control the high rates of inflation.

To conclude, it was argued in Chapter 3 that the growth process in all countries follows a logistic pattern, but the rate at which an economy moves from one phase of the logistic pattern to another, and the speed with which it grows within each phase varies from country to country. One of the factors which influences these variations is government expenditure. One way in which government expenditures may influence the growth process is through a supply effect, i.e. by improving the productive capacity of the economy. If this was the principal way in which government expenditures affected economic growth, it would have been shown by a strong positive relationship between the *level* of government expenditures and the *growth* of GDP. But this relationship has not been very strong, or even positive.

But there is another way in which government expenditures may have influenced the growth of GDP, that is through the demand effect. According to this effect, an increase of aggregate demand resulting from an increase in government expenditures would affect the growth of GDP not only by utilising existing productive capacity more fully, but also by inducing faster growth of productive capacity. To the extent that there is such a demand effect, it would be shown by a strong positive relationship between the *growth* of government expenditures and the *growth* of GDP. And this is what we find from the data.

One way in which government expenditures influence the growth process is through its sectoral impact. A large part of government expenditures consists of payment of wages and salaries, i.e. the purchases of services. Hence, the faster the growth of government expenditures, the faster will be the growth of the service sector. If the expansion of the service sector is at the expense of the industrial sector, there will be a slowing down of the growth of GDP. This is the central feature of the Bacon–Eltis explanation for the slower growth of the British economy, discussed in Chapter 7. But if the growth of the industrial sector is constrained for other reasons, such as those leading to de-industrialisation, then the faster the growth of service sector, the more fully will labour be employed, and the faster the growth of GDP. The most successful countries have been those in which the growth of demand from government expenditures or other sources of demand have induced a faster growth of productive capacity, and also helped demand to keep pace with the growing productive capacity.

10 Exports

10.1 VARIATIONS IN EXPORT RATIOS

In this chapter, we consider the relationship between exports and income. As in the case of investment and government expenditures, the relationship between exports and income can be considered in at least three forms, namely (a) the relationship between the *level* of exports, say as a proportion of GDP, and the *level* of income; (b) the relationship between the *level* of exports and the *growth* of income, and (c) the relationship between the *growth* of exports and the *growth* of income. It is important to distinguish these three relationships, because they differ in their underlying mechanism.

We first consider the relationship between exports as a proportion of GDP and the level of income. In a sense, exports are a much clearer case of an exogenous source of demand than investment and government expenditures, because they are influenced much more by the incomes of the importing countries than by the income of the exporting countries. However, individual countries can influence the volume of their exports by the policies they pursue with respect to trade controls, inflation and exchange rates. Some countries, often described as inward looking countries, have reduced their export ratios by imposing various impediments to the free export of their goods to foreign countries, or by following other policies which have the same effect. On the other hand, other countries, often described as outward looking countries, have increased their export ratios by giving special privileges to exporters. It has been observed that outward looking countries have generally grown faster than inward looking countries, and therefore economists have generally advocated that countries should participate as intensively as they can in international trade in order to achieve a rapid growth of their GDP. However, we must first investigate why exports have this favourable effect.

Individual countries can influence their export ratios by the policies they pursue, but the extent to which countries participate in international trade is not *entirely* at their choice. It must depend, at least to some extent, on the balance between their endowment of productive resources and the pattern of their demands. The endowment of productive resources is likely to be more varied in large countries;

therefore, they are more able to meet their demand for goods and services out of their own resources, and therefore have a smaller participation in international trade. The endowment of resources is likely to be less varied in small countries, which therefore tend to have a greater participation in international trade. Therefore, the size of countries has been considered as one of the main determinants of their export ratios (see e.g. Marshall, 1919; Lloyd, 1968). There is indeed a tendency for export ratios to decline with size measured as the geographical area of countries, but the relationship is not a particularly strong one, especially among LDCs (Sundrum, 1983, table 11.19, p. 213).

A more meaningful measure of size from the economic point of view is the national income of countries. But in relating export ratios of countries to their national income, we must note that the national income of countries is the product of two variables, their population size and their per capita income. When we consider these two variables separately, we find that they influence export ratios in different ways. Tables 10.1 and 10.2 show the export ratios in each of the post-war decades of LDCs and DCs, grouped both according to population size and income level.

According to these tables, export ratios tend to decline with population size, but to increase with per capita income, the latter relationship being weaker than the former. This is confirmed by the regression result obtained by Chenery and Syrquin (1975, p. 38) using both cross-section and time series data; they found the relationship:

$$XR = .038 + 062(\log Y) - .003(\log Y)^2 - .015(\log N) - .006(\log N)^2 \text{ etc.}$$
$$(0.41) \quad (1.95) \quad\quad (1.07) \quad\quad\quad (1.76) \quad\quad\quad (3.60)$$

$$(R^2 = .22) \tag{10.1}$$

where Y is per capita income in US dollars and N is population in millions. However, the positive relationship between export ratios and level of income does not necessarily mean that it is income which influences the export ratio; it is more likely that it is the export ratio which influences the level of income. Therefore, exports can generally be taken as an exogenous source of demand, i.e. one which can be influenced to a considerable degree by government policies.

Table 10.1   Export ratios by population size and income level: LDCs

1981 Per capita income (in US$)	Average export ratios in countries with population (millions)					
	Below 10	10–30	30–50	50–100	100 and over	Total
(a) 1950s						
Below 250	20.9	22.6	–	–	7.5	19.9
250–500	37.8	15.4	–	–	–	25.3
500–750	26.9	13.1	16.2	5.6	–	22.9
750–1000	32.5	13.4	–	–	–	27.8
1000 & over	26.0	29.7	–	–	–	27.0
Total	26.8	17.9	16.2	5.6	7.5	23.2
(b) 1960s						
Below 250	17.5	24.7	–	10.2	4.6	17.6
250–500	20.9	12.9	–	–	–	17.9
500–750	27.3	16.1	–	15.1	–	23.9
750–1000	29.0	12.8	–	6.2	–	22.5
1000–2000	49.3	23.6	9.1	–	–	36.3
2000 & over	36.7	–	–	–	–	36.7
Total	26.7	18.5	–	–	4.6	23.3
(c) 1970s						
Below 250	18.1	16.9	–	6.6	13.6	16.1
250–500	22.5	20.1	20.7	11.1	26.2	21.2
500–750	29.0	19.1	–	25.0	–	28.0
750–1000	31.6	34.1	8.1	–	–	30.5
1000–2000	34.7	30.5	–	9.2	–	29.4
2000 & over	89.5	55.5	–	–	–	78.2
Total	31.4	27.1	16.5	12.2	13.3	27.9

Source: World Bank (1984).

10.2 EXPORTS AND GROWTH OF INCOME: THE STATISTICAL EVIDENCE

(a) Level of Exports and Growth of Income

In examining the statistical evidence, the first question to consider is whether there is any relationship between the *level* of exports (say as

Table 10.2   Export ratios by population size and income level: DCs

1981 Per capita income (in US$)	Average export ratios in countries with population (millions)					
	Below 10	10–30	30–50	50–100	100 and over	Total
(a) 1950s						
Below 2000	18.1	21.6	12.6	10.9	–	17.9
2000–4000	27.4	–	16.2	22.8	–	24.9
4000–6000	–	19.0	–	–	–	19.0
6000 & over	–	–	–	–	4.9	4.9
Total	23.8	21.0	15.0	16.9	4.9	20.7
(b) 1960s						
Below 2000	16.4	14.7	–	10.2	–	14.4
2000–4000	30.7	14.2	–	18.9	–	26.0
4000–6000	29.5	15.2	–	–	–	25.9
6000 & over	30.0	20.6	–	–	5.2	18.6
Total	28.2	15.9	–	16.7	5.2	22.5
(c) 1970s						
Below 2000	24.0	19.6	–	–	–	21.8
2000–4000	34.8	–	15.1	–	–	27.6
4000–6000	37.4	49.9	–	24.5	12.8	32.3
6000–8000	36.1	16.2	–	25.2	–	29.9
8000 & over	28.7	25.7	–	–	8.3	20.9
Total	34.6	27.9	15.1	24.1	10.6	28.8

Source: World Bank (1984).

a ratio of GDP) and the growth of GDP. The data for the post-war period are summarised in Table 10.3. The relationship between the two variables is positive for the LDCs, but is consistently negative for the DCs. In both DCs and LDCs, there was an increase in the export ratio in the 1970s, but there was a decline in the growth rate of GDP. These conflicting patterns suggest that there is no systematic pattern, either positive or negative, between the export ratio and the growth of income.

(b) Growth of Exports and Growth of Income

In fact, most authors who have investigated the statistical evidence

Table 10.3 GDP growth rates by export ratios

Export ratios (XR)	Average GDP growth rates (GY) in					
	LDCs			DCs		
	1950s	1960s	1970s	1950s	1960s	1970s
Below 5	5.7	3.4	4.2	3.2	–	–
5–10	4.0	4.9	5.6	6.0	5.6	2.9
10–15	3.6	4.0	4.8	6.7	7.4	4.5
15–20	4.1	4.4	4.5	4.9	5.3	4.2
20–25	4.0	5.2	5.0	4.2	5.0	3.5
25 & over	5.7	5.7	3.7	2.8	4.5	2.8
Average GY	4.6	4.9	4.5	4.7	5.3	3.2
Average YR	24.1	23.6	27.4	21.3	22.5	28.8
Correlation between GY and XR	.363	.386	.216	.429	−.394	−.123
Number of Countries	49	78	82	22	23	23

Source: World Bank (1984).

have concentrated on the relationship between the *growth* of exports and the *growth* of income. The data for the post-war period are summarised in Table 10.4. Now we see a consistently positive relationship between GYs and GXs, and except for the LDCs in the 1950s, a statistically much stronger relationship than that between GYs and XRs. The nearly perfect correlation in the DCs in the first two decades is particularly remarkable; the much weaker relationship in the DCs in the 1970s is probably due to the disturbed conditions of that decade as a result of the oil crises. The high correlation between the growth rates of income and the growth rates of exports has been noted by a number of economists writing in the 1960s and 1970s (see e.g. Balassa, 1978; Emery, 1967; Michaely, 1977).

But in studying the relationship between the growth of income and the growth of exports, we must allow for the effect of other variables such as the growth of capital and labour. We therefore refer to the results obtained by a number of authors, who have regressed GDP growth rates of LDCs on the growth of exports and a number of other variables as well, using cross section data (Table 10.5).

In the first two equations, Tyler (1981) included the growth rates of labour (GL) and of investment (GI) in addition to the growth rate of

Table 10.4   GDP growth rates by growth of exports

Growth of Exports (GX) (%)	Average GDP growth rates in					
	LDCs			DCs		
	1950s	*1960s*	*1970s*	*1950s*	*1960s*	*1970s*
Below 3	4.3	3.5	2.6	2.4	–	4.4
3–4	4.2	4.0	3.2	2.8	–	2.6
4–5	5.0	3.9	3.8	–	2.9	2.7
5–6	3.5	5.7	5.5	3.4	3.6	3.5
6–7	–	3.8	6.2	3.5	4.6	3.0
7–8	5.7	4.6	6.7	4.3	4.4	3.4
8–10	5.8	5.7	5.1	4.6	4.9	4.0
10 & over	5.9	7.2	6.6	7.1	7.0	4.5
Average GY	4.8	4.9	4.5	4.7	5.3	3.2
Average GX	5.2	6.4	4.6	8.3	8.8	5.7
Correlation between GY & GX	.311	.502	.583	.927	.917	.371
Number of countries	34	76	81	22	23	23

Source: World Bank (1984).

Table 10.5   Regression of GY on GX and other variables
(t-ratios in parenthesis)

Source/sample	Dependent variables					
	GL	*GI*	*IR*	*GX*	*Other*	R^2
Tyler (1981)						
(1) 43 Middle Income LDCs: 1960–77	.981 (2.58)	.254 (5.92)		.570 (1.69)		.69
(2) 43 Middle Income LDCs: 1960–77	1.014 (2.70)	.236 (5.27)			.045 *GMX* (2.23)	.71
Kavoussi (1984)						
(3) 73 LDCs: 1960–78	.400 (1.69)	.241 (5.84)		.105 (3.72)		.57
(4) 36 Middle Income LDCs: 1960–78	.124 (0.50)	2.43 (4.53)		.163 (3.00)		.65

Table 10.5 continued

Source/sample	GL	GI	IR	GX	Other	R^2
			Dependent variables			
(5) 37 Low Income LDCs: 1960–78	.900 (1.91)	.231 (3.83)		.077 (2.47)		.57
Ram (1987) (6) 88 LDCs: 1960–72	.515 (2.20)		.090 (3.25)	.180 (4.59)		.38
(7) 82 LDCs: 1960–72	.304 (1.39)		.079 (3.05)	.186 (4.70)	.217 GZ (4.19)	.49
(8) 54 Middle Income LDCs: 1960–72	.242 (1.06)		.018 (.54)	.243 (5.49)		.41
(9) 34 Low Income LDS: 1960–72	1.343 (2.00)		.110 (2.06)	.087 (1.34)		.42
(10) 88 LDCs: 1973–82	.457 (1.51)		.134 (3.95)	.302 (6.17)		.44
(11) 79 LDCs: 1973–82	.396 (1.44)		.056 (1.68)	.314 (6.53)	.285 GZ (4.59)	.56
(12) 54 Middle Income LDCs: 1973–82	.559 (1.58)		.235 (4.72)	.281 (4.26)		.50
(13) 34 Low Income LDCs: 1973–82	1.475 (2.04)		−0.003 (−.06)	.331 (5.01)		.51

Notes: GMX = growth of manufactured exports; GZ = growth of government consumption expenditures.

exports in his regression of GDP growth rates in LDCs for the period 1960–77. In equation (1) GI is the most significant variable influencing GY, while the influence of GX is barely significant. But this is partly because of the multi-collinearity due to the high correlation between GX and GI, to be noted below. Equation (2) shows that there is a much stronger effect of the growth of manufactured exports.

Kavoussi (1984) undertook a similar analysis for a larger sample of LDCs for about the same period, distinguishing between low income and middle income countries. In all cases, he found that the regression coefficient of export growth was highly significant. Both the regression coefficient and its level of significance was higher for the middle income countries; this was probably because manufactures were a larger proportion of the exports of these countries.

Ram (1987) analysed the relationship for two sub-periods, also distinguishing between low income and middle income LDCs. However, he has taken the investment ratio (*IR*) rather than the growth rate of investment (*GI*) to represent the role of investment. He found that the regression coefficients of *GX* are larger than in the other studies, and also more significant. One reason is because the correlation between *GX* and *IR* is weaker than that between *GX* and *GI*. He also finds that the regression coefficients are higher for the period 1973–82 than for the period 1960–72, and in the period 1960–72, the regression coefficient for the low income countries is smaller and less significant than for the middle income countries. The coefficients are not much affected when the growth rate of government expenditure is also included as an additional explanatory variable. Ram also carried out a similar analysis of time series data for the period 1960–82 for a large sample of 88 LDCs, and found the same type of results.

Another study which is worth noting is that by Feder (1983), who estimated the following equation both for LDCs and DC's for the period 1964–73:

$$GY = a + b_1(IR) + b_2(GL) + b_3(KX) + b_4(GX) \qquad (10.2)$$

where GX is growth rate of exports, while KX is the export component of the growth rate of GDP. This equation is based on a model in which the factors by which export growth influences income growth are distinguished into two parts, namely δ' the differential in productivity between the export and domestic sectors, and θ the elasticity of domestic sector output with respect to volume of exports. As explained in the previous chapter, where the same model was applied to government expenditures, the coefficient of KX is interpreted as $(\delta' - \theta)$ while the coefficient of GX is interpreted as θ. His results are shown in Table 10.6.

These results indicate that in both DCs and LDCs, domestic output was influenced by volume of exports, the elasticity being much higher

Table 10.6   Regression of *GY* on *KX*, *GX* and other variable: 1964–73
(t-ratios in brackets)

Explanatory variable	31 semi-industrialised LDCs	19 DCs
Constant	.006 (0.60)	−.030 (2.61)
IR	.124 (3.01)	.141 (2.87)
GL	.696 (3.40)	.660 (1.48)
KX	.305 (4.57)	−.240 (1.31)
GX	.131 (4.24)	.494 (5.48)
R²	.809	.815

Source: Feder (1983), table 3, p. 68.

in DCs than in LDCs; the productivity differential in favour of the export sector was greater in the LDCs than in the DCs.

10.3 EXPORTS AND GROWTH OF INCOME: THEORETICAL EXPLANATIONS

(a) Gains from Allocative Efficiency

Ever since the foundations of modern economics were laid by the classical economists, one of the main themes of the subject has been the advantages that a country derives from free trade and the adverse effects of the governmental control of foreign trade that had prevailed before. However, there have been many different explanations of how countries benefit from free trade. One of the most popular of these is the explanation derived from Ricardo's theory of comparative advantage. According to this theory, different countries have a comparative advantage in different commodities, and free trade permits countries to specialise in different commodities according to their comparative advantage. Then, consumers benefit by being able to buy the commodities they want at the cheapest price, because they are produced in the countries which are most efficient in producing them. Much of modern trade theory consists of a much more general formulation of Ricardo's theory. An important new development has been the Heckscher-Ohlin theory which identifies the source of comparative advantage in the nature of each country's factor endowment. But the essential argument is still that the advantage of free trade lies in the gains from allocative efficiency. This is the case illustrated in Figure 1.2 as a movement along the transformation curve.

There can be no question that part of the growth of countries in the past has been due to the gains from allocative efficiency resulting from the great expansion of world trade in the past two countries. But the gains from allocative efficiency alone are not sufficient to explain the findings from the statistical evidence. While free trade is better than no trade, what we have to explain is whether more trade is better for economic growth than less trade. For example, in Ram's (1985, p. 418) argument that 'a high level of exports (and trade) leads to a better allocation of resources in terms of the simplest concepts of comparative advantage and production efficiency', the free trade that leads to the allocative gains does not necessarily mean more exports. Strictly speaking, there is an optimum amount of exports that maximises the gains of allocative efficiency due to free trade. While the governmental control of trade has reduced exports below this optimal level in some countries, it has led to more exports than this level in other countries. Thus, as Bhagwati and Krueger (1973) say, the export-oriented countries such as South Korea appear 'to have intervened virtually as much and as "chaotically" on the side of export promotion as others have done on the side of import substitution, and their success cannot be attributed to the presence of a neoclassically efficient allocating mechanism *in toto* in the system'.

There are a number of reasons why gains from allocative efficiency do not explain the observed relationship between exports and growth. First, as Harberger (1959) pointed out, the magnitude of the benefits from better allocation of resources under free trade may be quite small. Secondly, the rapid growth of exports of the DCs in the post-war period until 1973 consisted largely of intra-industry trade, i.e. a trade in which both imports and exports consist of the same type of goods (Grubel and Lloyd, 1975). It is unlikely that the comparative advantage of these countries differed greatly between their exports and their imports in such trade; therefore, their growth could not have been mainly due to the gains from improvement in allocative efficiency.

The most serious problem with this explanation is that improvements in allocative efficiency only explain why a greater participation in world trade may lead to a higher level of welfare than otherwise, i.e. it only explains the relationship between the level of exports and the level of income. An increase in the export ratio may increase the national income, but this is a once-over effect, though the benefits may last for a considerable period of time, if countries which were previously isolated from world trade are suddenly opened up to world trade, as happened in many LDCs during the nineteenth century. But once a country has been engaged in world trade for some time, the improvement of allocative efficiency is unlikely to account for countries with high export ratios having faster growth of their national income. As Krueger (1981, p. 4) pointed out:

> On the one hand, the classical free-trade arguments while indicating the superiority of free trade, do not provide any hint as to why that superiority should be demonstrated in a more rapid rate of growth (as contrasted with a higher level of income after sustaining once-and-for-all losses associated with protection). On the other hand, even if the losses from first-best optimality were several times as great as traditional theory would suggest, the differences in growth rates seem to be greater than can conceivably be accounted for by the exporting sector of the economy.

Similarly, Myint (1987, p. 116–7) has pointed out that:

> attempts to quantify the gains or losses associated with the trade distortions tend to come out as a 'small' percentage of the aggregate income. There may be some dispute about the exact magnitude of these gains or losses in particular cases, but the general order of magnitude is unlikely to change so long as we interpret them strictly as direct static gains or losses, without bringing in factors outside the formal framework of the neoclassical theory, such as X-efficiency or improved productivity as the result of induced technical changes . . . The gains from the removal of the static distortions seem to be too small to explain the rapid growth of the (export-oriented) countries which have grown as rapidly as they have.

We must therefore consider other explanations for the observed relationship between export growth and GDP growth.

(b) Dynamic Advantages of Trade

One such explanation is based on the dynamic, rather than the static, advantages of trade. The argument that the gains from trade were due to improvements in allocative efficiency was based on an assumption that the comparative advantage of countries in different commodities was fixed over time. By contrast, the argument underlying the dynamic advantages of trade is based on changes in these comparative advantages brought about by an expansion of trade. For example, in his explanation for the rapid growth of Japan after the Meiji Restoration based on export growth, Lockwood (1954, p. 320) argued that trade had a favourable effect on growth over time through gaining knowledge of new products and new techniques, and hence spoke of trade as a 'highway of learning'. Similarly, Myint (1958) stressed the 'educative' effects of foreign trade in introducing new wants, new technology, and new forms of economic organisation into an underdeveloped country. Haberler (1959, p. 705) considered trade as 'the most important vehicle for the transmission of technological know-how' and Johnson (1977, p. 427) argued that trade influenced growth 'through the educational effects of exposure to foreign competition and foreign ways of doing things'.

A particularly important form of the dynamic advantages of trade is that arising from increasing returns to scale. As exports grow, there is an increase in the scale of production with its attendant economies, leading to a continuous increase in the efficiency with which resources are used. This is the type of advantage that was stressed by Adam Smith in his dictum that 'the division of labour depends on the extent of the market'. It is this advantage that explains the large and growing volume of intra-industry trade among the DCs in the postwar period. However, such economies of scale are particularly important in the manufacturing sector; therefore the dynamic advantages of trade in the form of increasing returns is particularly important in the case where it is the export of manufactured exports which increases over time.

(c) Relaxation of Foreign Exchange Constraint

Another way in which exports might contribute to economic growth is by relaxing the foreign exchange constraint on growth. The foreign exchange constraint arises if countries seeking a high rate of growth can save enough to finance the required rate of investment, but cannot domestically produce the capital goods needed for that amount or type of investment. Then, an increase of exports helps these countries to earn more foreign exchange to import the capital goods from abroad, and hence achieve a higher rate of growth. The

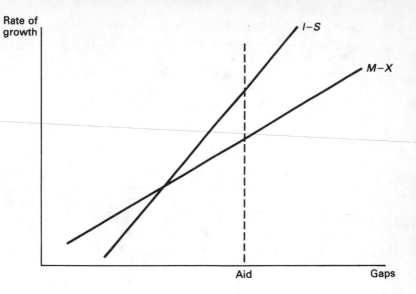

Figure 10.1

argument can therefore be considered as a special case of the gains from allocative efficiency in which countries benefit by exchanging their exports for capital goods which can only be produced by other countries.

This argument has been spelt out in the two gap theory of Chenery and Bruno (1962) and Chenery and Strout (1966). One gap is the excess over savings of the investment needed for a target rate of growth. The other gap is the excess over exports of imports at that rate of growth. In the national accounts estimates, these two gaps must be equal *ex post*, but they may not be equal *ex ante* (see Thirlwall, 1978, pp. 292–8 for derivation of these gaps). The relationship between the *ex ante* gaps and the rate of growth is illustrated in Figure 10.1. The theory was developed to estimate the foreign aid needed to assist countries to achieve a target rate of growth. It was argued that the amount of foreign aid needed should equal the larger of the two gaps.

The theory has also been used to determine the constraints on growth. Thus, the foreign exchange constraint is said to be binding if the foreign exchange gap is greater than the investment savings gap. Then, for a given amount of foreign aid, the rate of growth determined by the foreign exchange gap will be lower than that determined by the investment savings gap. Because the two gaps must be equal *ex post*, some of the savings which the country could have made will be frustrated. Then, an increase in exports will avoid the frustration of the savings propensity, and enable the country to achieve a higher rate of growth.

The theory has been criticised on the ground that it underestimates the extent to which savings can be used to reduce a deficit in the balance of payments by such means as the adjustment of prices and/or the exchange rate (Findlay, 1971). If these adjustments work efficiently, the two gaps will be equal *ex post* and *ex ante*, and there will be only one gap. However, there are more serious problems with the theory. One is that the level of investment is not determined only by savings and any foreign capital inflow. It may also be financed by the banking system. Therefore, it is more likely that it is savings which adjust to the level of investment undertaken by entrepreneurs. Another problem is that a foreign exchange constraint is not only due to the need to import capital goods from abroad. This may be the case in some LDCs, but in other countries, the foreign exchange constraint may be due to the import demand for consumer goods at a high rate of growth. It is the latter which is usually the case in DCs. The rapid growth of exports has relaxed the foreign exchange constraint on growth in some countries such as South Korea, but this is because it has improved the creditworthiness of the country and enabled it to borrow more internationally to finance its investment.

(d) The Accounting Effect

It is sometime argued that the high correlation that is generally observed between the growth rates of exports and of GDP is, to some extent at least, a spurious one, because as the OECD report (1968, p. 127) put it: 'This conclusion is not entirely unexpected considering that export earnings constitute for many developing countries a significant part of GDP. Expanding exports thus not only provide earnings with which to purchase needed imports, but their production directly adds to GDP growth.'

Similarly, Michaely (1977, p. 50) argued that 'Since exports are themselves part of the national product, a positive correlation of the two variables is almost inevitable, whatever their true relationship'.

Table 10.7   Regression of *GY* and *KD* on KX
(R^2 values in parentheses)

Countries/ period	Regression coefficients of:	
	GY on KX	KD on KX
LDCs		
1950s	.6154 (.14)	−.3846 (.06)
1960s	.6137 (.28)	−.3863 (.14)
1970s	.7224 (.19)	−.2776 (.04)
DCs		
1950s	.8935 (.16)	−.1065 (.02)
1960s	.1870 (.01)	−.8130 (.14)
1970s	.2030 (.03)	−.7970 (.29)

In order to overcome this problem, he went on to correlate GDP growth rates with the change in the ratio of exports to GDP, but this does not solve the problem as the change in the ratio of exports to GDP is simply the difference between the growth rates of the two variables.

However, the correlation between the growth of exports and the growth of GDP cannot be dismissed as spurious on this ground, because the growth of exports will be a part of the growth of GDP only if it is not accompanied by a corresponding reduction in the growth of output for domestic use. In order to examine this possibility, Heller and Porter (1978) correlated the growth rate of exports with the growth rate of production for domestic use D, defined as $Y - X$. An even better solution, suggested by Kleimen (1980), is in terms of K-ratios, where the K-ratio of a component of GDP is that part of the growth rate of GDP which is due to the growth of that component. Thus the K-ratio of exports $KX = (\Delta X)/Y$ and the K-ratio of domestic output $KD = (\Delta D)/Y$. The K-ratios of investment and government expenditures were used in previous chapters. Kleimen suggested that, to assess the influence of export growth on GDP growth independently of any accounting effect, we must regress KD on KX. The results of such a regression analysis are presented in Table 10.7.

These results may be interpreted as follows. If the growth of exports has no effect on the growth of GDP, then the growth of exports must be accompanied by a corresponding decline in domestic output, and the regression coefficient of KD on KX must be negative and numerically equal to 1. In fact, this regression coefficient is

Table 10.8   Regression of KD in KX: 1950–73

	Total sample	Groups A[a]	Group B
No. of countries	41	7	34
Regression coefficient	.5349	−1.0210	−.0498
R^2	.0093	.4801	.0010

Note: [a] The countries in this group are Greece, Israel, Portugal, South Korea, Spain, Taiwan and Yugoslavia.

negative but greater than 1 in both DCs and LDCs in all three decades. Therefore, the growth of exports must have contributed to some part of the growth of GDP. This contribution was particularly large in the LDCs, and in the DCs in the 1950s.

In Kleimen's own (1980) application of the method to per capita data from a sample of 41 countries in the period 1950–73 (the same sample as that used by Heller and Porter, 1978), he actually found that the regression coefficient of KD on KX was *positive* implying that the growth of exports actually *increased* domestic output. He called this the spillover effect, and was surprised at its magnitude. However, his surprising result was due to the fact that his sample consisted of two very different groups of countries, one group of 7 countries being much more developed than the other larger group of 34 countries. It is more appropriate to do the regressions separately for the two groups of countries, as shown in Table 10.8.

Then, we see that the regression coefficient is negative for each of these groups, indicating that in both cases, the growth of exports was to some extent at the expense of the growth of domestic output. This effect was very large in the case of the more developed countries of the sample (group A) indicating that it was mainly a case of the growth of exports substituting for the growth of domestic output. The effect was much smaller in the case of the less developed countries of the sample (group B) indicating that the growth of exports made a real contribution to the growth of GDP with very little reduction in the growth of domestic output.

(e) Demand Effects: Vent for Surplus

The simplest explanation for the regression coefficients of KD on KX being negative but less than 1 in Table 10.7 is that the economy had under-employed resources to begin with. Then, to the extent that exports were increased by utilising these under-employed resources more fully, there was no corresponding reduction in domestic output, and a net increase in GDP. On this explanation, exports promote growth by providing a 'vent for surplus'. This was, in fact, one of the arguments used by Adam Smith in his advocacy of free trade. Though it was over-shadowed for a long time by the comparative cost theory (which assumed full employment) the vent for surplus theory was revived by Myint (1958). He has recently explained it as follows (Myint, 1987, p. 121):

> The vent for surplus theory was particularly suited to explain the rapid expansion of agricultural exports from the relatively sparsely populated countries of Southeast Asia and West Africa. After the initial opening up of these countries in the late nineteenth and early twentieth centuries, agricultural exports grew typically about 5 per cent a year for many decades. This happened without any important change in agricultural techniques, simply by bringing more land under cultivation. The additional labour was drawn from the subsistence sector. Unlike the situation in the densely populated countries, the underemployment was caused not by a shortage of land but by the limited local demand for the agricultural output that the existing underemployed labour could have produced with the existing uncultivated land. Hence the role of international trade as a vent for surplus. I believe that the vent for surplus theory provides a more powerful argument for free trade than the conventional comparative advantage theory. The direct gains from using the previously underutilized resources will be many times greater than the conventional gains from a more efficient reallocation of the given resources.

According to this theory, the growth of exports promotes the growth of GDP because it leads to a fuller utilisation of under-employed resources. Hence, this is an example of a demand effect. The growth of GDP is essentially due to the increase in demand brought about by the growth of exports.

(f) Interaction of Demand and Supply

In the theory considered above, the growth of GDP resulting from the growth of exports is mainly due to the fuller utilisation of existing productive capacity. As Myint has argued, this was certainly an important part of the explanation for the rapid growth of LDCs in the nineteenth and early twentieth centuries resulting from the great expansion of their exports after they were opened up to international trade under colonial governments. To some extent, this may have also operated in the post-war decades, especially in LDCs.

But the high values of the regression coefficients of KD on KX found in Table 10.7 show that the growth of exports was associated with a remarkably small decline in domestic output in the post-war decades, especially in the LDCs. It is unlikely that the growth of exports had this effect only because of the fuller utilisation of existing productive capacity. Instead, it is more likely that there was also a considerable increase in productive capacity, associated with the growth of exports. This is an example of the interaction between demand and supply.

One way in which the growth of exports promotes the growth of productive capacity is by inducing faster techonological progress. In other words, the growth of exports helped to trigger off the dynamic advantages of trade referred to above. It has been described by Myint (1987, p. 121–2) as the 'productivity theory of international trade' which is also attributed to Adam Smith:

This emphasized the role of international trade in widening the extent of the market and the scope for division of labour. These changes would raise the productivity of resources by improving the skill and dexterity of labour, by overcoming technical indivisi- bilities in production, and by encouraging technological inno- vations.

Another way in which the growth of exports leads to the growth of productive capacity is by expanding the opportunities for profitable investment and inducing higher levels of investment by increasing demand. To examine this effect, we consider the correlation between the growth of investment (GI) and the growth of exports (GX) (Table 10.9).

Except in the 1950s, there was a positive correlation between GI and GX. The correlation was particularly strong in the DCs in the 1960s. This was the decade in which the DCs experienced their highest rates of GDP growth as well as their highest rates of export growth. This relationship may therefore be explained as the result of rapid growth of investment induced by the rapid growth of exports.

Table 10.9   Correlation between growth of exports (GX) and growth of investment (GI)

Period	Correlation Coefficient between GX and GI in LDCs	DCs
1950s	−.079	−.377
1960s	.236	.641
1970s	.368	.187

Source: World Bank (1984).

(g) Structural Impact of Exports

In Chapter 3, it was argued that the growth process in all countries follows a logistic pattern, such that the growth process can be described by an S-curve. This pattern arises because there is an acceleration of growth as the centre of gravity of the structure of the economy shifts from agriculture to industry, and because there is a deceleration of growth when the centre of gravity shifts again from industry to services. However, the S-curve varies from country to country, because of differences in the speed of movement from one phase to another, and the speed of movement within each phase.

The variation of the S-curves between countries due to these differences is due partly to differences in the supply factors, such as the growth of labour and capital, and the progress of technology, discussed in Part II. It depends also on demand factors, such as investment and government expenditures, discussed in Chapters 8 and 9. In the same way, the growth of exports also has significant effects on the S-curve along which each country moves over time.

The way exports influence the shape of each country's S-curve, however, depends on the sort of commodities that a country exports There are two distinct patterns. If exports consist mainly of primary products, an increase of exports will extend the agricultural phase of the logistic pattern of growth, and therefore delay the industrial phase, and the growth acceleration associated with it. But during this phase, exports may accelerate growth if it provides a vent for surplus, i.e. if it provides demand for under-utilised resources. However, after such under-utilised resources are exhausted, the primary exporting countries revert back to the low rate of growth of countries in the agricultural phase of their development. This is because the export of primary products does not have as strong an interaction between demand and supply factors, such as higher investment and the improvement of technology, discussed above. This explains the typical growth history of LDCs, which experienced high rates of growth as a result of the great expansion of their primary exports during the nineteenth and early twentieth centuries, but emerged at the end of the Second World War as typical underdeveloped countries.

The other pattern is the case where exports consist largely of manufactures. In this case, a rapid growth of exports will speed the shift of the structure of production from agriculture to industry, and therefore advance the growth acceleration phase. The growth acceleration will be greater, if exports provide a demand for under-utilised resources, as when a labour surplus country exports highly labour-intensive manufactures. In addition, when exports consist largely of manufactures, there will be a greater interaction between demand and supply factors, which induces faster growth of investment and faster progress of technology as discussed above. Because of these indirect effects, such countries will be able to maintain high rates of growth even after exports stop growing at a high rate. These growth promoting effects are much stronger than those due to improvements in allocative efficiency, and are the main explanation for the rapid growth of the DCs in the first quarter century after the Second World War, and also the rapid growth of the middle income LDCs which expanded their manufactured exports rapidly during the same period.

10.4 THE TAIWAN EXPERIENCE

In Part II, we considered the role of various supply factors in economic growth. These are the factors which are emphasised in prevailing theories of growth. But in Part III, it was argued that various demand factors have played a more significant role in promoting economic growth, partly by leading to the full utilisation of existing productive capacity, and partly by inducing a faster growth of productive capacity. Thus, for example, we found that while GDP growth rates were correlated with levels of investment indicating the supply effects of investment, they were even more strongly correlated with the growth rates of investment indicating the demand effects of investment. Further, the growth rates of investment were in turn influenced by the growth rates of such demand factors as government expenditures (Table 9.10) and of exports (Table 10.9). Finally, these

Table 10.10 Growth performance of Taiwan: 1952–86
(at 1981 constant prices)

Period	Rate of growth of GDP
1952–60	7.41
1960–65	9.55
1965–70	9.71
1970–75	8.98
1975–80	10.58
1980–86	6.65
1952–86	9.01

Source: Republic of China, *Statistical Year book* (1987).

demand factors have played a significant role in the logistic pattern that economic growth has generally taken in practice.

The previous discussion of these themes was largely based on cross section analysis based on data from all countries for which they were available. It is therefore useful to consider also an analysis based on time series data. It is not possible to do this for many countries; therefore such an analysis is undertaken only for one country, which has experienced a particularly rapid growth in recent decades, namely Taiwan. Although Taiwan's experience has been studied intensively, there still remain a number of controversial features. Therefore, Taiwan's recent experience is a particularly suitable case for studying these controversial features.

(a) Rate of Growth

Taiwan's growth performance in the post-war period is summarised in Table 10.10. Starting from a lower base, Taiwan's growth performance before 1975 was as good as that of Japan, and even better after 1975. Even in this short period, the growth rate of Taiwan shows symptoms of the logistic pattern, rising in the early phase and declining thereafter. Some of the reasons for this pattern are discussed below.

(b) Investment

The growth of capital is usually considered to be the most important supply factor in economic growth. Therefore, we consider the rate of investment in the Taiwan economy in Table 10.11.

Table 10.11   Rate of investment in Taiwan: 1952–86

| Period | Investment as % of GDP at 1981 constant prices | % Financed by: | |
		Domestic saving	Foreign capital inflow
1952–55	12.1	59.6	40.4
1956–60	12.0	60.0	40.0
1961–65	15.9	83.3	16.7
1966–70	21.6	95.0	5.0
1971–75	28.6	103.9	−3.9
1976–80	30.0	108.3	−8.3
1981–86	23.6	157.8	−57.8

Source: *Taiwan Statistical Data Book, 1987*. Cited in Tsiang (1988), table 8, p. 35.

There was a steady rise in investment as a proportion of GDP for most of the post-war period. A large part of investment was financed by foreign capital in the early years, but since the mid-1960s, it was entirely financed by domestic savings.

For analysing the role of capital in the growth process, it may be useful to have estimates of capital stock. There are no official figures available, but a rough estimate can be made as follows. We start with a figure of 3.7 for the capital–output ratio in 1960, as suggested by Tsiang and Wu (1985, p. 321). Then, estimates for the following years can be derived by adding gross investment and subtracting depreciation for each year, as given in the national accounts. The depreciation figures are published only at current prices; we have therefore estimated the figures at 1981 prices by assuming that the ratio of depreciation to investment at constant prices is the same as at current prices. The results are shown in Table 10.12.

We note that the depreciation rate (i.e. depreciation as a percentage of capital stock) increases more or less steadily from 1.33 in 1960 to 4.47 in 1986. It is therefore reasonable to assume a lower depreciation rate of, say, 1.2 per cent for the period before 1960. This assumption combined with the official figures of fixed investment at 1981 constant prices was used to estimate the capital stock before 1960.

The growth rates of capital stock, the capital–labour ratio and the productivity of labour, derived from these estimates, are shown in Table 10.13.

Table 10.12   Growth of capital stock in Taiwan: 1952–60

Year	Capital stock K (million NT $) at 1981 prices	Depreciation rate δ	Capital output ratio K/Y	Capital per worker K/L	GDP per worker Y/L
				(thousand NT $ at 1981 prices)	
1952	901,480	1.20	6.18	308	49.8
1953	904,535	1.20	5.67	305	53.8
1954	911,566	1.20	5.22	301	57.7
1955	919,964	1.20	4.87	296	60.8
1956	925,539	1.20	4.65	294	63.3
1957	933,178	1.20	4.36	289	66.3
1958	940,370	1.20	4.12	282	68.4
1959	950,959	1.20	3.87	278	71.8
1960	966,769	1.33	3.70	278	75.2
1961	986,909	1.38	3.53	282	79.7
1962	1,008,559	1.55	3.35	285	85.1
1963	1,030,358	1.74	3.13	287	91.7
1964	1,056,502	1.90	2.86	289	101.0
1965	1,082,994	1.95	2.64	288	109.2
1966	1,119,055	2.07	2.50	290	116.1
1967	1,167,088	2.34	2.36	288	122.3
1968	1,228,322	2.55	2.27	291	127.9
1969	1,304,275	2.75	2.22	297	134.1
1970	1,388,203	3.07	2.12	303	143.2
1971	1,482,239	3.37	2.01	313	160.0
1972	1,600,038	3.67	1.91	323	169.1
1973	1,736,771	3.52	1.84	326	177.3
1974	1,892,518	3.04	1.98	345	174.1
1975	2,081,994	3.22	2.06	377	181.3
1976	2,314,324	3.48	2.03	408	200.7
1977	2,539,333	3.69	2.03	425	209.2
1978	2,765,356	3.93	1.95	444	228.0
1979	3,017,399	3.73	1.96	470	239.1
1980	3,316,841	3.43	2.01	507	251.8
1981	3,679,727	3.74	2.10	552	262.2
1982	4,036,203	3.84	2.25	593	264.0
1983	4,372,864	3.92	2.26	619	273.9
1984	4,676,108	4.06	2.20	640	290.3
1985	4,972,748	4.28	2.25	669	297.9
1986	5,185,499	4.47	2.12	671	316.4

Table 10.13   Growth of capital and output in Taiwan: 1952–86
(constant 1981 prices)

Period	*Growth rate (%) of*		
	Capital-stock K	Capital per worker (K/L)	Output per worker (Y/L)
1952–60	0.85	−1.39	5.02
1960–70	3.54	0.65	6.80
1970–78	9.22	5.23	5.18
1978–86	8.46	5.64	3.91

Source: See table 10.12.

There are three notable features about the growth of capital in Taiwan. First, the capital–output ratio declined for most of the period until the late mid-1970s. Although the capital–output ratio varied greatly even in other countries, the neoclassical growth theory is based on a constancy of this ratio, assumed to be a stylised fact of the growth experience of DCs. Secondly, the capital–labour ratio actually declined in the early period 1952–60, rose slowly at only 0.65 per cent annually in 1960–70, and rapidly at over 5 per cent only thereafter. Thirdly, output per worker was growing all the time, at around 5 per cent even in 1952–60, above 5 per cent until 1978, falling to about 4 per cent after 1978. The growth of labour productivity was faster than the growth of capital per worker for most of the period, and nearly as fast after 1978. The rapid growth of output in Taiwan cannot be attributed solely to the high rate of investment, on any reasonable estimate of the elasticity of output with respect to capital. Instead, it must be attributed to a high rate of technological progress and a substantial structural transformation of the economy. The growth of capital did play a part, but mainly in facilitating these processes.

However, the rapid rise in the investment rate in Taiwan itself needs to be explained. In the early years, a large part of investment was financed by foreign capital inflow, but foreign financing of investment declined rapidly and disappeared during the 1960s, after which it was Taiwan which was exporting capital. Hence, for most of the period of rapid growth, the investment was financed by domestic savings. Just how rapid was the rise in the savings rate in Taiwan may be seen by comparing with the change in the savings rate of some

Table 10.14   Net domestic savings rate in four countries

Country	Average savings rate in	
	1961–70	*1971–80*
Taiwan	16.7	31.9
Japan	27.5	23.0
UK	11.4	8.1
USA	9.5	6.4

Source: Tsiang (1985), table 3.6, p. 48.

developed countries (Table 10.14). The growth of the savings rate in Taiwan from the 1960s to the 1970s is truly phenomenal, occurring at a time when the savings rate declined in many DCs.

An explanation of the rapid growth of Taiwan (and other Asian NICs) in terms of savings and demographic behaviour has been offered by Tsiang (1985, 1988) and Tsiang and Wu (1985) by a modification of the neo-classical theory of growth discussed in section 4.3. In that theory, it was assumed that the savings ratio s and the population growth rate n were given constants. Then, there is a particular value of the capital-labour ratio k^* for which $sf(k^*) = nk^*$. As k rises whenever $k < k^*$, and falls whenever $k > k^*$, the economy converges to a stable equilibrium growth path at k^*.

In the case of Taiwan, there was a steady rise in the savings ratio s and a steady fall in the population growth rate n, as shown in Table 10.15. The implications of these variations for growth are illustrated in Figure 10.2. This figure is a modification of Figure 4.1 in two respects. On the one hand, because the rate of growth of population and the labour force rises with per capita income up to a point and falls thereafter, nk is no longer a straight line through the origin but a curve with two points of curvature. Then, any given savings curve S cuts the curve nk at three points 1, 2 and 3, of which only 2 is a point of stable equilibrium. On the other hand, there is a steady rise in the S curve to a higher position such as S' because of the rise in the savings ratio. As S' rises above S, the points 2 and 3 approach each other until they coincide when S' is tangential to the nk curve. This point, however, is an unstable equilibrium. Once past this point, the capital labour ratio will go on increasing because $sf(k) > nk$, or equivalently because $s > n(K/Y)$ and there will be a steady accelera-

Table 10.15   Growth of savings, capital and labour in Taiwan

Year	K/Y	n	s	s − (K/Y)n
1952	6.0	3.3	5.2	−14.6
1955	4.8	3.8	4.9	−13.3
1960	3.7	3.5	7.6	−5.4
1961	3.6	3.3	8.0	−3.9
1962	3.4	3.3	7.6	−3.6
1963	3.2	3.2	13.4	3.2
1964	2.9	3.1	16.3	7.3
1965	2.7	3.0	16.5	8.4
1966	2.6	2.9	19.0	11.5
1967	2.5	2.3	20.1	14.3
1968	2.4	2.7	19.8	13.3
1969	2.3	2.5	22.1	16.3
1970	2.2	2.4	23.8	18.5
1972	2.0	2.0	31.6	27.6
1974	2.1	1.8	31.5	27.7
1976	2.2	2.2	32.2	27.4
1978	2.0	1.9	35.2	31.4

Source: Tsiang (1985), table 3.7, p. 49.

tion of the growth rate, which is described as a 'take off'. From the data of Table 10.15, Tsiang and Wu have dated the year of this take off as 1963. Similarly, they have dated the take-off of Korea in 1966–67, of Hong Kong in 1965 and of Singapore in 1968.

The theory, however, is only a description of what happened, rather than an explanation of it. The falling rate of population growth in Taiwan may be attributed to the family planning programme in the country. But there is no explanation for the phenomenal rise in the savings ratio or the high rate of technological progress, which played a crucial role in the rapid growth of Taiwan. We must therefore consider other explanations.

(c) Structural Transformation

The rapid growth of Taiwan during the post-war period was accompanied by a remarkable structural transformation (Table 10.16). The levels and growth of labour productivity derived from these data are shown in Table 10.17.

From these estimates, we can decompose the overall growth of

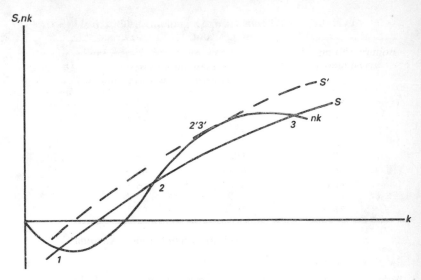

Figure 10.2

Table 10.16   Structural transformation of Taiwan economy, 1952–86

Year	% Employment in			% GDP from:		
	Agriculture	Industry	Services	Agriculture	Industry	Services
1952	56.1	16.9	27.0	35.9	18.0	46.1
1960	50.2	20.5	29.3	32.8	24.9	42.3
1970	36.7	27.9	35.4	16.7	39.2	44.1
1978	24.9	39.3	35.8	8.9	50.5	40.6
1986	17.0	41.5	41.5	5.5	51.6	42.9

Source: Republic of China: Taiwan *Statistical Data Book* (1987).

Table 10.17   Labour productivity by sectors, Taiwan, 1952–86

Year	Labour productivity (1981 NT $000 per worker)				Growth of labour productivity since last date shown			
	Agriculture	Industry	Services	Total	Agriculture	Industry	Services	Total
1952	31.9	53.0	84.9	49.8	–	–	–	–
1960	49.2	91.3	108.6	75.2	4.63	7.19	3.01	5.02
1970	65.1	201.0	178.7	143.2	4.19	8.17	4.46	6.80
1978	80.9	293.2	259.1	228.0	2.60	4.04	4.37	5.18
1986	102.5	293.6	327.1	316.4	2.15	3.73	2.93	3.91

Source: Republic of China, *Taiwan Statistical Data Book* (1987).

Table 10.18   Components of growth of labour productivity in Taiwan, 1952–1986 (percentage contributions in brackets)

Period	Growth of labour productivity	Due to growth of labour productivity in			Due to reallocation of labour
		Agriculture	Industry	Services	
1952–60	5.02	1.91	1.26	1.27	0.58
	(100)	(38)	(25)	(25)	(12)
1960–70	6.80	0.80	2.25	2.23	1.52
	(100)	(12)	(33)	(33)	(22)
1970–78	5.18	0.36	1.57	1.73	1.52
	(100)	(7)	(30)	(34)	(29)
1978–86	3.91	0.24	1.74	1.14	0.79
	(100)	(6)	(45)	(29)	(20)

labour productivity into various components, according to the following formula of Chapter 3:

$$\dot{q} = \Sigma k_i \dot{q}_i + \Sigma(\lambda_i' - \lambda_i)\, q_i'/q \tag{10.3}$$

The various components are shown in Table 10.18, which indicates that there was a significant growth of labour productivity in each sector, in addition to a significant contribution from the reallocation effect. This effect increased both absolutely and relatively up to a point and declined thereafter. This is one important reason for the slower growth of the later period. Another reason has been the smaller contribution from the agricultural and service sectors in the later period. The Taiwan experience is thus a striking example of the acceleration of growth in the middle phase of the logistic, and also of the deceleration of growth in the later phase.

(d) Growth of Exports

The most striking feature of Taiwan economic performance, however, was the growth of exports in the post-war period, summarised in Table 10.19. Starting from a low ratio of GDP in the 1950s, exports became more than half of GDP in the 1980s. The most rapid growth occurred in the 1960s; the growth rate declined thereafter, while remaining high by international standards.

   The rapid growth of exports started in the early 1960s when Taiwan

Table 10.19   Export performance of Taiwan, 1952–86 (at 1981 constant prices)

Period	Average % share of GDP	Average annual growth rate
1952–60	8.3	8.98
1961–70	17.7	22.09
1971–78	42.7	14.23
1979–86	55.8	10.78

Source: Republic of China, *Taiwan Statistical Yearbook* (1987).

accepted the advice of an IMF mission headed by Professors S.C. Tsiang and T.C. Liu (Tsiang, 1985, pp. 35–6) to devalue the currency and liberalise foreign trade. But apart from these measures, the government also followed an active policy of encouraging exports by controlling financial allocations, labour relations, administrative guidance, close collaboration between government and business, and promoting foreign capital (C. Johnson, 1987).

Export growth was certainly a key factor in Taiwan's rapid growth. Comparing Tables 10.10 and 10.19, there was a parallel movement of the two rates. But the relationship between the two rates must be considered in more detail. The tremendous expansion of exports cannot be attributed only to the exploitation of an initial comparative advantage and the consequent improvement in allocative efficiency brought about by a liberal trade policy. Instead, there was a dramatic improvement of Taiwan's comparative advantage in the production of manufactures.

First recall that the growth of exports is itself part of the growth of GDP, so that it is more relevant to consider how far the growth of exports was associated with a growth of domestic output. As suggested above, the most convenient way to study this relationship is by regressing the K-ratios of domestic output D and of exports X, i.e. their respective contributions to the overall growth rate of GDP. The results are shown in Table 10.20.

As discussed above, the regression coefficient of KD on KX indicates the extent to which the growth of exports was at the expense of the growth of domestic output. There are two ways in which the growth of exports might not have significant adverse effects on the

Table 10.20   Regression of *KD* on *KX*, Taiwan, 1952–86

Period	Regression of KD on KX	R^2
1952–60	−1.324	.65
1969–70	−0.609	.34
1970–86	−0.339	.42

Source: Republic of China, *Taiwan Statistical Yearbook* (1987).

growth of domestic output. One way is if there are considerable under-utilised resources to begin with, as considered in the vent for surplus theory. The other way is if the growth of exports leads to a sufficient increase in productive capacity. In the Taiwan case, we see that the growth of exports had a large negative effect on the growth of domestic output in the early period of the 1950s, and to some extent also in the 1960s. Therefore, the growth of exports in this period was not mainly due to the exploitation of under-utilised resources. But the growth of exports had only a small negative effect on the growth of domestic output after 1970. It is unlikely that this was due to under-utilised resources after two decades of rapid growth. Therefore, this small negative effect may be explained as due to the rapid growth of productive capacity induced by the growth of exports.

A large part of the growth of productive capacity was due to technological progress, associated with the rapid structural transformation of the economy, noted in Table 10.16. This structural transformation in turn was induced by the changing composition of exports, summarised in Table 10.21.

In the 1950s, the bulk of Taiwan exports consisted of agricultural products, but by the 1980s, they consisted almost exclusively of manufactures. The 1960s were a period in which exports of all types of commodities increased rapidly, due to the devaluation and trade liberalisation, but the fastest growth was in manufactured exports. In the 1970s and 1980s, manufactured exports continued to grow rapidly, though at lower rates than in the 1960s. As a result of the rapid growth of manufactured exports, there was a shift of labour from agriculture to industry, where it was able to take advantage of the faster growth of labour productivity, and thus contribute to the rapid growth of labour productivity in the economy as a whole.

Finally, we consider the interaction between exports and investment. Table 10.22 shows the correlation between the growth rates of exports and investment during 1961–84, which was the period in

Table 10.21 Changing composition of Taiwan Exports, 1952–86

Period	Agricultural products	Processed Agricultural products	All Agricultural products	Manufactures	Total
(a) *Percentage shares*					
1952–60	19.0	65.8	84.8	15.2	100.0
1961–70	14.3	29.8	44.1	55.9	100.0
1971–78	6.0	8.8	14.8	85.2	100.0
1979–86	2.3	5.2	7.5	92.5	100.0
(b) *Average annual growth rate (%)*					
1952–60	8.53	4.85	5.63	27.42	8.98
1960–70	18.33	6.36	9.75	31.98	22.09
1970–78	8.21	7.16	7.63	17.71	14.23
1978–86	−7.10	7.90	2.63	10.86	10.78

Source: Republic of China, *Statistical Yearbook* (1987).

Table 10.22 Correlation between growth of exports and growth of investment

Lag of investment growth behind export growth	Correlation between growth of export and growth of Investment
−2	.077
−1	.317
0	.156
1	.153
2	.706
3	.397

which there was the most rapid growth of manufactured exports.

This table enables us to compare two possible relationships. On the one hand, it may be argued that it was the growth of investment which led to the growth of exports. But we see that the correlation between lagged export growth and investment growth is relatively small. Further, this relationship alone does not explain the rapid growth of investment. On the other hand, it may be argued that it was the growth of exports which induced the growth of investment, because the growth of exports, especially of manufactures created profitable opportunities for investment. This relationship is supported by the much higher correlation between lagged investment growth and export growth.

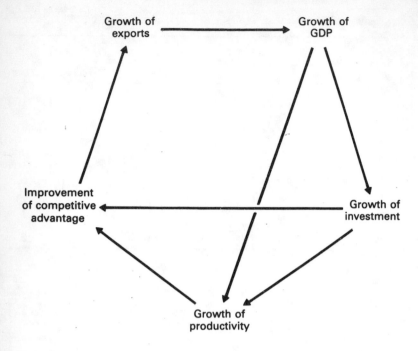

Figure 10.3

Source: Adapted from Cornwall (1977) chapter 9.

In fact, the two relationships have operated at the same time. To begin with, the devaluation of the currency and the liberalisation of trade in the late 1950s led to a growth of exports, initially of primary products and labour intensive manufactures. The growth of exports in turn induced a growth of investment and technological progress. Hence, Taiwan's competitive position improved steadily, as her export prices fell relative to other countries, and led to a further expansion of exports, increasingly of capital intensive and high technology manufactures. Hence, there was a cumulative process, which may be described as the virtuous cycle of export-led growth, illustrated in Figure 10.3.

On this view, the rapid growth of the Taiwan economy in the post-war period was due, not so much to the improvement of allocative efficiency associated with the liberalisation of trade and the expansion of exports, but rather to the interaction between demand and supply as discussed above.

Part IV
Inflation, Income
Distribution and Growth

Growth in the Service Sector

CHARACTERISTICS OF SERVICES

Services, they are defined as the residual, covering that produced which is not classified and generally allocated in national accounts, all production other than those which clearly belong to the agricultural or primary industrial sectors is put into the category of services. While we define the service sector on the negative criterion that they do not belong to the commodity producing sectors, one of the main characteristics distinguishing them from other goods is that of intangibility—a related characteristic that they are generally not storable. For example, they cannot be embodied in investment or durable consumer goods which can serve over a long period. It is for this reason that classical economists considered the hiring of labour by the ...

Nature of Service Sector

The category of goods defined in this category, within the sector, is made up of a number of sub-sectors, including in many cases those of intangibility, which are more or less direct and lot by investment ...

11 Inflation and Growth

11.1 THE STATISTICAL EVIDENCE

The various supply and demand factors influencing growth were discussed in previous chapters in real terms. But these factors themselves may be influenced by monetary forces, such as those occurring during inflation. Therefore, in the present chapter, we consider the relationship between inflation and growth. In elementary expositions, inflation and growth are treated as separate phenomena to be explained by different theories. But in fact there are a number of ways in which the two phenomena may be related. Before discussing these interactions, we first consider the statistical evidence of the relationship as it has occurred in practice.

This relationship, however, is a complex one, partly because both inflation and growth are essentially dynamic phenomena, and partly because they are both influenced by a variety of factors. It has sometimes been argued that the very complexity of the subject makes the statistical evidence useless. For example, Johnson (1966, p. 283) wrote that 'To be relevant, historical and comparative analysis would have to go beyond the simple correlation of growth rates and rates of price change into an analysis that would seek to isolate the influence of inflation of growth from other contemporary growth-promoting or growth-inhibiting influences'. Similarly, Lewis (1964, p. 30) asked statisticians to 'stop boring us with irrelevant comparisons between rates of inflation and growth in different countries'.

At the same time, we cannot ignore the great deal of empirical information that has now become available on the experience of growth and inflation. The dangers of statistical analysis involved in the above criticisms refer particularly to the concentration on short period changes in inflation and growth. Some of these difficulties are overcome to some extent by considering both growth rates and inflation rates over fairly long periods, such as a decade at a time. Such data for the post-war decades for a large number of DCs and LDCs are summarised in Table 11.1.

In all cases, the correlation between growth rates and inflation rates are rather low. Further, the correlation coefficients are uniformly negative in LDCs but uniformly positive in DCs.

One reason for these disappointing results is that the correlation

Table 11.1   Decades rates of growth and inflation

Countries/ decade	Number of countries	Average growth rate of GDP	Average rate of inflation	Correlation coefficient
LDCs				
1950s	40	5.1	7.3	−.195
1960s	80	4.9	7.9	−.098
1970s	83	4.4	19.5	−.203
DCs				
1950s	22	4.7	5.1	.397
1960s	23	5.3	4.7	.176
1970s	23	3.2	12.5	.336

Source: World Bank (1984).

coefficients measure only the strength of the *linear* relationship
between variables. But the relationship between inflation and growth
rates may not be linear or even monotonic. In fact, a number of
studies have found that among countries with high rates of inflation,
the relationship between inflation rates and growth rates is negative,
i.e. countries with higher rates of inflation tend to have slower
growth, but among countries with low or moderate rates of inflation,
the relationship is positive, i.e. countries with higher rates of inflation
tend to have higher growth rates (Tun Wai, 1959; Dorrance, 1966;
Thirlwall, 1974). Recent data for the post-war decades from a larger
sample of countries are summarised in Table 11.2. (The two DCs
with high rates of inflation in the 1950s are Israel and Yugoslavia,
which are included among the DCs for this analysis.) This table again
confirms a tendency for an inverted U-shaped relationship between
inflation and growth. This curvilinear relationship is part of the
explanation why the simple (linear) correlation coefficients are so low
and have different signs for DCs and LDCs.
    This result emphasises the need for caution in using the statistical
evidence. For example, IMF (1982, p. 134 and Table 73) compared
the growth performance of 112 non-oil LDCs divided into two equal
groups according to their rates of inflation in the period 1965–81 and
concluded that 'For the most part it has been found that relatively
low inflation rates have been associated with relatively high growth
rates and that reductions, or at least relative reductions, in inflation
have been associated with improvement, or relative improvement, in

Table 11.2   GDP growth rate by rate of inflation

Rates of inflation (%)	Rates of growth of GDP (%)					
	LDCs			DCs		
	1950s	*1960s*	*1970s*	*1950s*	*1960s*	*1970s*
below 5	5.2	5.1	3.5	4.0	4.9	0.7
5–10	5.1	4.0	4.0	5.4	6.1	3.4
10–15	7.0	3.7	5.0	11.3	5.8	2.8
15–20	6.9	8.6	5.4	–	–	4.1
20 and over	3.5	4.2	3.3	5.6	–	4.0

Source: World Bank (1984).

growth rates'. While this finding is consistent with the fact that countries with very high inflation tend to have lower growth rates than countries with moderate or low inflation, it does not take account of the fact that some countries with moderate rates of inflation have experienced faster growth than countries with low rates of inflation. This interesting fact has some important implications both for analysis and for policy.

In view of the well-known limitations of cross-section analysis, it is necessary to consider also the historical relationship between the two rates as shown by time series data. Then, we see that while there are many cases where a rise in inflation rates is associated with a fall in growth rates, there are also cases where a rise in inflation rates is associated with a rise in growth rates.

Conversely, we may also consider what happened to growth rates in countries where there was a significant fall in inflation rates. This question was examined in two recent studies which, however, reached opposite conclusions. On the one hand, Gordon (1982) found in an analysis of 14 historical episodes that stopping inflation usually resulted in a slow-down of growth. On the other hand, Sargent (1982) in his analysis of four inflationary episodes found that stopping inflation led to some rise in growth rates. These divergent results were, at least partly, due to the fact that the cases considered by Gordon were those of countries experiencing relatively moderate rates of inflation, while the cases considered by Sargent were those of countries experiencing high rates of inflation, amounting to hyper-inflation. Thus, both these conclusions are consistent with the curvilinear relationship suggested by the cross-section data of Table 11.2.

Table 11.3   Average growth rates of LDCs by inflation rates (number of countries in brackets)

Inflation rate (%)	1950s Slow	1950s Rapid	1960s Slow	1960s Rapid	1970s Slow	1970s Rapid
Below 5	3.5(15)	7.4(11)	3.4(33)	7.1(28)	2.8(2)	5.0(1)
5–10	3.4(2)	5.7(4)	3.2(5)	5.4(3)	2.5(15)	7.5(6)
10–15	–	7.0(2)	3.2(3)	5.1(1)	2.8(18)	7.1(19)
15–20	–	6.9(1)	–	8.6(1)	1.5(2)	7.0(5)
20 and over	3.1(4)	5.1(1)	3.4(5)	8.2(1)	0.6(9)	7.5(6)
Total	3.5(21)	6.9(19)	3.4(46)	7.0(34)	2.2(46)	7.2(37)

Note: Slow: growth rate <5%; rapid: growth rate >5%.
Source: World Bank (1984).

Although there is a curvilinear relationship, it does not mean that countries with a given rate of inflation have the same rate of growth. In fact, countries with the same rate of inflation vary greatly in their growth rates. Some indication of this variation of growth performance is given in Table 11.3 for LDCs.

From this table, we see that at each inflation rate, there are both fast growing and slow growing countries, the difference in growth rates being quite considerable in each case. In particular, we see that there are many countries with low inflation rates and also low growth rates, and also that there are many countries with both high inflation rates and high growth rates. This, however, does not mean that there is no relationship between inflation and growth. Instead, it only indicates that there are a number of other factors which also influence both inflation and growth. Some of these factors are discussed below.

Table 11.1 showed that, in the case of DCs, low inflation rates were associated with high growth rates for the 1950s and 1960s, but in the 1970s, growth rates fell quite sharply, while inflation rates more than doubled. Table 11.4 gives GDP growth rates, inflation rates and unemployment rates on an annual basis for the period since 1966. There was a steady acceleration of inflation rates until 1974, and a slow decline since then. There was a sharp decline of growth rates in 1975; though the growth rates recovered in the next year, they remained at about half the level enjoyed before 1974. Unemployment rates also started rising in 1974 and reached high levels by developed country standards during the 1980s. This catastrophic

Table 11.4   Inflation rates and growth rates of DCs, 1967–86
(averages of 19 DCs)

Year	Inflation rate	Growth rate	Unemployment rate
1967	3.9	4.0	–
1968	5.2	4.2	2.8
1969	4.5	6.1	2.6
1970	5.8	5.4	3.1
1971	7.2	3.9	3.6
1972	7.6	5.1	3.7
1973	10.1	5.7	3.3
1974	12.2	4.3	3.5
1975	11.6	1.1	5.2
1976	11.4	2.9	5.3
1977	9.8	2.3	5.3
1978	9.1	2.9	5.2
1979	9.1	3.5	5.1
1980	10.7	2.2	5.8
1981	10.2	0.8	6.7
1982	9.5	0.7	8.1
1983	7.3	2.0	8.6
1984	6.7	3.0	8.0
1985	6.3	2.6	7.8
1986	5.6	2.0[a]	7.7

Note: [a] excluding Denmark.
Source: Inflation and growth rates from World Bank (1984); Unemployment rates (averages of OECD countries) from OECD *Economic Outlook* (Dec. 1988).

change is often attributed to the oil shocks of 1973 and 1979, but it needs more detailed analysis.

11.2 CAUSES OF INFLATION

Having considered the relationship between inflation and growth as observed in practice, we next proceed to consider the underlying reasons for this relationship. The first point to note is that the relationship between inflation and growth depends on the causes of inflation. This is because inflation due to some causes may have a different effect on growth than inflation due to other causes. Further, the relationship between inflation and growth may also be due to third factors which influenced both inflation and growth. Therefore, in the present section, we consider some of the causes of inflation.

(a) Monetary Expansion

According to the traditional Quantity Theory of Money, the main cause of inflation is the expansion of money supply. This theory has been greatly refined in modern monetarist analysis, but the basic argument is still the same.

According to the Equation of Exchange, the extent to which the price level rises when money supply increases depends on what happens to real income and the velocity of circulation. Thus, if real income and velocity are constant, the price level rises in the same proportion as the money supply. Over time, however, there will be a rise in real income, but in classical theory, it is typically assumed that all resources are fully employed, so that the growth of real income will be determined by real factors such as the growth of factor endowments, and the expansion of money supply will have no effect on real income growth. Then, the rate of inflation will be equal to the rate of monetary expansion less the rate of growth of real income. In particular, if the supply of money increases at the same rate as real income, there will be no inflation of prices.

(b) Expectations

The velocity of circulation depends partly on the financial institutions of the country. These institutions change only slowly over time; therefore, in the short run, they will have only a small effect on the velocity of circulation, or its inverse, the proportion of incomes that people wished to hold in the form of cash balances. But in the short period, the proportion of assets which people wish to hold in the form of cash balances, and hence the velocity of circulation, depends also on people's expectations about future changes in the value of money, relative to the returns from holding assets in other income-earning forms. Hence, in modern monetarist theory, the demand for real cash balances is taken as a function of the expected rate of inflation and the rate of return from income earning assets. The equilibrium between this demand and the supply of money then determines the rate of inflation from any given expansion of money supply.

The expected rate of inflation represents people's confidence in money. When people lose confidence in money, they prefer to hold assets in the form of other assets, and the flight from holding assets in the form of money to holding other assets leads to the very rise in prices that is expected. In most monetarist exposition, the expected rate of inflation is assumed to depend in part on the prevailing and past rates of inflation. Thus, if there is an inflation due to any cause, the inflation becomes cumulative, as people revise their expectations about future inflation. In practice, however, revisions of expectations may occur due to a variety of other causes as well.

(c) Cost-Push Factors

In the Quantity Theory analysis, the causation runs from increases in money supply to rises in the price level. The increase in the money supply is then explained by such exogenous changes as the discovery of gold in the days of the gold standard, the printing of money by governments, the expansion of credit by banks, or a surplus in the balance of payments. However, it is also possible that an inflation may begin without any increase in the money supply. This may happen, for example, if there is a rise in some key prices, especially prices which enter into the cost of production of many commodities, and these initial rises in some prices are then transmitted to other prices, leading to a cost-push inflation. Then, there may be an endogenous increase in the money supply to validate the rise in the price level. In this case, the causation runs from increases in the price level to the expansion of the money supply. The typical example of such a cost-push factor in LDCs is a reduction in food supply due to a bad harvest. Then, food prices rise sharply because of the low elasticity of demand for food. Because food is a basic item of consumption, the rise in food prices is transmitted to other prices as well, and there is a general inflation. The process as it has occurred in India has been vividly explained by Jha (1980, pp. 80–1), a former Governor of the Indian central bank, as follows:

> Time and again bad monsoons have led to shortfalls in agricultural production, generating all-round shortages of basic foodstuffs, oil seeds, cotton; these set off declines in supplies of agro-based industrial products such as oils, sugar vanaspati, cloth, etc. Such scarcities generate irresistible demands among workers for monetary compensations to offset price-rises. In the organized sectors, dearness allowances have to be granted, pushing up costs and raising prices generally. As higher dearness allowance has to be

paid to government servants also, the budgetary deficits grow, augmenting the money in circulation. Relief operations in drought-hit areas make unforeseen demands on the exchequer, enlarging the deficit envisaged in the budget. The higher cost of raw materials arising out of basic scarcities, and consequently of finished goods, makes it necessary for industry and trade to borrow more from the banks by way of working capital. In Indian conditions, therefore, larger budgetary deficits and credit expansion by banks often are the result, and not the cause, of rising prices.

An example of a cost-push inflation which occurs in DCs is a rise in wages brought about by such causes as trade union pressure. As prices in a number of markets of these countries are determined as a mark-up over costs, the rise in wages will lead to a rise in the general price level.

A third important example of cost-push inflation is that which occurs in countries which depend heavily on imports of both consumer goods and raw materials. In such cases, a rise in the prices of imports, brought about either by a rise in foreign prices or by a sharp devaluation, is transmitted to domestic prices, and leads to a general inflation. The most important example of such inflation in recent times occurred when the OPEC countries raised the price of oil sharply in 1973, and again in 1979. As Rostow (1980, p. 194) put it,

> If there is a large movement in the relative price of a major commodity (for example, a quadrupling of the oil price) and the monetary system fails to impose the grotesque deflation required to hold the price level constant by lowering other prices, then a rise in relative prices can yield a rise in the price level.

The initial rise in prices due to such cost-push factors then continues because monetary authorities will be under great pressure to expand the money supply to validate the price rise. In such cases, monetarists argue that the inflation is due to the increase in the money supply, rather than to the cost-push factors. That is, they would argue that if the money supply is not increased, the inflation would be curbed, and the price level would fall back to its initial position. However, once prices have risen because of the cost-push factor, keeping the money supply constant may not lower the price level; instead it may only reduce the level of economic activity, and the real income of the country. This is in fact the main reason why most governments and monetary authorities are reluctant to keep the money supply constant and instead yield to the popular pressure to expand the money supply. As a result, the money supply becomes an endogenous variable.

In the two approaches distinguished above, the causal link between money supply and prices runs in opposite directions. A number of studies have been carried out to test the validity of each theory on the basis of econometric tests of causality. However, it is not the case of one theory being right and the other wrong. Rather, one theory may be valid in one country at one time, while the other is valid in other countries or even in the same country at a different time, depending on the nature of monetary policy followed. Thus, while there have been cases where inflation was due to an expansion of money supply by the monetary authorities, there have been other cases where inflation was due to an initial rise in some key price, followed by an endogenous expansion of money supply.

(d) Initiation and Propagation of Inflation

As Lewis (1964) pointed out, we must also distinguish between factors which initiate an inflation, and those which keep it going. The initiating factors may be an expansion of money supply or a reduction of supply. But once an inflation has begun, other forces come in to keep it going.

The typical example of such a propagating mechanism is the case of the wage–price spiral. For example, if for any reason there is a rise in the prices of consumer goods, it will be followed by intense pressures to raise wages. In some countries, this mechanism is built into measures for indexing wages to the cost of living in order to maintain the real value of wages. Then, the rise in wages in turn leads to a further rise in prices, and the process becomes cumulative. It has been argued that the steady rise in inflation rates in DCs during the 1960s was of this type, brought about by changes in labour market institutions (Cornwall, 1983).

Another propagating mechanism, especially relevant in LDCs, operates through the government budget. Once an inflation has started, there is a tendency for government expenditures to rise as rapidly as the inflation, because these expenditures are based on the current level of prices. But government revenues tend to rise more slowly, because they are based on the price level of an earlier date. Hence, the inflation leads to a budget deficit, or to an increase in the deficit. Attempts to finance such a deficit by money creation then leads to further inflation, which again becomes cumulative (Sundrum, 1973; Aghevli and Khan, 1978). By contrast, in DCs, inflation tends to increase government revenues rapidly, because of the progressive system of income taxes.

(e) Latin American Type of Inflation

Many of the countries experiencing high rates of inflation (say, over 20 per cent per year) tend to be in Latin America, four out of five in the 1950s, four out of six in the 1960s, and seven out of 15 in the 1970s. It is therefore useful to distinguish this type of inflation from others.

Monetarist economists explain this inflation also as the result of excessive expansion of the money supply. However, an alternative view, known as the structuralist theory, has been advanced explaining these high rates of inflation as the inevitable consequence of promoting growth in economies subject to severe structural rigidities such as inelastic supply of food from the agricultural sector, a severe foreign exchange constraint in the balance of payments, or a fiscal constraint on the government budget. It is possible that a greater monetary stimulus may be needed in countries subject to such structural rigidities than in other countries. However, countries experiencing such high rates of inflation have not been particularly notable for high rates of growth. Further, even if the structural rigidities had been an important source of inflation in the early phase of their development, it is surprising that they have persisted for so long and led to the high rates of inflation which have been in vogue for a number of decades (see Kirkpatrick and Nixson, 1987, for a recent survey of the theory and its statistical tests).

Most versions of the structuralist theory of Latin American inflation are based on the inelasticity of supply of important types of commodities such as agricultural production for domestic consumption or exports. However, a more plausible explanation is that suggested by Lewis (1964) that it is the share of national income claimed by influential groups in society which are rigid at incompatible levels. Thus, there is less surplus labour in Latin America, labour is better organised especially in urban areas, the trade unions have little sympathy with their governments, and therefore are more powerful in insisting on maintaining the wage share of national income. If the share of income claimed by labour is incompatible with the claims of other groups such as the employers, these incompatible income claims provide a powerful propagating mechanism for inflation, once it gets under way for any reason. Under these conditions, inflation is largely a political problem, which cannot be solved just by manipulating prices or the money supply.

Having surveyed the various causes of inflation, we next consider how inflation due to these causes has influenced growth.

11.3 INFLATION AND GROWTH: SUPPLY FACTORS

There are many ways in which inflation might affect the growth process. Just as we distinguished between supply and demand factors of growth in previous chapters, it is useful to make a similar distinction among the effects of inflation on growth. The effects operating through supply factors are discussed in this section, and those operating through demand factors are discussed in the next section.

(a) Monetary Efficiency

One way in which inflation might affect growth is through its effects on monetary efficiency, i.e. its effects on the various roles that money plays, such as the unit of account, the store of value and the medium of exchange. Because of the great popular concern with these aspects of monetary efficiency, Phelps (1972, p. 171) has facetiously suggested that another role of money is as a source of anxiety!

From the point of view of monetary efficiency, the adverse effect of inflation is that it will 'disturb seriously the general confidence in the stability of the value of money' leading to 'serious social consequences' and 'significant misallocations of resources' (Johnson, 1966, p. 253). Also, it is argued that 'the costs of rational economic calculations will be less with price stability than when prices are expected to change at the same rate, even when these expectations are held with certainty' (Johnson, 1968, p. 111). These costs will be greater if there is uncertainty about future prices changes.

On these grounds, price stability is often taken as an end in itself. There is a problem in that, during a period of technological progress, there must be a fall in the prices of goods relative to the wages of labour. Then, it is sometimes suggested that it is wages which should be kept stable, leading to a gently falling level of the prices of goods in accordance with the rising productivity of labour.

However, our present concern is with the effects of inflation on growth. Therefore, we have to consider how far the adverse effects of inflation on monetary efficiency might also affect the growth process. These effects might be quite significant if inflation is proceeding at a high rate. This is one explanation for the negative relationship between inflation and growth at high rates of inflation. But even in these cases, the negative relationship may not be due only to the deterioration in monetary efficiency; instead, it may also be due to the fact that both the high rates of inflation and the slow growth of GDP are due to other causes, such as wars and other military disturbances, or natural disasters affecting many LDCs. When inflation is proceeding at a more moderate rate, the growth effects of inflation through monetary inefficiency may be less significant.

(b) Mobilisation of Resources

One way in which inflation might actually promote growth is if it is used to mobilise resources for investment in the form of forced savings. Because the tax system and the banking system are relatively under-developed in many LDCs, these countries have often resorted to inflation to finance development expenditures, especially through the budget. In fact, the case for such inflationary finance of investment has a long and distinguished ancestry starting with David Hume (Thirlwall, 1974, Chapter 2). This has also been recognised by Johnson (1966, pp. 251–2) who agreed that 'a moderate degree of inflation is likely to be an inevitable concomitant of a development policy that seeks efficiently to mobilise an economy's resources for economic growth'. However, he estimated that what this involved was 'inflation at an annual percentage rate that can be counted on the fingers of one or at most two hands', and hence that 'a policy of deliberately promoting development by inflationary means, though it has theoretical and practical attractions, is likely in fact to retard rather than foster economic growth'.

A more rigorous analysis of the role that inflation can play in mobilising resources has been given by Friedman (1953, 1971) and Mundell (1971). The argument in Mundell's version may be summarised as follows. The central idea is that if the government increases the money supply by a given percentage, it will not be able to command the same proportion of real resources in the economy, because the expansion of money supply will raise the price level and reduce the purchasing power of the newly created money. To analyse such effects, suppose the money supply expands at a constant rate m, as the government increases the supply of reserve money and uses the proceeds to finance investment. Let k be the reserve money ratio, q the productivity of capital, and V the velocity of circulation. Then, the rate of growth r will be given by:

$$r = (kq/V)m \tag{11.1}$$

The rate of inflation Π will then be given by:

$$\Pi = m - r \tag{11.2}$$

But when there is such inflation, the velocity of circulation based on the demand for money to hold will not be constant but will change according to the rate of inflation. The relationship between V and Π may then be represented by:

$$V = V_0 e^{a\Pi} \tag{11.3}$$

where a is a constant, the functional form used by Cagan (1956). From these equations, we get:

$$r = (kqm)/V_0 e^{a\Pi} \tag{11.4}$$

Defining the function $f(x) = xe^{-ax}$ and using (11.2), equation (11.4) can be written in the more convenient form:

$$f(r) = (kq/V_0)f(m) \tag{11.5}$$

Then, the maximum growth rate achievable by monetary expansion can be derived diagrammatically as shown in Figure 11.1. In this figure, the curve $OQPX$ represents the function $f(x)$. From (11.5), $f(r)$ will be maximised when $f(m)$ is maximised. The maximum of $f(m)$ occurs at the point P where the rate of monetary expansion m^* is given by:

$$m^* = 1/a \tag{11.6}$$

On the vertical line at this point, take N so that $(MN/MP) = kq/V_0$ and take the point Q on the curve such that $QR = MN$. Then, QR is the

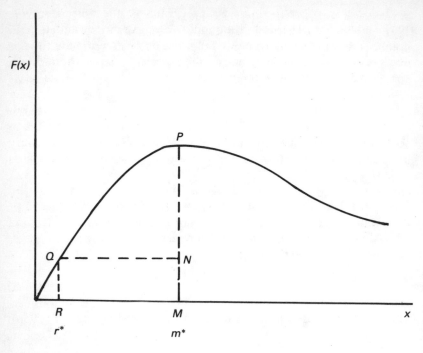

Figure 11.1

maximum value of f(r). Between O and M, $f(x)$ increases with x. Therefore, the maximum value of $f(r)$ at the point Q gives the maximum growth rate r^* attainable by monetary expansion.

This derivation shows how the parameters k, q and V_0 determine r^*. The main conclusion drawn from this analysis is that the extent to which growth can be accelerated by inflation is very limited. As Mundell (1971, p. 39) put it, 'Even in the case where the values of the parameters are purposely chosen to make the inflation argument favourable, inflation rates of over 50 per cent are necessary to add 1 per cent to the growth rate'. However, Friedman (1971) has shown that the contribution of inflation might be higher if superimposed on other sources of growth.

Equation (11.6) is a remarkable result, showing that the growth maximising rate of monetary expansion depends only on the co-efficient a of the velocity function. This is partly due to the particular velocity function assumed in the analysis. For other functions, m^* depends also on the rate of growth of income, and the income elasticity of demand for money (Friedman, 1971, p. 550; Mundell, 1971, pp. 36–9). The result also depends on the fact that the analysis is conducted in continuous time. When a period analysis is followed, we find that m^* depends on those other factors, even with the same velocity function (Sundrum, 1976, p. 195).

What the above analysis shows is that there is a limited, and usually quite small, share of the national income that a government can acquire by a constant rate of inflation. This raises the question why governments, especially in LDCs, resort so frequently to inflationary methods of raising resources. The reason is that the above analysis is based on steady rates of inflation, whereas if rates of inflation are allowed to vary in the short period, then it is possible that the government can acquire a larger share of the national income than indicated in the above analysis (Friedman, 1971). Thus, if there is only a low rate of inflation to begin with, the government may be able to increase its share of the national income by raising the rate of inflation for a short period. On the other hand, if the rate of inflation is high to begin with, the government has to reduce the rate of inflation to increase its share of the national income (for a detailed analysis, see Sundrum, 1976).

The general conclusion of this analysis is that, while inflation may help governments to raise resources for investment and thus accelerate growth for short periods of time, the maximum amount of resources that can be raised by following this method over a long period is quite limited. However, the analysis has been confined to the role of inflation in influencing the supply factors underlying the growth process. But as we have argued in Part III, the growth process depends also on various demand factors. Therefore, we must consider also the relationship between inflation and growth operating through these demand factors.

11.4 INFLATION AND GROWTH: DEMAND FACTORS

(a) The General Case

We first consider the general case of the relationship between inflation and growth operating through demand factors. Then, we apply the analysis to deal with various special cases.

In elementary expositions of Keynesian theory, it is sometimes implied that, when there are under-utilised resources, an increase in aggregate demand will raise output by fuller utilisation of these resources without any rise in prices. In practice, however, the process of bringing even under-employed resources into productive activity will involve some rise in prices. Therefore, we may take the general case as one in which an increase in aggregate demand will lead to both some inflation and some growth.

The question to consider then is how much inflation and how much growth will result from a given increase in demand. An increase in demand occurs first in the form of an increase in monetary demand. Then, the increase in real demand depends on the rise in prices. We have already considered this effect in discussing how much real resources can be mobilised by a government when it increases the money supply. There we considered a simple model in which the increase in prices was determined by a particularly simple velocity function. In practice, the price effect of a monetary expansion is likely to be determined by other factors as well. It is convenient to separate price rises due to the monetary expansion itself from price rises due to other factors, such as people's expectations about future price changes and cost-push factors. When inflation is due to these other factors, the money supply has to expand just to transact business at the higher price level. The monetary expansion will then not represent any increase in aggregate demand in real terms, and hence will not have any effect on the growth rate. In order to consider the effects on the growth rate itself, it is convenient to define the concept of the increase of demand in real terms as the increase in monetary demand less an allowance for inflation due to these other factors.

After allowing for such exogenous increases in prices, the amount of output growth that results from an increase in aggregate demand in real terms depends on the elasticity of supply. The more elastic the supply, the greater will be the growth effect, and the smaller the inflation due to the growth of demand, and conversely. In the extreme case where the elasticity of supply is zero, the result will be only inflation and no growth.

In LDCs, the elasticity of supply depends not only on the extent of under-utilised resources but also on a number of technological and institutional factors, which are discussed below. But in DCs, one of the most important factors influencing the elasticity of supply is the extent of under-utilised resources, especially the level of unemployment of labour. Therefore, there will be an inverse relationship between the level of unemployment and the rate of inflation. This was the relationship that Phillips (1958) derived from a century of

British experience from the middle of the nineteenth century onwards. According to this relationship, as an economy reaches the full employment level, attempts to reduce unemployment even further will tend to accelerate inflation rates sharply. Hence, classical economists who believe in a natural tendency for the economy to operate at full employment levels argue that the Phillips curve will be vertical at an unemployment rate representing a natural rate of unemployment due to frictional causes only (for a detailed review, see Cornwall, 1983).

The Phillips curve showing an inverse relationship between inflation and unemployment presents countries with a menu of alternative combinations of rates of inflation and levels of unemployment from which they can make a choice of what suits them best. Thus, countries suffering from high rates of unemployment might choose to expand demand while countries experiencing high rates of inflation might choose to adopt contractionary demand policies.

However, we cannot expect the same Phillips curve to hold in all countries at all times. One of the main factors influencing the position and shape of the Phillips curve are the institutions of the labour market. In some countries, the labour market works to stress wage increases of employed workers more than the provision of employment for unemployed workers, while labour markets in other countries may rank these objectives in the opposite order. The resulting shape of the Phillips curve then determines the rate at which countries trade growth for price stability. Under some conditions, the trade-off may be so favourable that countries follow expansionary demand policies. Under other conditions, the trade-off may be deemed so unfavourable that countries follow contractionary demand policies.

It is sometimes argued (e.g. Barro, 1984, ch. 17) that the empirical evidence, for example, that of some developed countries in the inter-war and post-war periods, does not show any systematic relationship between inflation and growth. But, because of the variety of factors influencing each variable, it cannot be expected that the same relationship will hold for all countries at all times. Therefore, we consider instead a number of cases showing different relationships between the two variables, and discuss the factors operating in each case.

(b) Inflation without Growth: LDCs

First, we consider the case of LDCs which have experienced high rates of inflation with low rates of growth. In some of these cases, both the high rates of inflation and the low rates of growth were due to other factors such as wars, civil disturbances and natural disasters. In other cases, the explanation is that, although there was much under-employment of labour, the elasticity of supply was also low. A common explanation is that the under-employment of labour was not due to a deficiency of demand, but rather to the fact that the proportions in which labour could be combined with cooperating factors such as land and capital were rigidly fixed under the prevailing technology in LDCs, and these other factors were already fully utilised.

In most cases, however, factor proportions are not as rigidly fixed, and land and capital not as fully utilised as assumed in this argument. Even in agriculture, the labour intensity with which land is cultivated varies considerably between countries, being much lower in South Asia than in Northeast and Southeast Asia (Chapter 5). Further, labour with very limited quantities of capital can be used to improve the land and construct much needed small irrigation works, and hence increase output (Booth and Sundrum, 1984, ch. 5). Factor proportions are even more flexible in other sectors, especially if the composition of output can be shifted towards labour intensive commodities, and if more suitable capital goods can be manufactured in LDCs.

A more important reason why an increase of demand in this group of countries might trigger off an inflation without growth is that stressed by Kalecki (1954), which is also a part of the structuralist theory of inflation. According to this explanation, the increase of demand leads to a sharp increase in the demand for food, but the supply of food from the agricultural sector is very inelastic, being governed by institutional constraints to growth, and does not respond to the growth of demand (for a more detailed analysis, see Rakshit, 1982).

(c) Growth without Inflation: LDCs

The case considered in the above sub-section is sometimes taken as the typical case of LDCs. Hence the opinion often expressed that Keynesian theory is not applicable to LDCs, in particular that any increase of demand will only lead to inflation without growth because of a low elasticity of supply. However, as shown in Table 11.3, there are also a number of LDCs which achieved rapid growth with relatively low rates of inflation. In many cases, the rapid growth was associated with the growth of export demand rather than with the growth of domestic demand. These cases are considered further in section 11.4(f) below. But there are also cases in which the growth was due to an increase of domestic demand.

This case is best illustrated by the experience of Indonesia in the period 1967–81. During this period, the trend rate of growth was 8 per cent per annum. This rapid growth is often attributed to the great increase in Indonesia's foreign exchange earnings from oil exports. But the big increase in earnings from oil exports occurred only after 1973, whereas Indonesia experienced a high trend rate of growth (8.7 per cent at 1973 constant prices) even during the period 1967–73. Further, the increase in export earnings after 1973 was due more to higher prices than increased quantities; therefore, the increase in export earnings does not explain the rapid growth of GDP in real terms.

The more important reason for the rapid growth was that the government's improved budgetary position induced it to follow an expansionary demand policy, which in turn led to rapid growth by fuller utilisation of under-utilised resources, including labour. In other LDCs, the growth of employment was constrained by a limited stock of capital, but Indonesia was able to expand its capital stock substantially by imports of capital goods. At the same time, the potential inflationary effect was avoided by a very rapid growth of food supply, both from domestic production and from imports.

During this period, the government was particularly concerned to maintain price stability. The speed with which the high rate of inflation prevailing in the mid-1960s was brought under control within a short period is one of the most remarkable stabilisation experiences ever achieved in any country. This was achieved in spite of quite large increases in the money supply. The reduction in the rate of inflation was mainly due to the policy of stabilising the price of rice, the staple food item (Sundrum, 1973). After 1973, however, there were some inflationary episodes, but they were due to cost-push factors, such as the drastic harvest shortfall of 1972–3 and the devaluation of 1975, rather than to the expansionary demand policies (Sundrum, 1986).

Indonesia's rapid growth in 1967–81 may be contrasted with its slow growth (4 per cent at 1973 constant prices) in the period after 1981. The slow growth cannot be explained only by the fall in the price of oil exports. Instead, it was due to the contractionary demand policies followed by the government in response to the deterioration in the terms of trade (Sundrum, 1988).

(d) Low Inflation and Slow Growth: LDCs

In sub-section (b), we considered the case of LDCs with high rates of inflation and low rates of growth. But there have also been LDCs with low rates of inflation and low rates of growth. This case may be explained by the argument that these LDCs did not pursue active policies of expanding aggregate demand to utilise their resources more fully, mainly for fear of inflation.

This case is best illustrated by the experience of India. Indian planners were mainly concerned with supply factors as the means of promoting growth, rather than demand factors. Hence, at least until 1970, they followed a rather conservative monetary policy. For example, the average growth rate of money supply was ony 7.8 per cent (average of annual rates) in the two decades 1951–70. Further, this inflation was mostly due to sharp increases in the price level due to periodic harvest shortfalls. During these episodes, the monetary authorities reacted to the harvest shortfalls by reducing aggregate demand in order to reduce inflation. This policy response then transmitted the fluctuations of the agricultural sector to other sectors of the economy; thus for example there was a severe deceleration of industrial growth for a long period after the drastic harvest shortfalls of the mid-1960s (Sundrum, 1987).

(e) Rapid Growth and Inflation: LDCs

Contrary to the widespread opinion that high rates of inflation, say at double digit levels, are incompatible with rapid growth, we have seen in Table 11.3 that there have been many cases in the 1970s and even in the 1950s and 1960s of LDCs which achieved high rates of growth even with these rates of inflation. In many of these cases, the growth of GDP was due to a rapid growth of exports, but there were also a number of countries which achieved high rates of growth of GDP with only a slow growth of exports. Of LDCs with double-digit inflation and growth rates of over 5 per cent per annum, two out of four in the 1950s, two out of three in the 1960s, and 12 out of 30 in the 1970s had export growth rates of less than 6 per cent per annum. Further, among these countries, those with slower export growth rates had average GDP growth rates nearly as high as those with faster export growth rates, namely 6.6 per cent compared with 6.4 per cent in the 1950s, 6.7 compared with 8.6 in the 1960s, and 6.8 compared with 7.4 in the 1970s. Hence, in these cases, the rapid growth of GDP even with high rates of inflation may be attributed to the growth of aggregate domestic demand. One of the most interesting examples of this category of countries is the case of Brazil. Brazil had a growth rate of 6.9 per cent in the 1950s with an inflation rate of 15.8 per cent and an export growth rate of only 1.7 per cent. In the 1960s, the growth rate was 5.4 per cent, with an inflation rate of 46.6 per cent and export growth rate of 5.4 per cent. During these decades, the main source of demand growth was from investment and government consumption expenditures.

(f) Inflation and Export-led Growth: LDCs

In the last chapter, it was argued that the rapid growth of exports is an important demand factor leading to the rapid growth of GDP, partly because it leads to fuller utilisation of under-utilised resources and partly because it induces a faster growth of productive capacity. The growth of exports, in turn, depends on countries having a competitive advantage in international markets. One way in which countries may gain a competitive advantage is by having a low rate of inflation. Many of the countries which had rapid GDP growth with low rates of inflation, shown in Table 11.3, had achieved these results by having a rapid growth of their exports. Some of the typical examples in this category are Hong Kong, Singapore, Taiwan, Thailand, Malaysia and Mexico.

But, as we saw in the previous sub-section, there were also many countries in the 1970s which were able to expand their exports rapidly and achieve high rates of GDP growth, even with high rates of inflation. To some extent, this was because the effect of high inflation on their competitive position was offset by changes in the exchange rates. Thus, it has been argued that one of the main reasons which led to the acceleration of export growth in Taiwan since the late 1950s was a significant devaluation of the currency at that time. However, the effects of devaluation are usually short-lived. For example, based on a survey of a number of devaluations in LDCs, Connolly and Taylor (1976) estimated that the favourable effects of devaluation on relative prices and export prospects tended to be eroded within two years.

Another way in which countries have been able to expand their exports rapidly over a long period, even with high rates of inflation, is by giving exports special privileges in the access to scarce resources. Two of the most important examples of such countries are Brazil in the 1970s and South Korea since the 1960s.

(g) Rapid Growth with Mild Inflation: DCs

We now turn to consider the experience of DCs. We first consider their experience in the post-war period until 1973. As shown in Table 11.4, up to this year, these countries experienced high rates of GDP growth with only low, though rising, rates of inflation. This was also the period in which these countries had low rates of unemployment. The experience of DCs may therefore be explained as a case of the Phillips curve offering a very favourable trade-off between growth and price stability, and of countries generally moving up such a Phillips curve.

The movement up the Phillips curve represented a steady rise in the level of aggregate demand. One of the most important reasons for the growth of demand in these countries was the growth of exports, mostly among the industrial countries themselves. The growth of exports was facilitated by the significant liberalisation of trade under GATT auspices, and an orderly adjustment of international payments under the Bretton Woods system.

(h) Slow Growth with Severe Inflation: DCs

Since 1973, however, there has been a drastic fall in the growth rate of DCs as shown in Table 11.4. There was also a sharp increase in the rate of inflation for a few years, combined with a rise in the level of unemployment. Severe inflation with slow growth was a well known phenomenon among LDCs, but its appearance in the DCs was greeted with considerable surprise, and described by the special term of 'stagflation'. It was even thought that the situation represented a breakdown of the concept of the Phillips curve and a serious weakness of Keynesian theory.

A more plausible interpretation is that the rise in the rate of inflation was mainly due to cost-push factors emanating from the rise in oil prices in 1973 and again in 1979 (Bruno and Sachs, 1985). This cost-push factor led to an outward shift of the Phillips curve, representing a more unfavourable trade-off between growth and price stability. At the same time, conservative governments came to power in the major OECD countries, and combined with the more unfavourable trade-off between growth and price stability, followed contractionary demand policies. The underlying argument was that the contractionary policies were needed to control the inflation, and that once inflation was controlled, these countries would revert back to their previous pattern of rapid growth. However, while the contractionary policies led to a continuous rise in unemployment rates, they failed to reduce inflation to their previous levels (for a more detailed analysis of DC performance in this period, see Cornwall, 1990).

Another reason for the slow growth of DCs after 1973 was a drastic fall in the growth of their exports. The fall in the growth of exports, in turn, was due to the increasing instability of flexible exchange rates and the breakdown of the Bretton Woods system. As Cooper (1987, p. xvi) says, 'movements in real exchange rates are too great to be tolerable with relatively free trade and capital movements'. Partly because of such instability, the DCs have begun to follow protectionist policies which have further reduced the growth of world exports.

(i) Conclusions

Inflation and growth are often treated as separate phenomena determined by different mechanisms, the rate of growth being determined by the expansion of productive capacity which is fully utilised at all times, while the rate of inflation is determined by monetary forces, especially the expansion of the money supply. But as argued in Part III, the rate of growth is also determined by demand factors which influence both the utilisation of existing productive capacity, and the rate at which it expands over time. Further, the rate of inflation is determined not only by money supply but also by cost push factors. As a result, there are a number of ways in which the rate of growth is influenced by the rate of inflation, and in which both are influenced by third factors. In particular, inflation might influence growth either through supply factors or through demand factors.

It is generally assumed that, while a certain amount of inflation is inevitable in the course of rapid growth, the rate of inflation that is required is quite small. However, this argument is based only on the relationship between inflation and growth operating through supply factors. Then, it is argued that inflationary methods of financing growth are inefficient, because the maximum amount of resources that can be mobilised by inflation is very small, and the rate of inflation required to mobilise even this amount of resources is very high.

However, inflation may also influence growth through demand factors. This may occur even in LDCs where aggregate supply is not as inelastic as often assumed. Consequently, some LDCs have grown quite rapidly even with relatively high rates of inflation, while others have grown more slowly even with low rates of inflation. The drastic fall in the growth rate of DCs since 1973 was mainly due to the failure of these countries to follow expansionary demand policies for fear of their effects on inflation.

12 Income Distribution and Growth

12.1 THEORETICAL ARGUMENTS AND STATISTICAL EVIDENCE

The relationship between income distribution and the level and growth of national income has been studied intensively in the recent literature. However, the main concern of this literature has been with the influence of income levels on the inequality of income distribution. Thus, there have been many studies examining the extent to which the way income is distributed in countries at different income levels follows Kuznets' Law that income inequality increases with the level of per capita income up to a point and declines thereafter, i.e. that the relationship between inequality and income level is positive at low levels of income and negative at higher levels. The influence of different rates of growth of income on inequality has also been examined, but as pointed out by Ahluwalia (1976, pp. 335–7), the available data do not show any significant relationship.

Most studies, however, have been based on cross section analysis. Hence, they have been particularly affected by the limitations of such analysis, especially the fact that, apart from any influence that the level and growth of income may have, the distribution of income in a country is also affected by many other factors, especially the institutional factors affecting the working of factor markets and the distribution of productive assets among individuals and households. Thus, the general tendency for inequality to be lower in DCs than in LDCs is due, not only to the difference in income levels, but also to other factors, such as the higher levels of education and training of workers, and their greater bargaining power in the determination of wages in DCs. Similarly, the tendency for inequality to be greater in middle income LDCs than in low income LDCs is due, not only to the differences in income levels, but also to other factors such as the distribution of land, capital and other productive assets (for a critical review of the literature on the role of income in influencing the distribution of income, especially in LDCs, see Sundrum, 1990).

While there has been much discussion of the influence of income level on the distribution of income, our present concern is with the influence of income distribution on the level and growth of national income. On this topic, there has been much less discussion in the literature. The limited discussion of the subject consists largely of some broad judgements of some writers often based on their ideological positions. One view, characteristic of much of prevailing growth theory, is that the level and growth of national income are determined by the total factor endowments of countries, so that the distribution of income has no part to play. The very phrase 'income distribution' evokes the picture of a given volume of income having been produced, which is then 'distributed' among the members of society.

There is also another view based on the influence of income distribution on growth operating through political factors. According to this view, a very unequal distribution of income will lead to such serious political instability that it will disrupt the growth process, and hence that a more equitable distribution of income is a minimum condition of economic growth. In fact, the empirical evidence on this proposition is very mixed, some countries with a very unequal distribution of income being remarkably stable, while political disturbances have occurred in many countries with a more equal distribution of income.

On the other hand, there is the contrary view often advanced by neo-classical economists. According to this view, 'there is a conflict between rapid growth and an equitable distribution of income; and a poor country anxious to develop would probably be well advised not to worry too much about the distribution of income' (Johnson, 1958, p. 153). One reason for this conclusion may be the positive relationship between inequality and income level in the early stages of growth implied in Kuznets' Law. The argument is also based on the desirability of the market mechanism as the preferable instrument of economic development; hence it has been claimed that 'the remedies for the main fault which can be found with the use of the market mechanism, its undesirable social effects, are luxuries which under-developed countries cannot afford to indulge in if they are really serious about attaining a high rate of development' (Johnson, 1958, p. 153).

It is with respect to such arguments that Sen (1973, p. 70) remarked, 'I have heard it argued that equality is a "luxury" that only a rich country can "afford", and while I cannot pretend to understand fully this point of view, I am impressed by the number of people who

Table 12.1   Rates of growth and income inequality: LDCs, 1970–81 (figures in brackets are rates of growth 1970–81 and Gini coefficients for latest available year respectively).

Income inequality	Low		Rates of growth Medium		High	
Low	Bangladesh El Salvador India Sri Lanka Taiwan	(4.1; .37) (3.1; .40) (3.7; .40) (4.3; .41) (9.2; .28)	Pakistan	(5.0; .33)	Egypt Hong Kong S. Korea Thailand	(8.1; .47) (10.0; .39) (9.0; .37) (7.2; .42)
Medium	Argentina Venezuela	(1.9; .43) (4.5; .49)	Costa Rica Philippines Trinidad and Tobago Turkey	(5.2; .48) (6.2; .45) (5.5; .43) (5.4; .49)	Indonesia Malaysia	(7.8; .42) (7.8; .49)
High	Peru Zambia	(3.1; .56) (0.4; .53)	Ivory Coast Kenya Mauritius Panama Colombia	(6.2; .55) (5.8; .55) (6.2; .52) (4.5; .56) (5.6; .56)	Brazil Mexico	(8.4; .60) (6.5; .52)

Source: World Bank (1984, 1988). For Gini index of Colombia (income recipients) and Pakistan (households), Jain (1975).

seem prepared to advocate such a position'. In fact, it seems also to have been the position of Marx himself, when he discussed the role of the capitalist system with all its inequities in developing the productive forces of society, and criticised the 'utopian' socialists of his time for advocating the premature implementation of redistributive policies.

Given this wide variety of opinion on the subject, it may be thought that the problem can be resolved by reference to the empirical evidence. Unfortunately, such statistical data as are available do not throw any clear light on the subject. Consider, for example, the cross section data on income inequality and economic growth among LDCs in the post-war period, summarised in Table 12.1. The table does not show any significant relationship between the two variables. Countries with the same degree of income inequality have widely differing rates of economic growth.

It is possible that it is not the degree of income inequality at a point of time, but rather the change in income inequality over a period of

Table 12.2   Classification of LDCs by trends in income inequality and
rate of GDP growth

Trends in income inequality	Growth rate of GDP		
	Low	*Medium*	*High*
Rising	Bangladesh	Argentina Philippines	Brazil Colombia Mexico Thailand
Mixed	India Sri Lanka	Malaysia Indonesia	S. Korea
Falling	–	Costa Rica Pakistan	Peru Taiwan

Source: Sundrum (1990), table 5.3.

time, which influences the rate of growth. In order to examine this
possibility, LDCs for which data are available are classified according
to trends in income inequality and rates of growth in Table 12.2.
Again, we do not observe any systematic relationship between trends
in inequality and rates of growth. Particularly notable is the contrast
between countries such as Brazil, Mexico and Thailand, which combined high rates of growth with rising degrees of inequality, and
countries such as Taiwan which combined high rates of growth with
falling degrees of inequality.

The recent experience of DCs is described in Table 12.3. In the
DCs also, there is no systematic relationship between income inequality and economic growth.

On some reflection, however, there are many reasons why even if
income distribution has some influence on the rate of growth, this
influence may not be revealed by the data considered above. In the
first place, while data on rates of growth are reasonably accurate
these days, the data on income distribution are much less reliable and
much less comparable between countries and over time. Secondly,
the above data do not by themselves show the direction of causation
between the two variables. While income distribution may have some
effect on economic growth, economic growth may also have some
effects on income distribution. Thus, the above data show the net
result of the two effects. For example, the two effects may have

Table 12.3   Income inequality and rates of growth: DCs

Country	Gini index	GDP growth rate: 1960–70	GDP growth rate: 1970–81
Netherlands	.27	5.2	2.7
Belgium	.27	4.7	3.0
Japan	.28	10.4	4.5
West Germany	.30	4.4	2.6
Switzerland	.30	4.3	0.7
Finland	.31	4.3	3.1
Ireland	.31	4.2	4.0
Norway	.31	4.3	4.5
UK	.32	2.9	1.7
Spain	.32	7.1	3.4
Sweden	.32	4.4	1.8
Denmark	.33	4.5	2.1
Israel	.33	8.1	4.0
USA	.34	4.3	2.9
Canada	.34	5.6	3.8
France	.35	5.5	3.3
Italy	.36	5.5	2.9
New Zealand	.38	3.6	2.0
Australia	.40	5.6	2.8
Portugal	.41	6.4	4.2

Source: World Bank (1984, 1988).

worked in the same direction in countries such as Taiwan, but in opposite directions in other countries such as Brazil.

Thirdly, while a country's rate of growth may change rapidly over time as shown, for example, by the acceleration of growth in many LDCs in the post-war period and the drastic deceleration of growth in DCs between the 1960s and 1970s, the distribution of income in a country depends so much on deep-seated economic institutions that it is likely to be fairly stable and change only slowly over time. Fourthly, there is the related point that it is only fairly large changes in income distribution which are likely to have any significant effects on economic growth. Finally, the sort of changes in income distribution which have occurred in the countries considered in the above tables may have had such small effects on the rate of growth that these effects have been swamped by the more powerful and quickly transmitted effect of other variables on the rate of growth. Thus, the rapid growth of exports has been the main cause of the rapid growth of countries such as Taiwan in the 1960s and 1970s and Brazil in the 1970s, and this effect has dominated any influence that their very different income distributions may have had on their growth rates.

Therefore, the lack of any systematic relationship in the statistical evidence summarised above does not necessarily mean that income distribution has no influence on economic growth. In fact, individuals in different income classes differ so much in their consumption behaviour and their productive activities that it is much more likely that the distribution of income has some influence on the way a country utilises its productive capacity and responds to new opportunities, and hence on the level and growth of national income.

As in the study of the relationship between inflation and growth in the last chapter, it is useful to distinguish the influence of income distribution on growth according to whether it operates through supply factors or demand factors. When growth is constrained by supply factors, any influence that the distribution of income may have in augmenting productive capacity will be favourable to economic growth, and conversely. On the other hand, where growth is constrained by demand factors either in the economy as a whole, or in particular sectors, any influence that the distribution of income has in augmenting demand will be favourable to economic growth, and conversely.

First, we consider some effects which operate mainly on the supply side. In the case of the agricultural sector, the experience of many countries has been that small farms make more productive use of land than large estates (Booth and Sundrum, 1984, ch. 5). This is mainly because small farmers apply their family labour more intensively on their land than large farmers using hired labour. Also, in countries where land is distributed more equally, there is a greater prevalence of the 'community principle', i.e. the tendency for farmers to cooperate in collective projects benefiting all of them and promoting growth of output. In some countries, it has been found that large farmers have adopted modern techniques faster and increased output to a greater extent than small farmers, but this is mainly because the large farmers have better access to these techniques and the credit to purchase the modern inputs characteristic of these techniques. In the industrial sector also, small and medium enterprises may use labour more intensively than large firms. This has been an important feature of industrial growth in Taiwan. Against this, however, eco. omies of scale are much more important in this sector, giving an advantage to the larger units. Large firms may also be able to undertake more expenditure on research and development. More generally, although the expansion of education may initially worsen the distribution of income, as more and more workers get a high level of education and training, it will lead to a more equal distribution of income in the long run and a faster growth of national income. This has been one of the main reasons for the decline of income inequality in the DCs since the beginning of this century.

Turning next to effects operating on the demand side, there are many cases in which economic growth is constrained by demand factors. Thus, it has been argued that one reason for the slow industrial growth of India especially in the later 1960s was the lack of demand, due to the lack of purchasing power among the lower income groups, especially in rural areas. A growth of demand will then lead, not only to fuller utilisation of existing productive capacity, but may also lead to faster growth of productive capacity. Then, any change in the distribution of income which expands demand will lead to faster growth of national income. We have already noted in Chapter 6 the argument that one reason why modern economic growth began first in Britain in the late eighteenth century was the relatively more egalitarian distribution of income in that country at that time, a distribution which was favourable to the growth of demand for the new industrial products that became available with the technological progress.

In neo-classical economics, it is typically argued that attempts to raise wages, however desirable from the point of view of income distribution, would have adverse effects on economic growth, either because it would affect the competitive position of countries in export markets, or because it would lead to the substitution of capital for labour, and hence to unemployment and slower growth. However, higher wages also have an effect in raising aggregate demand, and in cases where growth is constrained by demand, this effect may offset the effect through substitution (Hicks, 1973; Malinvaud, 1977, p. 67). In recent years, the experience of many DCs has shown that reductions in unemployment, which improves the distribution of income, also helps to speed up the rate of growth, as formalised, for example, in Okun's Law.

Thus, there are many ways in which the distribution of income might affect the rate of economic growth, depending in particular on how it affects supply or demand factors, and on which of these factors are the main constraints on growth. There are, however, two particular types of interaction, namely the effect through the rate of saving and that through the structure of production, which need special consideration. These are discussed in the following sections.

12.2 RELATIONSHIP THROUGH THE RATE OF SAVING

One of the relationships most stressed in the literature is the influence of income distribution on the rate of savings. As household surveys of income and expenditure all over the world have shown, rich households save a higher proportion of their income than poor households. Therefore, it follows that, other things being equal, the average rate of savings in a country will be higher, the more unequal the distribution of income.

The argument is often expressed in terms of the wages and profit shares of income. As persons earning profit incomes are usually richer than wage earners, the rate of savings out of profit incomes is higher than that out of wages. Therefore, the average rate of savings will be higher, the greater the profit share of total income. This was the central theme of Lewis's dualistic model of development. The distribution of income between wages and profits also plays a key role in Kaldor's theory of growth.

In practice, especially in LDCs, this effect, while positive, may not be very significant. This is because, as incomes rise from very low levels, even rich households do not save a high proportion of their incomes, but spend much of the increase of incomes on consumption, often in the form of durable consumer goods, especially more lavish houses. Therefore, a considerable part of what is often classified as investment consists of conspicuous consumption expenditures, which have little effect on the growth of productive capital (see e.g. Dasgupta, 1975).

However, we must also consider the influence of savings on the rate of growth. It is often assumed in growth theory that a higher rate of saving will lead to a faster growth of national income. But this will be true only under certain conditions. One of these conditions is that existing capital stock is fully utilised, so that a rapid growth of output depends on a high rate of investment. Another condition for the rate of saving to influence the rate of growth is that it is savings which determines the level of investment.

It is true that a higher rate of growth depends on a rapid accumulation of capital but as argued in Part II, the accumulation of capital by itself has only accounted for a relatively small part of economic growth. A more important factor has been the rate of technological progress, which not only increases the productivity of given capital stock and other resources but has also been an important factor in inducing faster capital accumulation. Further, the more important role of capital accumulation has been as a vehicle for technological progress.

In countries where the capital market is very underdeveloped, a considerable part of investment is financed by the own savings of the investors. But where the capital market is more developed, the people who invest are usually different from those who do the saving. In classical theory, it is then argued that the rate of interest adjusts to an equilibrium level, through which the volume of savings determines the volume of investment. Then, it follows that the more unequal the distribution of income, the greater will be the volume of savings and investment. But even in the modern theory of growth derived from this neo-classical assumption, the rate of saving does not affect the long term rate of growth, which is determined instead by the rate of growth of labour supply and technical progress. Rather, the rate of saving only determines the *level* of per capita income on the resulting steady state path of the economy.

A more serious weakness of the classical theory, however, is the assumption that it is the level of savings which determines the level of investment. In fact, according to the Keynesian multiplier theory discussed in Chapter 9, the level of investment is determined by many other exogenous factors, and in turn it is the level of investment which determines the level of savings through changes in the level of income. This effect of investment on the level of income depends on the rate of savings, but in the opposite direction to what is usually assumed in classical theory, because the smaller the rate of saving, the higher is the multiplier. This relationship is known as the 'paradox of thrift'; it is paradoxical only in comparison with the model of the fully employed economy. In an economy with under-utilised resources, therefore, a more equal distribution of income might be more favourable to the rate of growth precisely because it reduces the rate of saving.

12.3 RELATIONSHIP THROUGH THE STRUCTURE OF PRODUCTION

In Chapter 3, we noted the great influence of the structure of production on the growth of an economy, and particularly how changes in the structure of production played a crucial role in bringing about the logistic pattern of growth. In the present section, we consider how the distribution of income might affect the growth process through its influence on the structure of production.

This influence is rather complex. Therefore, we shall only consider the principles involved by considering a simple model to show how the interaction between consumption patterns of people at different income levels and the distribution of income within individual sectors jointly determine both the structure of production and the overall distribution of income. It is well known from a long series of household expenditure surveys that households at different levels of income have different patterns of consumption. Poor households generally spend a high proportion of their income on food, while rich households spend a high proportion in manufactures and services. These patterns of consumption will influence the demand for the output of the various sectors. Through such demand effects, the distribution of income will have a powerful influence on the structure of production. On the other hand, the structure of production will also have important effects on the distribution of income. This is because different sectors employ the factors of production in different combinations, and the markets for these factors may also work in different ways in different sectors.

To study this two way relationship between income distribution and the structure of production, consider an economy divided into three sectors called agriculture, industry and services, and the population divided into three income groups – the rich, middle and poor – each containing a third of the population. Let X be a (3 x 1) column vector of the outputs of the three sectors, and let Y be a (3 x 1) column vector of incomes accruing to the three income groups. Then, there are two relationships between X and Y. On the one hand, there is the process of income generation, showing how the income generated in each sector is distributed among the different income groups, shown by the equation:

$$Y = AX \tag{12.1}$$

where A is a (3 x 3) matrix of elements a_{ij} representing the income accruing to the i-th income group from a unit output of the j-th sector. On the other hand, there is the pattern of expenditure showing how the income of each income group is spent on the output of the various sectors, shown by the equation

$$X = BY \tag{12.2}$$

where B is a (3 x 3) matrix of elements b_{ij} representing the expenditure on the output of the i-th sector from a unit of income of the j-th income group.

In practice, not all the value of output of a sector is distributed as incomes to the factors of production, and not all the output is available for final use. But for the sake of simplifying the analysis, we neglect all inter-industry transactions, and assume instead that the value of output in each sector is fully distributed as incomes of the various groups and that all incomes are fully spent on the output of the various sectors. Then, we get

$$X = BAX \qquad (12.3)$$

This is a set of homogeneous equations which will have a non-trivial solution, because the matrix $(I-BA)$ will be singular, on the assumption that the columns of A and B add up to unity. Equation (12.3) therefore completely determines the structure of outputs up to a scale factor. Similarly, we have

$$Y = ABY \qquad (12.4)$$

another set of homogeneous equations which completely determines the distribution of incomes, again up to a scale factor. In this model, the distribution of income and the structure of production are determined by the coefficients of the A and B matrix, describing both the composition of demand of different income groups and the process of income generation in the different sectors.

To illustrate the method, consider a numerical example where the matrices A and B have the following values:

$$A : \begin{bmatrix} .10 & .20 & .15 \\ .25 & .33 & .25 \\ .65 & .47 & .60 \end{bmatrix} \quad B : \begin{bmatrix} .80 & .51 & .40 \\ .13 & .29 & .36 \\ .07 & .20 & .24 \end{bmatrix}$$

Then, solving equations (12.3) and (12.4), we get for X and Y (in percentage terms):

$$X : \begin{bmatrix} 48.7 \\ 30.8 \\ 20.5 \end{bmatrix} \quad Y : \begin{bmatrix} 14.1 \\ 27.5 \\ 58.4 \end{bmatrix}$$

The argument can be used to study the demand for industrial

products in LDCs. If the distribution of income is very unequal, so that the incomes of the lower income groups are very low, they will have little surplus of purchasing power over the requirements for buying basic foods to spend on manufactures. The demand for manufactures from the middle and higher income groups alone may not be sufficient to achieve a rapid growth of the industrial sector. This argument is often used to explain the slow growth of industry in some LDCs, after an initial phase of rapid industrial growth based on import substitution. A particularly striking example of this phenomenon is the case of the deceleration of industrial growth in India since the mid-1960s (Sundrum, 1987, pp. 133–4; for a contrary view, see I.J. Ahluwalia, 1985, ch. 4).

The solution, of course, depends on the values of A and B. To show how A and B determine the overall distribution of income and the structure of production, consider another example with a different and more equal distribution of income within the agricultural sector, so that now we have:

$$A : \begin{bmatrix} .15 & .20 & .15 \\ .30 & .33 & .25 \\ .55 & .47 & .60 \end{bmatrix}$$

Then, the new solutions are:

$$X : \begin{bmatrix} 49.9 \\ 29.2 \\ 20.9 \end{bmatrix} \qquad Y : \begin{bmatrix} 16.5 \\ 29.9 \\ 53.6 \end{bmatrix}$$

As may be expected the overall distribution of income is now more equal, and there is an increase in the agricultural share of total output. But there is also an increase in the service sector share of total output, due to the complex interactions between the variables of the two matrices. These structural changes brought about by the change in the distribution of income within the agricultural sector will then have further effects on the growth of the economy, along the lines discussed in Chapter 3.

So far, we have only been considering what is known as the primary distribution of income, i.e. the distribution of incomes earned by participating in the production process. But individuals may also receive part of their income in the form of transfer payments. Especially in the developed countries, and to some extent also in the less-developed countries, there is a considerable amount of such transfers from the rich to the poor. The primary distribution of income modified by such transfers is the secondary distribution of income. The above model may be adjusted to take account of such redistributive policies. Such a model has been estimated for India and some Latin American countries (see e.g. Sinha *et al*. 1979 for the application to India).

An interesting point is that such transfer payments, exogenous to the process of income generation, would generally affect the structure of production, and hence would also lead to changes in the primary distribution of income. The final effect depends on the extent to which the poor consume the products of the sector from which they earn the major part of their income. In most cases, the poor earn their incomes from the agricultural sector, on which they spend most of their incomes. Then, income transfers from the rich to the poor improves the incomes of the poor in two ways, both by the direct effect of the transfers and by the indirect effect on their primary incomes. In fact, it may even be possible to achieve a permanent shift in the primary distribution of income in favour of the poor by a finite period of transfers of income. But, under other conditions, transfers from the rich to the poor may have a perverse effect of making the primary distribution of income more unequal. This result will occur particularly if the rich spend a large part of their income on services provided mainly by the poor; then, a reduction in the disposable income of the rich may reduce the employment of the poor so much as to reduce their primary incomes.

The distribution of income may also be affected by the provision of public goods and services to different income groups. The distribution of income modified in this way may be described as the tertiary distribution of income. Such changes in income distribution would then have further effects on the structure of production in favour of the goods and services provided by the government.

One limitation of this simple model is that all demands for the outputs of the various sectors are endogenous, influenced only by the incomes of different sections of the community, and all incomes are spent on domestic production. However, there may also be some exogenous sources of demand, say from exports or investment, and correspondingly, some leakages of demand in the form of savings or imports. Then, changes in these exogenous sources of demand and their sectoral composition will lead to changes in the structure of production and the distribution of income. These effects can be derived by constructing a matrix multiplier model analogous to the usual multiplier model (for a more detailed discussion, see Booth, Chaudhri and Sundrum, 1979).

Although the model developed above is a very simple one, it is useful to emphasise the close interaction between the distribution of income and the structure of production. But we have already seen (Chapter 3) that the structure of production has a significant influence on the rate of growth. Therefore, in considering the influence that the distribution of income has on the rate of growth, we must consider not only the effect through the rate of saving but also the effect through the structure of production. In particular, this mechanism explains why a more equal distribution of income may lead to a faster rate of growth. This is particularly important for the growth of the industrial sector. In many countries, the rate of industrial growth is constrained by lack of demand, which in turn is due to the prevailing distribution of income. Thus, one reason for the slackening of industrial growth in the DCs since 1973 has been the high and rising rate of unemployment. Another example is the deceleration of industrial growth in many LDCs after an initial phase of rapid growth due to the import substitution, because the demand for industrial goods from the upper income groups has been exhausted and there is less demand from the lower income groups because of the unequal distribution of income. Under these conditions, policies which lead to a more equal distribution of income will help to sustain and increase the demand for industrial goods, and hence prolong the industrial phase of rapid growth.

13 Conclusions

13.1 FACTORS IN LONG-TERM GROWTH

Although the causes of economic growth have been studied since classical times, the theories which are currently fashionable derive mainly from the neo-classical interest in the subject in the 1950s and 1960s, when there was a veritable explosion of articles and books on the subject for well nigh two decades. Since then, however, interest in the subject waned in the 1970s, when economists shifted their attention to the short-term macroeconomic problems affecting most countries in that decade. The theory of growth developed in the 1950s and 1960s is now relegated to chapters in the fashionable textbooks, and forms the main diet on which successive generations of students continue to be fed.

This is most unfortunate because this stale theory of growth suffers from a number of major defects. In the first place, it makes too sharp a distinction between the growth process in the developed and the less-developed countries, as if economic growth in these two groups of countries is due to entirely different forces, and different theories are needed to explain them. One part of the subject, generally known as growth theory, is confined to the study of economic progress in the DCs, while another part of the subject, generally known as development economics, deals with the problems of growth in LDCs.

Another serious weakness of the prevailing theory of growth is that it has been more interested in the logical analysis of conveniently chosen assumptions than with explaining the growth process as it has occurred in practice. To the extent that growth theory is concerned with facts at all, it relies only on a few stylised facts assumed to characterise growth since the late nineteenth century in a few countries which had already achieved a high level of development by then. In particular, it is assumed that this experience showed that growth occurred at steady rates; therefore, much of the growth theory is only concerned to find the conditions under which such steady state growth could occur.

Finally, another weakness of growth theory is its intense preoccupation with supply factors, i.e. it tries to explain the growth of national income solely in terms of the growth of productive capacity and the gains in the allocative efficiency of these resources, on the assumption that whatever productive capacity exists at any time is always fully utilised. Already, in the wake of the Great Depression, Keynes had shown the importance of demand factors in explaining the changes in the extent to which productive capacity was actually utilised, and hence in the determination of actual output. While Keynes had advanced his theory to explain short period changes, the demand factors which he stressed are clearly relevant also to the growth process in the long run.

It is therefore time to make a new start in growth theory. This has been the aim of the preceding chapters. By way of recapitulation, some of the main features of the present approach may be briefly summarised as follows. First, the main concern of the present study is with the growth process as it has occurred in practice. Therefore, we have referred extensively to the substantial amount of empirical evidence on the subject. In particular, we have taken full account of the remarkable episodes of economic growth that occurred in post-war decades in a large number of countries, both developed and less-developed, for which statistical data are available.

Secondly, by covering a wider range of countries, the present approach views the process of economic growth in its entirety, from very low levels of income all the way to the highest levels. Hence, this approach takes a more unified view of growth occurring both in the DCs and the LDCs, in contrast to much of the prevailing theory which has been concerned with the growth experience of a small group of countries in a particular phase of their development.

Finally, in contrast to prevailing theories, it was argued in the previous chapters that supply factors, such as the growth of productive capacity and changes in the allocative efficiency with which resources are used, alone are not sufficient to explain many important episodes of economic growth as they have actually occurred in practice, and further that the usual arguments in terms of savings behaviour and exogenous technological progress are not adequate to explain changes in these supply factors. Instead, we find that the economic growth of countries is a complex process influenced by a wide variety of factors both on the supply and demand side. It is clearly not a process that can be fully explained by a few basic relationships, as in modern growth theory, even though they are analysed by highly sophisticated techniques. Instead, the present approach gives more weight to the demand effects of such variables as investment, government expenditures and exports, in explaining both the utilisation of existing productive capacity, and the growth of this capacity over time.

The first result of this approach is that the 'stylised facts' which were believed to characterise economic growth and which modern growth theory has been concerned to explain do not correspond even to a first approximation to the actual experience of economic growth, especially when this process is viewed in a more comprehensive way. In particular, it was argued in Chapter 2 that growth is not characterised by steady rates, but rather follows a logistic pattern of slow growth at low levels of income, accelerating to high rates of growth at medium levels of income, falling back to slower growth again at the highest levels of income.

A second important feature of growth as it has actually occurred in history is that it was closely associated with a significant structural transformation of the growing economies, namely the steady decline of the agricultural share of GDP and of employment, a rapid increase of the industrial share up to a point, and then the great expansion of the service sector at the highest levels of income. The structural transformation of the economy has, of course, been well documented in the researches of economic historians, especially Kuznets. But in spite of its significant magnitude and its close association with the growth process, this structural transformation has not been taken into account in the standard theories of growth as it is generally taught at present. Therefore, Chapter 3 provides a model in which structural transformation plays a central role in explaining the logistic pattern of growth, according to which the growth process typically follows an S-curve.

While economic growth in all countries follows an S-curve, all countries do not necessarily follow the same S-curve. Instead, the S-curve is squeezed in some countries, and stretched out in others; in other words, countries differ in the rates at which they move from one phase to another of the logistic pattern, and the rates at which they move within each phase. Therefore, an important requirement of growth theory is to explain differences in the S-curve followed by different countries at different times.

Part II dealt with one set of factors influencing the S-curve of growth, namely the supply factors, the growth in the stocks of the factors of production – land, labour and capital, and the improvement in the state of technology. These are the factors which have been most intensively studied in prevailing growth theories, summarised in Chapter 4. Because of the importance assigned to the role of structural transformation in the present approach, the working of the various supply factors is studied with special reference to the three major sectors of the economy. Chapter 5 dealing with the agricultural sector was specially concerned with the relationship between land and labour. Chapter 6 dealing with the industrial sector was specially concerned with the relationship between capital accumulation and technological progress, while Chapter 7 on the service sector was specially concerned with the role of labour.

Part III of the book then dealt with another set of factors, the demand factors. Some sources of demand are endogenous in the sense that they depend on the growth of income, and cannot be used to explain growth. But other sources of demand are exogenous in the sense of being independent of the growth of income; instead, the growth of these exogenous sources of demand has an important influence on the growth of income. One of these is investment; as discussed in Chapter 8, investment plays a dual role, both in increasing productive capacity and as a source of demand. Chapters 9 and 10 then dealt with the two other exogenous sources of demand, government expenditure and exports. In these chapters, it was pointed out that these three variables – investment, government expenditures and exports – had important influences on growth, not so much through their effects on the efficiency of resource allocation, but rather through their effects in stimulating demand for these resources and in further inducing the growth of supply factors. An important indication of the greater importance of demand effects compared with supply effects is the fact that growth rates of GDP are generally more highly correlated with the *growth rates* of these variables than with their *levels* measured as ratios to GDP.

In Part IV, we considered two other processes which are also associated with economic growth both through supply and demand effects. One is the role of inflation, discussed in Chapter 11, which plays a part both in mobilising resources and as a vehicle for expanding demand. The other is the distribution of income, discussed in Chapter 12, which also affects economic growth in many ways, especially through its effects on the saving rate and the structure of production.

13.2 MAJOR EPISODES OF ECONOMIC GROWTH

In the previous section, we recapitulated the argument of the preceding chapters in terms of the various factors influencing economic growth. In the present section, we recapitulate that argument by considering the role of these factors in the major episodes of economic growth identified in Chapter 2.

(a) Modern Economic Growth

The first major episode of rapid growth in modern times was the onset of modern economic growth in western countries beginning from the late eighteenth century. It was a decisive break from the traditionally low rates of growth that had prevailed before in all countries. In terms of the logistic pattern of growth, this episode may be interpreted as the movement from the first phase of slow growth based mainly on agricultural development to the second phase of rapid growth based mainly on industrial development. In accordance with this pattern, this transition occurred only in a limited number of countries which had already attained a higher level of development.

The main force which triggered off this transition was an unprecedented rate of technological progress. The technological progress consisted, not only of the development of new techniques of production and the invention of new products, but also 'much social invention' involved in the development of new economic institutions. An important characteristic of these new developments was the increasing use of capital. Therefore, capital accumulation also played a part but it was more a case of capital accumulation racing to catch up with the rate of technological progress.

While these supply factors played a significant part, they were assisted by favourable demand factors. Thus, in the case of Britain, the leader of the Industrial Revolution, an important source of demand was the relatively egalitarian distribution of income in that country. In addition, another major source of industrial growth in Britain and other European countries during the period of their modern economic growth was a great expansion of world trade, giving rise to the view of trade as the 'engine of growth'. In the course of this trade expansion, these countries became the main suppliers of industrial products to the rest of the world.

Although modern economic growth of the western countries in the eighteenth and nineteenth centuries was a sharp break from previous rates of growth, it was a relatively slow process by comparison with the subsequent industrialisation of other countries, in more recent times. This was because the later entrants to this process were able to exploit the backlog of technology which had already been built up in other more advanced countries, whereas the pioneers of modern economic growth had to depend on a much slower progress of technology, which was being simultaneously invented.

(b) Tropical Development of LDCs

Concurrent with modern economic growth in the western countries, many tropical countries also experienced high rates of growth. The main reason for the high rates of growth of these tropical countries was the expansion of demand for their exports. The rapid growth of some of these countries has sometimes been interpreted as a 'take off', similar to that which occurred in the western countries. But while modern economic growth was based on the development of industry, the tropical development of LDCs was based mainly on the export of primary products. In particular, the expansion of such primary exports was not based on any significant development of new technology; instead, it was based much more on the utilisation of surplus resources of land and labour, using traditional technology, except for cases of mineral exploitation and plantation development based on some new techniques and a limited investment of capital. Hence, the acceleration of growth which occurred in the tropical countries was not a case of a transition from the early phase of slow growth in the logistic pattern to the middle phase of rapid growth.

The main reason was that the export growth of LDCs consisted of primary products rather than manufactures. The exports of manufactures contributes to growth in two ways, one by providing the demand for the more intensive utilisation of existing productive capacity, and the other by inducing the growth of productive capacity itself. By contrast, the exports of primary products affects growth only by providing a vent for surplus. What was missing in the case of the tropical development of the present-day LDCs was the growth of productive capacity. Therefore, in retrospect, it has to be interpreted as a case of a temporary period of rapid growth within the first phase of the logistic pattern, even though it was a long drawn process in some countries. Eventually, with the exhaustion of surplus resources and the decline in the growth of primary exports, the expansion of primary exports became a much less significant source of growth in these countries, and they emerged at the end of the Second World War as typical less-developed countries.

(c) Rapid Growth of DCs: 1950–73

The first quarter century of the post-war period was marked by a great spurt in the growth of the DCs, which has been described as the 'golden age of capitalism' (Cornwall, 1990). It was a remarkable episode, coming as it did after the slow growth of the prolonged depression and the disruption of growth during the war years. Economists again became interested in the causes of economic growth, leading to new theories on the subject, especially the neo-classical theory of growth, and to attempts to explain why growth rates differed between countries in terms of such sources of growth as the contributions of the various factors of production and of technological progress, i.e. in terms of what we have described as the supply factors.

It was only after this period of rapid growth of the DCs was over and economists could look at the whole episode in its entirety that it became apparent that there was a systematic pattern in the growth rates of different DCs, namely that countries which started out at a lower level generally had a higher growth rate. It therefore seemed as if there was a tendency for per capita incomes to converge to a common level. A particular instance of this pattern was that the two countries which were most damaged by the war experienced the highest rates of growth, for a long period in the case of Japan and for a shorter period in the case of West Germany.

This in turn led to the theory that the rapid growth of the DCs was due to a catching up process. According to this theory, countries which were more backward in their technology compared with industrial leaders like the United States were able to grow faster, because they had a greater backlog of technology to absorb. But countries do not grow more rapidly simply because they have a greater backlog of technology to catch up. After all, arguably the LDCs have a much greater backlog of technology to catch up, but this does not seem to have made much difference to their growth rates. To some extent, the ability to borrow advanced technology depends on certain supply factors, such as the existence of scientific and technological manpower, or institutional conditions favourable to the absorption of foreign technology, which have been described as 'social capability' in the Japanese context.

But these supply factors alone are not sufficient to explain the catching up process. In addition, it was due also to certain demand factors. In most cases, the demand stimulus was provided by the growth of exports, especially of manufactures, among the industrial countries themselves. Hence, we observe a high correlation of growth rates of GDP and of investment with growth rates of exports, induced by the liberalisation of trade under GATT auspices. In countries like the United States where exports were a smaller proportion of GDP, there was also an interaction of demand and supply factors, as explained in great detail by Cornwall (1972). In terms of the logistic pattern of growth, this episode can therefore be interpreted as a case of demand factors extending the middle phase of rapid growth over a longer period, after its disruption during the 1930s and 1940s.

(d) Growth Acceleration of LDCs: 1950–80

The post-war period also saw an acceleration of the average growth rate of LDCs, which took the world by surprise (Lewis, 1970a). In fact, on the average, the LDCs grew faster even than the DCs at a time when the latter were growing at an unprecedented rate. However, there was a much greater diversity in the growth experience of LDCs than of DCs. In fact, the growth acceleration was particularly marked in only some of the LDCs, especially countries which were relatively small in population size. So the population-weighted average of growth rates was generally smaller than the unweighted average.

Further, the growth rates of LDCs were highly correlated with the growth rates of exports. The superior growth performance of the countries with faster growth of exports was therefore attributed to the allocative advantages of outward looking policies. The star performers from this point of view were the NICs, especially in Asia. Reviewing this performance, Tsiang and Wu (1985, p. 329) claimed that 'In sum, the experience of rapid economic growth in Taiwan, Korea, Hong Kong, and Singapore during the past two or three decades was achieved not by economic tricks, but by sensible policies based on sound neo-classical economic principles'.

However, the advantages of outward looking policies stressed by neo-classical theory consist only of improvements in allocative efficiency in the form of gains from trade. Such gains are only once-for-all gains, which could not possibly explain the tremendous spurt in growth of these countries. Further, with the major exception of small countries like the city states of Hong Kong and Singapore, the hand of the government in the other NICs was much more visible than implied in neo-classical theory.

Instead, the experience of the NICs was an episode which fits more closely with the growth acceleration in the middle phase of the logistic pattern of growth. In particular, it was a case in which a prior agricultural development advanced the transition to the middle phase, and the demand stimulus provided by the rapid growth of exports of manufactures prolonged the middle phase and raised the grow⁺ʰ rate in that phase.

(e) Growth Slackening in DCs: 1973–56

A surprising development of the post-war period was that, after a quarter century of unprecedented rapid growth, the growth rates of DCs plunged downward to less than half the previous levels. This dramatic downturn cannot be explained only in terms of the supply factors, which had only a few years before been sufficient to enable these countries to grow so much faster and for such a long period. The explanation has, therefore, to be sought in the demand policies followed by these countries.

In fact, these countries were following highly contractionary demand policies in this period. One reason was the decline of Keynesian theory and a widespread resurgence of classical and neo-classical theory, especially monetarist theory, among many influential economists in these countries. Another reason was that there was a rise in inflation rates due partly to the rise in oil prices and partly to significant changes in labour market institutions which imparted an inflationary bias to these economies. Therefore, there was a rise in the inflation cost of full employment policies. At the same time, many of these countries came under conservative governments. The result was the adoption of contractionary demand policies, in the hope of first controlling inflation and then dealing with the unemployment problem. But in the event, these contractionary policies only led to a drastic fall in the levels of economic activity, and failed to reduce inflation to their previous levels.

The decline in domestic economic activity in turn led to slowing down in the growth rate of exports, which in turn led to further slackening of domestic production in a cumulative process. The decline in exports was also due to the breakdown of the Bretton Woods system of international payments, itself due at least in part to increasing diversity of inflation experience, which could not be offset only by flexible exchange rates.

The above explanation of the downturn of economic growth in the DCs has concentrated on relatively short-term macroeconomic factors. However, it should also be viewed against the longer term perspective offered by the logistic pattern of growth. In this pattern, there is a deceleration of growth in the final phase, associated with the shift of the centre of gravity of the economy to the service sector. On this argument, therefore, the slow down of economic growth in DCs in the recent period may be attributed, at least to some extent, to the shift of resources, especially labour, from the industrial to the service sector of these economies, and the difficulty that they are having in achieving this shift, exacerbated by the macroeconomic problems mentioned above.

13.3 IMPLICATIONS FOR GROWTH POLICY

The most important lesson of the preceding analysis is that the growth of countries depends on both supply and demand factors. A sustained increase in the national income of a country is only possible if there is an increase in its productive capacity, brought about by the various supply factors discussed in Part II. However, an increase in productive capacity alone is not enough, for it only represents an increase in the potential output of the economy. For this potential to be realised, there must also be an increase in aggregate demand. The growth of production will itself generate an increase of incomes and a growth of demand associated with that increase of incomes. But in general, the growth of such endogenous sources of demand alone may not be sufficient to match the growth of productive capacity. Therefore, some growth of exogenous sources of demand, such as those discussed in Part III, will also be needed. In addition, there is also an interaction between supply and demand, such that an increase of demand induces an expansion of supply.

Hence, a country will have a high growth rate, if both supply and demand grow rapidly and in step with each other. If the growth of demand lags behind the growth of supply, then policies to stimulate demand will lead to faster growth. But if the growth of supply lags behind the growth of demand, then policies to expand supply will be needed to achieve faster growth.

An important consequence of this interplay of supply and demand factors is that the growth process typically follows a logistic pattern. Hence, growth rates of countries cannot be compared without reference to their place in the logistic pattern. This pattern is greatly influenced by the structural dimension of economic growth. On the demand side, an important influence leading to this pattern of growth is the systematic change in the pattern of consumer demand for the products of the various sectors in the process of economic growth. At low levels of income, demand is concentrated on food, the principal product of the agricultural sector. But in the agricultural sector, the growth of labour productivity is generally slow, especially because of the operation of diminishing returns due to limited supplies of land. Therefore, when agriculture is the dominant sector of the economy, the overall growth rate will be low.

When an economy reaches an intermediate level of income, the concentration of demand shifts to manufactures. A major characteristic of the industrial sector is the use of capital, not only as a substitute for labour but also as a vehicle of technological progress. Much of the capital is produced in the industrial sector itself. Further, industrial production is also subject to increasing returns to scale. Therefore, the productivity of labour is not only higher than in other sectors, but also grows faster. Hence, the rise of the industrial sector to a dominant position in the economy is associated with a significant acceleration of overall growth, both because of the faster growth of labour productivity in the industrial sector and because of the shift of resources from other sectors. In this phase, manufacturing becomes the main engine of growth.

In the final phase of growth, the concentration of demand shifts to the service sector at the highest levels of income, especially as a result of increased government expenditures. Because capital plays a smaller role in this sector, the growth of labour productivity generally lags behind that in the industrial sector. Therefore, the relative expansion of the service sector is generally associated with a deceleration of growth in the final phase of the logistic.

The logistic pattern of growth brought about by these systematic changes in the pattern of consumer demand will be modified by the effects of exogenous demand as they affect different sectors. Thus, investment demand will mainly affect the industrial sector while government expenditures will mainly affect the service sector. There is greater variation in the sectoral impact of the growth of exports. Where an increase of exports consists largely of primary products, there will be faster growth of the agricultural sector, which will delay the movement to the industrial phase of the logistic pattern. On the other hand, if the increase in exports consists largely of manufactures, it will prolong the industrial phase and the associated acceleration of growth, and postpone the transition to the service sector phase, and the associated deceleration of growth. It is against this analytical background that we now consider some problems of growth policy in LDCs and DCs.

(a) Growth Policy in LDCs

Although some LDCs have achieved high rates of growth, economic growth in most LDCs is still very slow, especially in the low income countries and in the most populous ones. These countries clearly need to accelerate their growth rates rapidly, especially to solve their pressing problems of mass poverty. Further, the experience of other LDCs has shown that such growth acceleration is feasible. Therefore, the main objective of policy in these countries is an acceleration of their growth rates. Some of the policy measures needed are discussed below.

Growth of Productivity

Most LDCs are trying to promote faster growth by raising their savings and investment rates. This is certainly necessary, but an even more important requirement is to raise the productivity of their resources. Further, an increase in productivity will itself attract more resources for investment.

The basic instrument for raising the productivity of labour is the rapid expansion of education and training. The goal to set is the expansion of education until all individuals get as much education as they can absorb. This is a big task, but it is a task which they can accomplish to a great extent with their own resources of manpower. What they must do, however, is to achieve this goal of educational development within as short a time as possible.

Once they have a sufficient stock of skilled manpower, the LDCs can exploit the backlog of technology that is already available in the advanced countries, as many DCs were able to do especially in the post-war period. However, foreign technology may not be entirely suitable for application to the LDCs. Therefore, the LDCs must also allocate sufficient research resources for adapting foreign technology to suit their own needs.

The growth of productivity, however, does not depend only on the technological gap and the allocation of resources for research. Technological progress may be inhibited by institutional bottlenecks. This is particularly the case in agriculture, which is the dominant sector of most LDC economies. It is only by overcoming the institutional bottlenecks that the agricultural sector can absorb new technology more rapidly. The sooner this is done, the sooner will agriculture fulfil its historical mission, and the economy move to its next phase of rapid growth based on industrialisation.

The Balanced Growth Doctrine

While policies dealing with supply factors have been widely discussed in the literature, those dealing with demand factors have received much less attention. Therefore, we discuss these policies in more detail. One of these policies is that concerned with the rates at which different sectors should be expanded. The expansion of a sector will not only increase the supply of its products, but the income generated in the process will also increase the demand for the products of other sectors. Therefore, the rates at which different sectors are expanded should be such that the increase in demand for the products of each sector will match the increase in their supply.

This is the central wisdom of the Balanced Growth doctrine advanced by Rosenstein-Rodan (1943), Nurkse (1952, 1958) and Lewis (1955). The argument has been explained by Lewis (1955, pp. 276–7, 283) as follows:

> Suppose there is considerable innovation in the agricultural sector producing food for the home market. The result is either a surplus of food to sell to the towns, or a surplus of labour in agriculture seeking non-agricultural employment, or some combination of both. If manufacturing industry is growing at the right rate, it can absorb both the surplus goods and the surplus labour. If it is not, the terms of trade will move against agriculture, and as there will be a surplus of farm labour as well as farm products, agricultural income will be depressed and further investment and innovation in this sector will be discouraged. Innovation in one sector of the economy is checked unless other sectors expand appropriately . . . Exactly the same difficulties arise if economic development is concentrated upon industrialisation to the neglect of agriculture, as happened in the USSR.
>
> A whole school of 'liberal' economists in the industrial countries urge upon the agricultural countries, usually in lofty moral tones, that they should concentrate upon agriculture and do nothing to advance their industry. The same school also extols the virtue of exporting and is horrified by programmes which might have the effect of reducing dependence on foreign trade. The follies of this school have their match in Marxist and nationalist dogmas,

according to which the road to economic progress lies through concentrating upon industrialisation. In the heat of the passions aroused by these controversies, it seems almost cowardly to take the line that all sectors should be expanded simultaneously but the logic of this proposition is as unassailable as its simplicity.

Since then, the doctrine has come under severe criticism. These criticisms have followed two lines, one that it is not necessary to expand sectors according to the growth of demand because, however sectors expand, their demand will be adjusted by changes in relative prices (see e.g. Findlay, 1959), and the other that instead of expanding sectors in this balanced fashion, resources should be allocated so as to equalise their marginal rates of return in all sectors (see e.g. Sheahan, 1958).

The first line of criticism is really a return to Say's Law that supply will create its own demand. In fact, relative prices, especially of broad groups of commodities, are not sufficiently flexible to bring about equilibrium of supply and demand in all sectors. It is because relative prices are sticky that the doctrine is usually interpreted as recommending the growth of sectors according to the respective income elasticities of demand. It is not a proposal for keeping relative prices constant, but rather a policy for promoting growth in conditions when relative prices are not sufficiently flexible to bring about full employment of resources in all sectors.

Regarding the second line of criticism, market forces without any policy interventions may allocate resources so as to equalise their marginal rates of return. This allocation may be optimal in the static sense of getting the maximum output from given resources, but the question addressed by the Balanced Growth doctrine is how an increase of resources should be allocated to different sectors in order to achieve the maximum growth of output. For this objective to be achieved, there must be sufficient demand for the increased supply from different sectors.

The most serious form of the second criticism is that such balanced growth is inconsistent with countries getting the full benefit of international trade according to comparative advantage. But because the Balanced Growth doctrine is only concerned to expand sectors in line with the growth of demand, it is quite consistent with the doctrine to expand a sector if an increase of demand is expected from export markets. The doctrine does not mean that countries should not take advantage of foreign trade, but rather is concerned with what they should do if export demand does not expand rapidly. The more important problem with reliance on foreign trade on the basis of comparative advantage is that a country's comparative advantage is not fixed immutably, but can be changed by policy efforts. The real question addressed by the Balanced Growth doctrine is how these comparative advantages should be changed.

Role of Government Expenditures

Some growth of government expenditures for public administration and the provision and maintenance of infrastructure is necessary for improving the productive capacity of an economy. This is particularly important in LDCs where the level of infrastructural development is low. These expenditures also increase aggregate demand, which promotes growth to the extent that they utilise under-employed resources and to the extent that they induce an expansion of productive capacity. But some LDCs have expanded government expenditures rapidly, especially in the area of public administration which has much less effect on the productive capacity of the country. When these expenditures are financed by money creation rather than by taxes, they may lead to rates of inflation so high as to have adverse effects on growth. Therefore, LDCs must ensure that government expenditures are increased only in areas which lead to an expansion of productive capacity.

Role of Exports

As we have seen, the growth of exports has been an important determinant of economic growth, especially through their demand effects in fuller utilisation of under-employed resources and in inducing faster growth of productive capacity. Therefore, LDCs wishing to accelerate their growth must take special efforts to promote their exports, especially by improving their competitive position in international markets, both by increasing their productivity and by their monetary and exchange rate policies. The extent to which countries can rely on exports for accelerating their growth depends partly on the growth of world trade and partly on the size of the countries. In particular, relatively smaller countries will be more successful in promoting growth on the basis of exports than the larger countries. Also, the possibilities of export-led growth are greater when world trade is expanding rapidly. In the post-war period until 1973, the biggest expansion of world trade was that among the DCs, but after

1973, the growth of trade among these countries has declined sharply. One solution is for LDCs to expand the trade among themselves.

Income Distribution

Under present conditions, it may not be possible for countries, especially the larger countries, to accelerate their growth on the basis of a rapid growth of exports. This does not, however, mean that they are doomed to slow growth. The main reason why export growth has been associated with rapid growth of GDP is because exports have provided an exogenous source of demand. An increase of exogenous demand can also be achieved by changes in the distribution of income, for example, by redistributive policies. Thus in countries whose growth is constrained by lack of capital and foreign exchange but which have under-employed labour, a redistribution of income in favour of the lower income groups will promote growth by reducing the demand for capital- and import-intensive commodities, mostly consumed by the upper income groups, and increasing the demand for labour-intensive commodities mostly consumed by the lower income groups.

(b) Growth Policy in DCs

The DCs have already attained a high degree of material affluence. Therefore, further growth of their national income is a less urgent priority of policy in these countries, especially in view of the high costs of growth in terms of environmental deterioration and social tensions. However, these countries are still pursuing economic growth, not so much as an end in itself, but as the means of solving other problems such as unemployment, balance of payments crises, and inflation. In particular, as Hirsch (1977, p. 7) pointed out, 'the compelling attraction of economic growth in its institutionalised modern form has been as a superior alternative to redistribution'.

The major problem of DCs is to achieve an acceptable distribution of income, especially one based on high levels of employment of their labour force. Under prevailing conditions, this problem cannot be solved only by accelerating their rate of growth. The slow growth of DCs at present cannot be blamed on limitations of supply factors. They already have a highly educated labour force, an abundant stock of capital and a high level of technology, so that they not only have a large productive capacity but also one which can be expanded rapidly in response to demand. Therefore, their prospects for a rapid recovery from their present stagnation and a solution to their serious problems of unemployment lies mainly in expanding aggregate demand. But in many DCs, policies of expanding aggregate demand are not being followed for fear of unacceptable rates of inflation due to the prevailing institutions of the labour market. The solution of these problems lies ultimately in new incomes policies based on institutional changes in the labour market.

The most advanced DCs are also going through a phase of deindustrialisation and moving into a predominantly service economy. This transition is part of the reason for the slackening of economic growth in DCs. It is also a factor which exacerbates the problem of unemployment, especially because the role of the government in expanding the service sector sufficiently to absorb the labour released from the other sectors raises serious problems of public finance. These problems must be solved for the DCs to achieve a soft landing in the third, and final, phase of the logistic pattern of growth.

Bibliography and Author Index

(*Figures in square brackets refer to pages in text where each work is cited.*)

ABRAMOVITZ, M. (1956) 'Resource and Output Trends in the United States Since 1870', *American Economic Review*, vol. 46, pp. 5–23. **[112]**

ABRAMOVITZ, M. (1986) 'Catching Up, Forging Ahead, and Falling Behind', *Journal of Economic History*, vol. 46, pp. 385–406. **[129–30]**

ACKLEY, G. (1961) *Macro-economic Theory* (New York, Macmillan). **[166–7]**

AGHEVLI, B.J. and M.S. KHAN (1978) 'Government Budget Deficits and inflationary process in developing countries', *IMF Staff Papers*, vol. 25, pp. 383–416. **[242]**

AHLUWALIA, I.J. (1985) *Industrial Growth in India* (Delhi, Oxford University Press). **[268]**

AHLUWALIA, M.S. (1976) 'Inequality, Poverty and Development', *Journal of Development Economics*, vol. 3, pp. 307–42. **[257]**

AHMAD, S. (1966) 'On the Theory of Induced Investment', *Economic Journal*, vol. 76, pp. 344–57. **[127]**

ALEXANDER, S. (1950) 'Mr. Harrod's Dynamic Model', *Economic Journal*, vol. 60, pp. 724–39. **[166]**

ALLEN, R.G.D. (1967) *Macro-Economic Theory* (London, Macmillan). **[116, 171]**

ASIMAKOPOULOS, A. (1986) 'Harrod and Domar on Dynamic Economics', *Banca Nazionale del Lavoro Quarterly Review*, no. 158, pp. 275–98. **[161]**

AYE HLAING (1965) *An Economic and Statistical Analysis of Economic Development of Burma under British Rule* (Unpublished PhD thesis, London University). **[83]**

BACON, R. and W. ELTIS (1976) *Britain's Economic Problem* (London, Macmillan). **[148, 198]**

BALASSA, B. (1978) 'Exports and Economic Growth', *Journal of Development Economics*, vol. 5, pp. 181–9. **[203]**

BARRO, R.J. (1984) *Macroeconomics* (New York, John Wiley). **[64–5, 249]**

BAUER, P.T. and B.S. YAMEY (1957) *The Economics of Underdeveloped Countries* (Cambridge, Cambridge University Press). **[68]**

BAUMOL, W.J. (1967) 'Macroeconomics of Unbalanced Growth', *American Economic Review*, vol. 57, pp. 415–26. **[144, 186]**

BAUMOL, W.J. (1986) 'Productivity Growth, Convergence and Welfare', *American Economic Review*, vol. 76(5), pp. 1072–85. **[129]**

BAUMOL, W.J., S.A.B. BLACKMAN and E.N. WOLFF (1985) 'Unbalanced Growth Revisited', *American Economic Review*, vol. 75, pp. 806–17. **[143]**

BELL, D. (1974) *The Coming of Post-Industrial Society* (London, Heinemann). **[138]**

BHAGWATI, J.N. and A.O. KRUEGER (1973) 'Exchange Control, Liberalization, and Development', *American Economic Review*, vol. 63(2) pp. 419–27. **[208]**

BICANIC, R. (1962) 'The Threshold of Economic Growth', *Kyklos*, vol. 15, pp. 7–28. **[107]**

BINSWANGER, H.P. and V.W. RUTTAN (1978) *Induced Innovation* (Baltimore, Johns Hopkins Press). **[92–3]**

BIRD, R.M. (1971) 'Wagner's Law' of Expanding State Activity', *Public Finance*, vol. 26, pp. 1–24. **[183]**

BIRD, R.M. (1978) 'Assessing Tax Performance in Developing Countries: A Critical Review of the Literature', in J.F.J. TOYE (ed.) *Tax and Economic Development* (London, Frank Cass), ch. 2, pp. 33–61. **[186]**

BIRNBERG, T.B. and S.A. RESNICK (1975) *Colonial Development* (New Haven, Yale University Press). **[21]**

BLACKABY, F. (ed.) (1979) *De-industrialization* (London, Heinemann). **[133]**

BOLNICK, B.R. (1978) 'Tax Effort in Developing Countries: What do Regression Measures Really Measure', in J.F.J. TOYE (ed.) *Tax and Economic Development* (London, Frank Cass), ch. 3, pp. 62–80. **[186]**

BOOTH, A.E., D.P. CHAUDHRI and R.M. SUNDRUM (1979) *Income Distribution and the Structure of Production* (Canberra, Australian National University, Seminar Paper). **[270]**

BOOTH, A.E. and R.M. SUNDRUM (1984) *Labour Absorption in Agriculture* (Oxford, Oxford University Press). **[95, 98, 250, 262]**

BOSERUP, E. (1965) *The Conditions of Agricultural Growth* (London, Allen and Unwin). **[59, 90]**

BRENNER, R. (1986) 'Agrarian class structure and economic development in pre-industrial Europe', in T.H. ASHTON and C.H.E. PHILPIN (eds) (1986) *The Brenner Debate* (Cambridge, Cambridge University Press). **[99]**

BRUNO, M. and J. SACHS (1985) *Economics of Worldwide Stagflation* (Cambridge, Mass., Harvard University Press). **[254]**

BUTT, D.M.B. (1960) *On Economic Growth* (Oxford, Oxford University Press). **[72–5, 93–9]**

CAGAN, P. (1956) 'The Monetary Dynamics of Hyper-Inflation', in M. FRIEDMAN (1956) *Studies in the quantity Theory of Money* (Chicago, University of Chicago Press). **[245]**

CALDWELL, J. (1976) 'Towards a Restatement of Demographic Transition Theory' *Population and Development Review*, vol. 2 (3–4), pp. 321–66. **[58]**

CHAYANOV, A.V. (1966) *The Theory of Peasant Economy* (Homewood, R.D. Irwin). **[86]**

CHELLIAH, R.J., H.J. BAAS and M.R. KELLEY (1975) 'Tax Ratios and Tax Effort in Developing Countries', *IMF Staff Papers*, vol. 22, pp. 187–205. **[186]**

CHENERY, H.B. (1977) 'Transitional Growth and World Industrialisation', in B. OHLIN, P. HESSELBORN and P.M. WIJKMAN (eds) *The Inter-*

national Allocation of Economic Activity (London, Macmillan), pp. 457–90. **[16, 36]**

CHENERY, H.B. and M. BRUNO (1962) 'Development Alternatives in an Open Economy: the Case of Israel', *Economic Journal*, vol. 72, pp. 79–103. **[211]**

CHENERY, H.B. and A. STROUT (1966) 'Foreign Assistance and Economic Development' *American Economic Review*, vol. 56, pp. 679–733. **[211]**

CHENERY, H.B., S. ROBINSON and M. SYRQUIN (1986) *Industrialization and Growth* (Oxford, Oxford University Press). **[16, 28–30, 113–15]**

CHENERY, H.B. and M. SYRQUIN (1975) *Patterns of Development 1950–70* (London, Oxford University Press). **[174, 184–5, 200]**

CHINA, REPUBLIC OF (1987), *Taiwan Statistical Yearbook, 1987* (Taipei, Council for Economic Planning and Development). **[25, 219–20, 225, 227–9]**

CLOWER, R.W. (1965) 'The Keynesian Counter-revolution', in F.K. HAHN and F.P.R. BRECHLING (eds) *The Theory of Interest Rates* (London, Macmillan). **[154]**

CONNOLLY, M. and D. TAYLOR (1976) 'Testing the Monetary Approach to Devaluation in Developing Countries', *Journal of Political Economy*, vol. 84, pp. 849–59. **[253]**

COOPER, R. (1987) *Essays in World Economics* (Cambridge, Mass, MIT Press). **[255]**

CORNWALL, J. (1972) *Growth and Stability in a Mature Economy* (London, Martin Robertson). **[45, 160, 169, 171–3, 278]**

CORNWALL, J. (1977) *Modern Capitalism* (London, Martin Robertson). **[27, 31, 45, 125, 133]**

CORNWALL, J. (1983) *The Conditions for Economic Recovery* (New York, M.E. Sharpe Inc.). **[26, 241, 249]**

CORNWALL, J. (1986) 'Stagnation, Innovational Investment and Patterns of Economic Growth' (Halifax, Dalhousie University Working Paper No. 86–03). **[20]**

CORNWALL, J. (1990) *The Theory of Economic Breakdown* (Oxford, Basil Blackwell). **[255, 276]**

DASGUPTA, A.K. (1954) 'Keynesian Economics and Under-developed Countries', *Economist Weekly*, vol. 6, pp. 101–5. **[157]**

DASGUPTA, A.K. (1975) *Economics of Austerity* (New Delhi, Oxford University Press). **[264]**

DEANE, P. and W.A. COLE (1962) *British Economic Growth, 1688–1959* (Cambridge, Cambridge University Press). **[105]**

DEMENY, P. (1968) 'Early Fertility Decline in Austria-Hungary: a Lesson in Demographic Transition', *Daedalus*, No. 97, pp. 502–22. **[58]**

DENISON, E.F. (1962) *The Sources of Economic Growth in the United States and the Alternatives Before Us* (New York, Committee for Economic Development). **[113]**

DOMAR, E.D. (1946) 'Capital Expansion, Rate of Growth and Employment', *Econometrica*, vol. 14, pp. 137–47. **[161]**

DORRANCE, G. (1966) 'Inflation and Growth: the Statistical Evidence', *IMF Staff Papers*, vol. 13, pp. 82–102. **[234]**

ECKHAUS, R.S. (1955) 'The Factor Proportions in Underdeveloped Countries', reprinted in A.N. AGARWALA and S.P. SINGH (eds) *The Economics of Underdevelopment* (London, Oxford University Press). **[157]**

ELVIN, M. (1973) *The Pattern of Chinese Past* (London, Eyre Methuen). **[103]**

EMERY, R.F. (1967) 'The Relationship of Exports and Economic Growth', *Kyklos*, vol. 20, pp. 470–84. **[203]**

FALVEY, R. and N. GEMMELL (1988) *Government Size and Economic Growth* (Canberra, Australian National University Working Paper – mimeograph). **[193]**

FEDER, E. (1983) 'On Exports and Economic Growth', *Journal Development Economics*, vol. 12, pp. 59–73. **[193, 206–7]**

FEI, J.C.H. and G. RANIS (1971) 'Development and Employment in Open Dualistic Economy', *Malayan Economic Review*, vol. 16(2), pp. 91–116. **[98]**

FINDLAY, R. (1959) 'International Specialisation and the Concept of Balanced Growth: comment', *Quarterly Journal of Economics*, vol. 73, pp. 339–46. **[284]**

FINDLAY, R. (1971) 'The Foreign Exchange Gap', in J.N. BHAGWATI, R.W. JONES, R.A. MUNDELL and J. VANEK (eds) (1971) *Trade, Balance of Payments and Growth* (Amsterdam, North-Holland). **[212]**

FRIEDMAN, M. (1953) 'Discussion of the Inflationary Gap', in M. FRIEDMAN (1953) *Essays in Positive Economics* (Chicago, University of Chicago Press), pp. 251–262. **[245]**

FRIEDMAN, M. (1971) 'Government Revenue and Inflation', *Journal Political Economy*, vol. 79, pp. 846–56. **[244–7]**

FUCHS, V. (1968) *The Service Economy* (New York, Columbia University Press). **[144, 186]**

FURNIVALL, J.S. (1931) *Introduction to the Political Economy of Burma* (Rangoon, Burma Book Club, 3rd edn published by People's Literature Committee and House, Rangoon, 1957). **[83]**

GEERTZ, C. (1963) *Agricultural Involution* (Berkeley, University of California Press). **[90]**

GEMMELL, N. (1986) *Structural Change and Economic Development* (London, Macmillan). **[148]**

GERSCHENKRON, A. (1962) *Economic Backwardness in Historical Perspective* (Cambridge, Mass., Belknap Press). **[67, 107]**

GERSCHENKRON, A. (1963) 'The Early Phases of Industrialization in Russia', in W.W. Rostow (ed.) (1963) *The Economics of Take-Off* (London, Macmillan), pp. 151–69. **[107]**

GOMULKA, S. (1971) *Inventitive Activity, Diffusion and the Stages of Economic Growth* (Aarhus, Aarhus University). **[128]**

GORDON, R.J. (1982) 'Why Stopping Inflation may be Costly', in R.E. HALL (ed.) (1982) *Inflation: Causes and Effects* (Chicago, University of Chicago Press), ch. 1, pp. 11–40. **[235]**

GRUBEL, H.G. and P.J. LLOYD (1975) *Intra-Industry Trade* (London, Macmillan). **[208]**

GUPTA, S.P. (1968) 'Public Expenditure and Economic Development – A

Cross-Section Analysis', *Finanzarchiv N.F.*, vol. 28, pp. 32–5. **[183]**

HABERLER, G. (1959) *International Trade and Economic Development* (Cairo, National Bank of Egypt), reprinted in G. MEIER (ed.) *Leading Issues in Economic Development* (3rd edn) (Oxford, Oxford University Press, 1975). **[210]**

HACCHE, G. (1979) *The Theory of Economic Growth* (London, Macmillan). **[66, 125, 128, 172]**

HAHN, F.H. and R.C.O. MATTHEWS (1964) 'The Theory of Economic Growth: A Survey', *Economic Journal*, vol. 74, pp. 779–902. **[66]**

HARBERGER, A.C. (1959) 'Using the Resources at Hand more Effectively', *American Economic Review*, vol. 49, pp. 134–46. **[208]**

HARRIS, J.R. (1972) *Industry and Technology in the Eighteenth Century: Britain and France* (Birmingham, University of Birmingham Press). **[106]**

HARROD, R.F. (1939) 'An Essay in Dynamic Theory', *Economic Journal*, vol. 49, pp. 14–33. **[161, 165]**

HARROD, R.F. (1959) 'Domar and Dynamic Economics', *Economic Journal*, vol. 69, pp. 451–64. **[166]**

HARROD, R.F. (1973) *Economic Dynamics* (London, Macmillan). **[164, 169]**

HAYAMI, Y. and V.W. RUTTAN (1985) *Agricultural Development: An International Perspective* (Baltimore, Johns Hopkins University Press). **[78–9, 92, 127]**

HELLER, P.S. and R.C. PORTER (1978) 'Exports and Growth', *Journal Development Economics*, vol. 5, pp. 191–3. **[213]**

HICKS, J.R. (1932) *Theory of Wages* (London, Macmillan). **[92, 127]**

HICKS, J.R. (1950) *Theory of the Trade Cycle* (Oxford, Oxford University Press). **[171]**

HICKS, J.R. (1969) *A Theory of Economic History* (Oxford, Oxford University Press). **[101, 103]**

HICKS, J.R. (1973) 'The Mainspring of Economic Growth', *Swedish Journal of Economics*, vol. 75, pp. 336–48. **[128, 263]**

HICKS, J.R. (1977) *Economic Perspectives* (Oxford, Oxford University Press). **[134]**

HIRSCH, F. (1977) *Social Limits to Growth* (London, Routledge and Kegan Paul). **[286]**

HOLLANDER, S. (1979) *The Economics of David Ricardo* (Toronto, Toronto University Press). **[57]**

INMAN, R.P. (1985) 'Introduction and Overview', in R.P. INMAN (ed.) (1985) *Managing the Service Economy* (Cambridge, Cambridge University Press). **[138, 144]**

INTERNATIONAL MONETARY FUND (1982) *World Economic Outlook* (Washington, DC, IMF). **[234]**

INTERNATIONAL MONETARY FUND (1985) *Government Finance Statistics Yearbook* (Washington, DC, IMF). **[187–8]**

ISHIKAWA, S. (1967) *Economic Development in Asian Perspective* (Tokyo, Kinokyniya Bookstore). **[89]**

ISHIKAWA, S. (1978) *Labour Absorption in Agriculture* (Bangkok, ILO–ARTEP). **[90–1]**

JAIN, S. (1975) *Size Distribution of Income* (Washington, D.C., World Bank). **[259]**

JHA, L.K. (1980) *Economic Strategy for the 80s* (New Delhi, Allied Publishers). **[239–40]**

JOHNSON, C. (1987) 'Political Institutions and Economic Performance: The Government-Business Relationship in Japan, South Korea and Taiwan', in F.C. DEYO (1987) *The Political Economy of the New Asian Industrialism* (Ithaca and London, Cornell University Press), ch. 4, pp. 136–64. **[227]**

JOHNSON, H.G. (1958) 'Planning and the Market in Economic Development', *Pakistan Economic Journal*, no. 2, pp. 44–55, reprinted in H.G. JOHNSON (1962) *Money, Trade and Economic Growth* (London, Allen and Unwin), ch. 7, pp. 151–63. **[258]**

JOHNSON, H.G. (1966) 'Is Inflation the inevitable Price of Rapid Development or a Retarding Factor in Economic Growth', *Malayan Economic Revue*, vol. 11, pp. 21–8. **[233, 244]**

JOHNSON, H.G. (1968) 'Problems of Efficiency in Monetary Management', *Journal of Political Economy*, pp. 971–90, reprinted in H.G. JOHNSON (1972) *Further Essays in Monetary Economics* (London, Allen and Unwin), ch. 3, pp. 88–112. **[243]**

JOHNSON, H.G. (1977) 'Trade, Growth and Economic Stability', in *Trade and Employment in Asia and the Pacific* (Manila, Council for Asian Manpower Studies). **[210]**

JORGENSON, D.W. and Z. GRILICHES (1967) 'The Explanation of Productivity Change', *Review of Economic Studies*, vol. 34, pp. 249–83. **[113]**

KAHN, H. (1979) *World Economic Development* (Boulder, Colorado, Westview Press). **[136]**

KALDOR, N. (1957) 'A Model of Economic Growth', *Economic Journal*, vol. 67, pp. 591–624. **[116, 172]**

KALDOR, N. (1961) 'Capital Accumulation and Economic Growth', in F.A. LUTZ and D.C. HAGUE (eds) (1961) *The Theory of Capital* (London, Macmillan). **[65, 116, 172]**

KALECKI, M. (1954) *Theory of Economic Dynamics* (London, Allen and Unwin). **[250]**

KAVOUSSI, R.M. (1984) 'Export Expansion and Economic Growth', *Journal of Development Economics*, vol. 14, pp. 241–50. **[178, 204–6]**

KENNEDY, C. (1964) 'Induced Bias in Innovation and the Theory of Distribution', *Economic Journal*, vol. 48, pp. 541–7. **[128]**

KEYNES, J.M. (1936) *General Theory of Employment, Interest and Money* (London, Macmillan). **[13, 154–5, 165]**

KINDLEBERGER, C.P. (1965) *Economic Development* (New York, McGraw-Hill). **[39]**

KIRKPATRICK, C. and F. NIXSON (1987) 'Inflation and Stabilization Policy in LDCs', in N. GEMMELL (ed.) (1987) *Surveys in Development Economics* (Oxford, Basil Blackwell) ch. 5, pp. 172–204. **[242]**

KLEIMEN, E. (1980) *Exports and Growth: Evidence and Interpretation*, (Canberra, Australian National University). **[213–4]**

KONDRATIEFF, N.D. (1935) 'The Long Waves in Economic Life', *Review of Economics and Statistics.* **[20]**

KRAUSS, M.B. and H.G. JOHNSON (1974) *General Equilibrium Analysis* (London, Allen and Unwin). **[6]**

KRAVIS, I.B., A.W. HESTON and R. SUMMERS (1983) 'The Share of Services in Economic Growth', in F.G. ADAMS and B.G. HICKMAN (eds) (1983) *Global Econometrics* (Cambridge, Mass., MIT Press). **[137, 139, 146]**

KRISTENSEN, T. (1974) *Development in Rich and Poor Countries* (New York, Praeger). **[15, 35]**

KRUEGER, A.O. (1981) 'Export-led Industrial Growth Reconsidered', in W. HONG and L.B. KRAUSE (eds) (1981) *Trade and Growth of the Advanced Developing Countries in the Pacific Basin* (Seoul, Korea Development Institute), ch. 1, pp. 3–27. **[209]**

KUZNETS, S. (1957) 'Quantitative Aspects of the Economic Growth of Nations: II. Industrial Distribution of National Product and Labour Force', *Economic Development and Cultural Change*, vol. 5, no. 4 (supplement). **[31]**

KUZNETS, S. (1966) *Modern Economic Growth* (New Haven, Yale University Press). **[19, 105]**

KUZNETS, S. (1971) *Economic Growth of Nations* (Cambridge, Mass., Belknap Press). **[19–20, 28, 31]**

KUZNETS, S. (1973) 'Notes on Japan's Economic Growth', in L. KLEIN and K. OKHAWA (eds) (1973) *Economic Growth: The Japanese Experience since the Meiji Era* (Homewood, Ill., Richard D. Irwin). **[130]**

KUZNETS, S. (1982) 'The Pattern of Shift of Labor Force from Agriculture, 1950–79', in M. GERSOVITL, C.F. DIAL-ALEJANDRO, G. RANIS and M.R. RESENZWEIG (eds) (1982) *The Theory and Experience of Economic Development* (London, George Allen and Unwin), pp. 43–59. **[34–5]**

LANDAU, D. (1986) 'Government and Economic Growth in the Less Developed Countries: An Empirical Study for 1960–80', *Economic Development and Cultural Change*, vol. 35, pp. 35–76. **[189–91]**

LANDES, D. (1969) *The Unbound Prometheus* (Cambridge, Cambridge University Press). **[19, 71–2, 106]**

LEIJONHUFVUD, A. (1968) *On Keynesian Economics and the Economics of Keynes* (Oxford, Oxford University Press). **[154]**

LEWIS, J.P. (1962) *Quiet Crisis in India* (Washington, DC, Brookings Institution). **[158]**

LEWIS, W.A. (1954) 'Economic Development with Unlimited Supplies of Labour', *Manchester School*, vol. 22, pp. 139–1, reprinted in A.N. AGARWALA and S.P. SINGH (eds) (1958). *The Economics of Underdevelopment* (London, Oxford University Press, 1958). **[68–9, 157–8]**

LEWIS, W.A. (1955) *Theory of Economic Growth* (London, George Allen and Unwin). **[58, 66–7, 283]**

LEWIS, W.A. (1964) 'Closing Remarks', in W. BAER and I. KERSTENETZKY (eds) *Inflation and Growth in Latin America* (Homewood, Ill., Richard D. Irwin), pp. 21–33. **[233, 241–2]**

LEWIS, W.A. (1969) *Aspects of Tropical Trade 1883–1965* (Stockholm, Almqvist & Wiksell). **[22]**

LEWIS, W.A. (1970a) *The Development Process* (New York, UN). **[278]**

LEWIS, W.A. (1972) 'Reflections on Unlimited Labour', in L.E. di MARCO (ed.) (1972) *International Economics and Development* (New York, Academic Press). **[71]**

LEWIS, W.A. (1978) *Growth and Fluctuations* (London, George Allen and Unwin). **[68, 83, 104, 134–5]**

LEWIS, W.A. (1982) 'The Growth of Mature Economies', in C.P. KINDLEBERGER and G. di TELLA (eds) (1982) *Economics in the Long View* (New York, New York University Press), vol. I, ch. 7, pp 105–15. **[67]**

LEWIS, W.A. (1984) 'The State of Development Theory', *American Economic Review*, vol. 74, pp. 1–10. **[4]**

LEWIS, W.A. and A. MARTIN (1956) 'Patterns of Public Revenue and Expenditure', *Manchester School*, vol. 24, pp. 203–44. **[186]**

LLOYD, P.J. (1968) *International Trade Problems of Small Nations* (Durham, SC, Duke University Press). **[200]**

LOCKWOOD, W.W. (1954) *The Economic Development of Japan* (Princeton, Princeton University Press). **[210]**

MADDISON, A. (1982) *Phases of Capitalist Development* (Oxford, Oxford University Press). **[23, 128, 154]**

MADDISON, A. (1987) 'Growth and Slowdown in Advanced Capitalist Economies', *Journal of Economic Literature*, vol. 25(2), pp. 649–98. **[119–21]**

MAGER, N.H. (1987) *The Kondratieff Wave* (New York, Praeger). **[20]**

MALINVAUD, E. (1977) *The Theory of Unemployment Reconsidered* (Oxford, Basil Blackwell). **[263]**

MARSHALL, A. (1919) *Industry and Trade* (London, Macmillan). **[200]**

MARSHALL, A. (1961) *Principles of Economics* (London, Macmillan). **[75, 122]**

MATTHEWS, R.C.O. (1968) 'Why has Britain had Full Employment Since the War', *Economic Journal*, vol. 78, pp. 555–69. **[156]**

MEIER, G.M. (1976) *Leading Issues in Economic Development* (Oxford, Oxford University Press). **[68]**

MICHAELY, M. (1977) 'Exports and Growth', *Journal of Development Economics*, vol. 4, pp. 49–53. **[203, 212]**

MINAMI, R. (1986) *The Economic Development of Japan* (London, Macmillan). **[99]**

MORISHIMA, M. (1969) *Theory of Economic Growth* (Oxford, Clarendon Press). **[6, 168]**

MUELLER, D.C. (1987) 'The Growth of Government: A Public Choice Perspective', *IMF Staff Papers*, vol. 34(1) pp. 86–114. **[185]**

MUNDELL, R.A. (1971) *Monetary Theory* (Pacific Palisades, Calif. Goodyear Publishing Inc.). **[244, 246–7]**

MUSGRAVE, R. (1969) *Fiscal Systems* (New Haven, Yale University Press). **[183, 187]**

MYINT, H. (1958) 'The "Classical Theory" of International Trade and the

Underdeveloped Countries' reprinted in H. MYINT (1971), ch. 5, pp. 118–46. **[210, 215]**

MYINT, H. (1987) 'Neo-classical Development Analysis: Its Strengths and Limits', in G. MEIER (ed.) (1987) *Pioneers in Development* (London, Oxford University Press). **[209, 215–6]**

NABSETH, L. and G.F. RAY (eds) (1974) *The Diffusion of Industrial Processes* (Cambridge, Cambridge University Press). **[125]**

NEEDHAM, J. (1970) *Clerks and Craftsmen in China and the West* (Cambridge, Cambridge University Press). **[102–3]**

NEF, J.U. (1940) *Industry and Government in France and England, 1540–1640* (Ithaca, NY, Great Seal Books). **[106]**

NURKSE, R. (1952) *Problems of Capital Formation in Underdeveloped Countries* (London, Oxford University Press). **[157, 283]**

NURKSE, R. (1958) 'The Case for Balanced Growth', in G. MEIER (1976) *Leading Issues in Economic Development* (Oxford, Oxford University Press). **[68, 283]**

O'BRIEN, D.P. (1975) *The Classical Economists* (Oxford, Oxford University Press). **[57]**

O'BRIEN, D.P. (1981) 'Ricardian Economics and the Economics of David Ricardo', *Oxford Economic Papers*, vol. 33, pp. 352–86. **[57]**

OKHAWA, K. and H. ROSOVSKY (1973) *Japanese Economic Growth* (Stanford, Stanford University Press). **[131]**

OECD (1968) *Development Assistance* (Paris, OECD). **[212]**

OECD (1985) *Twenty-five Years of Development Cooperation* (Paris, OECD). **[16, 24, 28]**

PASINETTI, L. (1982) *Structural Change and Economic Growth* (Cambridge, Cambridge University Press). **[45]**

PEACOCK, A.T. (1976) 'Welfare economics and Public Subsidies to the Arts' in M. BLAUG (ed.) (1976) *The Economics of the Arts* (London, Martin Robertson). **[148]**

PEACOCK, A.T. and J. WISEMAN (1961) *The Growth of Public Expenditure* (Princeton, Princeton University Press). **[186]**

PHELPS, E. (1972) *Inflation Policy and Unemployment Theory* (London, Macmillan). **[243]**

PHELPS BROWN, E.H. (1968) *Pay and Profits* (Manchester University Press). **[67]**

PHILLIPS, A.W. (1958) 'The Relation between Unemployment and the rate of change of Money Wage Rates', *Economica*, vol. 25, pp. 283–99. **[248]**

PIGOU, A.C. (1935) *The Stationary State* (London, Macmillan). **[75]**

PRATTEN, C.F. (1971) *Economies of Scale in Manufacturing Industry* (Cambridge, Cambridge University Press). **[123]**

RAKSHIT, M. (1982) *Labour Surplus Economy* (Delhi, Macmillan). **[158, 250]**

RAM, R. (1985) 'Exports and Economic Growth: Some Additional Evidence', *Economic Development and Cultural Change*, vol. 33, pp. 415–25. **[208]**

RAM, R. (1986) 'Government Size and Economic Growth', *American Economic Review*, Vol. 76, pp. 191–203. **[191, 193, 195–6]**

RAM, R. (1987) 'Exports and Economic Growth in Developing Countries: Evidence from Time Series and Cross-Section Data', *Economic Development and Cultural Change*, vol. 36(1), pp. 51–72. **[206]**

RAM, R. (1987a) 'Wagner's Hypothesis in Time Series and Cross-section Perspectives', *Review of Economics and Statistics*, vol. b9, pp. 194–204. **[184]**

RAMSEY, F.P. (1928) 'A Mathematical Theory of Saving', *Economic Journal*, vol. 38, pp. 543–59. **[74]**

RAO, V.K.R.V. (1952) 'Investment, Income and the Multiplier in India', reprinted in A.N. AGARWALA AND S.P. SINGH (eds) (1958) *The Economics of Underdevelopment* (London, Oxford University Press). **[157]**

ROBINSON, E.A.G. (1953) *The Structure of Competitive Industry* (Cambridge, Cambridge University Press). **[122]**

ROSE, H. (1959) 'The Possibility of Warranted Growth', *Economic Journal*, vol. 69, pp. 313–32. **[168]**

ROSENSTEIN-RODAN, P.N. (1943) 'Problems of Industrialisation of Eastern and Southeastern Europe', *Economic Journal*, vol. 53, pp. 202–11. **[283]**

ROSTOVTZEFF, M. (1957) *The Economic and Social History of the Roman Empire*, vol. 1, (Oxford, Oxford University Press). **[102]**

ROSTOW, W.W. (1960) *The Stages of Economic Growth* (Cambridge, Cambridge University Press). **[18–9, 107]**

ROSTOW, W.W. (1975) *How It All Began* (New York, MacGraw-Hill). **[20, 102–3, 105–6, 124]**

ROSTOW, W.W. (1978) 'Growth Rates at Different Levels of Income and Stages of Growth', in P. USELDING (ed.) (1978) *Research in Economic History*, vol. 3, pp. 47–86. **[15, 36]**

ROSTOW, W.W. (1980) *Why the Poor Get Richer and the Rich Slow Down* (Austin, University of Texas Press). **[15, 36, 240]**

SALTER, W.G. (1960) *Productivity and Technical Change* (Cambridge, Cambridge University Press). **[127]**

SAMUELSON, P.A. (1939) 'Interactions between the Multiplier Analysis and the Principle of Acceleration', *Review of Economics and Statistics*, vol. 21, pp. 75–8, reprinted in P.A. SAMUELSON (1966) *Collected Scientific Papers* (Cambridge, Mass., MIT Press), vol. 2, ch. 2, pp. 1107–1110. **[170]**

SAMUELSON, P.A. (1965) 'A Theory of Induced Innovation along Kennedy–Weizsacker Lines', *Review of Economics and Statistics*, vol. 47, pp. 343–56. **[128]**

SAMUELSON, P.A. (1980) *Economics* (New York, McGraw-Hill). **[66]**

SARGENT, T.J. (1982) 'The End of Four Big Inflations', in R.E. HALL (ed.) (1982) *Inflation: Causes and Effects* (Chicago, University of Chicago Press), ch. 2, pp. 41–98. **[235]**

SCHMOOKLER, J. (1966) *Invention and Economic Growth* (Cambridge, Mass., Harvard University Press). **[126]**

SCHUMPETER, J. (1934) *The Theory of Economic Development* (Cambridge, Mass., Harvard University Press). **[19, 67]**

SEN, A.K. (1959) 'The Choice of Agricultural Techniques in Underdeveloped countries', *Economic Development and Cultural Change*, vol. 7, pp. 279–85. **[97]**

SEN, A.K. (1970) *Growth Economics* (London, Penguin Books). **[6]**

SEN, A.K. (1973) *On Economic Inequality* (Oxford, Clarendon Press). **[258]**

SHEAHAN, J. (1958) 'International Specialisation and the Concept of Balanced Growth', *Quarterly Journal of Economics*, vol. 72, pp. 183–7. **[284]**

SHINKAI, Y. (1960) 'On Equilibrium Growth of Capital and Labour', *International Economic Papers*, vol. 1, pp. 107–11. **[64]**

SINGH, S.K. (1975) *Development Economics* (Lexington, Mass Lexington Books). **[71]**

SINHA, R., P. PEARSON, G. KADEKODI and M. GREGORY (1979) *Income Distribution, Growth and Basic Needs* (London, Croom-Helm). **[269]**

SOLOW, R.M. (1956) 'A Contribution to the Theory of Economic Growth', *Quarterly Journal of Economics*, vol. 70, pp. 65–94. **[63]**

SOLOW, R.M. (1957) 'Technical Change and the aggregate Production Function', *Review of Economics and Statistics*, vol. 39, pp. 312–20. **[112]**

SOLOW, R.M. (1970) *Growth Theory: An Exposition* (Oxford, Oxford University Press). **[65]**

SOLOW, R.M. (1977) 'Comment on Chenery's Paper', in B. OHLIN, P. HESSELBORN and P. WIJKMAN (eds) (1977) *The International Allocation of Economic Activity* (London, Macmillan), pp. 490–3. **[36, 136]**

SOLOW, R.M. (1988) 'Growth Theory and After', *American Economic Review*, vol. 78(3), pp. 307–17. **[61, 169]**

STIGLITZ, J.E. and H. UZAWA (1969) *Readings in the Modern Theory of Economic Growth* (Cambridge, Mass., MIT Press). **[170]**

SUMMERS, R. (1985) 'Services in the International Economy', in R.P. INMAN (ed.) (1985) *Managing the Service Economy* (Cambridge, Cambridge University Press), ch. 1, pp. 27–48. **[137, 140–2]**

SUMMERS, R. and A. HESTON (1988) 'A New Set of International Comparisons of Real Product and Prices: Estimates for 130 Countries 1950–85', *Review of Income and Wealth*, vol. 34, pp. 1–26. **[195]**

SUNDRUM, R.M. (1973) 'Money Supply and Prices', *Bulletin of Indonesian Economic Studies*, vol. 9(3), pp. 73–86. **[242, 251]**

SUNDRUM, R.M. (1976) 'Transitional Dynamics of Deficit Financing', *Indian Economic Review*, vol. 9(2) (New Series), pp. 193–203. **[247]**

SUNDRUM, R.M. (1983) *Development Economics* (Chichester, John Wiley). **[200]**

SUNDRUM, R.M. (1986) 'Indonesia's Rapid Economic Growth: 1968–81', *Bulletin of Indonesian Economic Studies*, vol. 22, pp. 40–6. **[119, 251]**

SUNDRUM, R.M. (1987) *Growth and Income Distribution in India* (Delhi, Sage Publications). **[83, 158, 252, 268]**

SUNDRUM, R.M. (1988) 'Indonesia's Slow Economic Growth', *Bulletin of Indonesian Economic Studies*, vol. 24(1), pp. 37–72. **[251]**

SUNDRUM, R.M. (1990) *Income Distribution in LDCs* (London, Routledge). **[257]**

SWAN, T. (1956) 'Economic Growth and Capital Accumulation', *Economic Record*, vol. 63, pp. 334–61. **[63, 159]**

TAIT, A.A. and P.S. HELLER (1982) *International Comparison of Government Expenditure* (Washington, DC, International Monetary Fund, Occasional Paper No. 10). **[183–4]**

THIRLWALL, A.P. (1974) *Inflation, Savings and Economic Growth* (London, Macmillan). **[234, 244]**

THIRLWALL, A.P. (1978) *Growth and Development* (London, Macmillan). **[211]**

TSIANG, S.C. (1985) 'Foreign Trade and Investment as Boosters for Take-Off: The Experience of Taiwan', in V. CORBO, A.O. KRUEGER, and F. OSSA (eds) (1985) *Export Oriented Development Strategies* (Boulder and London, Westview Press), ch. 3, pp. 27–56. **[223, 227]**

TSIANG, S.C. (1988) 'Taiwan's Economic Success Demystified', *Journal Economic Growth*, vol. 3, pp. 11–20. **[223]**

TSIANG, S.C. and WU, R. (1985) 'Foreign Trade and Investment as Boosters for Take Off: The Experiences of the Four Asian Newly Industrializing Countries', in W. GALENSON (ed.) (1985) *Foreign Trade and Investment* (Madison, University of Wisconsin Press). **[220, 223–4, 278]**

TUN WAI, U. (1959) 'The Relation Between Inflation and Economic Development', *IMF Staff Papers*, vol. 7, pp. 302–17. **[234]**

TYLER, W.G. (1981) 'Growth and Export Expansion in Developing Countries', *Journal of Development Economics*, vol. 9, pp. 121–30. **[177, 203–4]**

UNITED NATIONS (1964) 'Plant Size and economies of Scale' in U.N. (1964) *Industrialisation and Productivity Bulletin* No. 88, New York, UN. **[123]**

UNITED NATIONS (1970) *The Measurement of Development Effort* (New York, UN). **[187]**

UNITED NATIONS (1983) *Industry in a Changing World* (New York, UN). **[31–3]**

USHER, D. (1980) *The Measurement of Growth* (Oxford, Basil Blackwell). **[116]**

UZAWA, H. (1963) 'On a Two Sector Model of Economic Growth II', *Review of Economic Studies*, vol. 30, pp. 105–18. **[64]**

VAIDYANATHAN, A. (1978) 'Labour Use in Indian Agriculture', in P.K. BARDHAN (ed.) (1978) *Labour Absorption in Indian Agriculture* (Bangkok, ILO-ARTEP). **[87]**

WORLD BANK (1983) *World Development Report, 1983* (Washington D.C., World Bank). **[32]**

WORLD BANK (1984) *World Tables* (Washington D.C., World Bank). **[16, 24, 28, 173, 175–8, 185, 189, 192, 197, 201–4, 217, 234–7, 259, 261]**

WORLD BANK (1987) *World Tables* (Washington D.C., World Bank). **[16, 25]**

WORLD BANK (1988) *World Development Report, 1988* (Washington D.C., World Bank). **[32–3, 133–4, 259, 261]**

YEUNG, P. and T.L. ROE (1978) 'A CES Test of Induced Technical Change: Japan', in H.P. BINSWANGER and V.W. RUTTAN (eds) (1978) *Induced Innovation* (Baltimore, Johns Hopkins University Press). **[93]**

YOUNG, A. (1928) 'Increasing Returns and Economic Progress', *Economic Journal* vol. 38, pp. 527–42. **[123–4]**

Subject Index

acceleration principle, 170–2
accounting effect
  of exports, 212–14
  of government expenditure, 192–3
  of investment, 179–81
agricultural involution, 90
agricultural sector
  area extension, 80–5
  growth of, 77–100
  historical mission of, 98–100
  labour intensity in, 80–1, 83–6
  labour productivity in, 30, 80–1, 86–9, 102
  logistic pattern in, 33–4
  mechanisation process in, 93–8
  technological progress in, 59, 89–93
allocative efficiency, improvement of, 8–9, 271
  and exports, 207–9

balanced growth doctrine, 283–5
Butt theory of growth, 12, 72–6, 93–8
  limitations of, 75–6

capital
  circulating, 59–60
  deepening, 62, 117–19, 123
  in industry, 101, 105
  labour saving, 95–8
  land saving, 95–8
  stock of, 117–22, 219–22
  widening, 62, 117–9, 123
capital–output ratio, 61, 162–4, 221–3
capitalism, 105
catching-up process, 128–31, 277
classical theory of growth, 5, 9, 12, 54–60, 153–4
  limitations of, 5–6, 13, 56–60
colonial pattern of development, 21

commodities, hierarchy of, 44–5, 135
community principle, 90
cost-push factors, 239–41

de-industrialisation, 131–5, 287
demand factors, 13, 153–230, 272
  and income distribution, 106, 265–70
  and inflation, 247–9
  in industry, 105–6, 131
  in services, 139–42
demographic transition theory, 57–8
dualistic theory of growth, 12, 69–72
  limitations of, 70–2
dynamic advantages of trade, 209–10, 216
dynamic stability, 61, 63–4

economic development, 19
economic growth
  and structural transformation, 27–35, 273
  factors in long-term growth, 271–4
  in historical perspective, 15–26
  in post-war DCs, 22–3, 276–8
  in post-war LDCs, 23–5, 278–9
  major episodes of, 18–26, 274–80
  slackening of, in DCs, 25–6, 147–8, 270, 279–80
  stylised facts, 6, 65–6, 271, 273
  without inflation, 250–1
  see also logistic pattern, rates of growth
education, 141, 282
expectations, 238–9
  rational, 157
exports, 155–6, 199–230, 285–6
  and growth of income, 201–18
  and investment, 216, 228–30

growth of, 22, 202–7
K-ratio of, 206, 213–14, 227–8
structure of, 217–18
variations in, 199–201

foreign exchange constraint, 210–12

GDP, changing composition of,
27–30
government expenditure, 155–6,
182–98, 285
and growth of income, 188–98
and investment, 196–7
growth of, 191–7
K-ratio of, 192–5
variations in, 182–8
government revenues, 186–7
growth policy, 280–7
in DCs, 286–7
in LDCs, 282–6
growth theory
Butt, 12, 72–6, 93–8
classical, 5, 9, 12, 54–6, 153–4
and data, 6, 271
extant theory, 3–4, 53–76
Harrod–Domar, 61, 161–70
Kaldor, 116–17, 172
Lewis, 12, 69–72
Marxian, 6
neo-classical, 6, 60–8
objectives of, 3–5, 53
stages, 18

Harrod–Domar theory of growth,
61, 161–70
Heckscher–Ohlin theory of trade,
207
hierarchy of commodities, 44–5, 135
high-level equilibrium trap, 103
historical mission of agriculture,
98–100

imports, 155
income distribution
and growth, 55–6, 257–70, 286
and savings, 264–5
and structure of production,
265–70

income elasticity of demand, 40–5,
48
for food, 44, 46, 48, 98
for services, 46, 48, 139, 145
increasing returns, 105, 122–5
induced innovation
in agriculture, 92–3
in industry, 127–8
inducement to invest, 160
Industrial Revolution, 18
as take-off, 106–7
in Europe, 104–6
industrial sector
growth of, 101–35
in traditional societies, 101–4
labour productivity, 33
logistic pattern in, 32–3
sources of growth, 108–23
industrialisation
beginnings, 101–8
failure of, in traditional societies,
102–4
inflation, 14, 233–56
and export-led growth, 253
and growth, 233–7, 243–56
and mobilisation of resources,
244–7
causes of, 237–43
expectations and, 238–9
Latin American type, 242–3
propagation of, 241–2
without growth, 249–50
innovations, 125
autonomous, 126
diffusion, 126, 128–31, 277
induced, 59, 90, 92–3, 126–8
intra-industry trade, 208
inventions, 125
investment, 153–81
and exports, 216–17, 228–30
and government expenditures,
197–8
and growth of income, 61–2,
167–72
and income, 175–6
and savings, 66
dual role of, 161–72
growth of, 176–81, 216–17

in Taiwan, 220–4
K-ratio of, 162–3, 180–1
irrigation, 90–1

K-ratio
  of exports, 206, 213–4, 227–8
  of government expenditures,
    192–5
  of investment, 162–3, 180–1
Kaldor theory of growth, 116–17,
  172
Keynesian theory, 154–6
  and LDCs, 157–8
Kondratieff cycles, 20

labour
  changing allocation of, 29–32,
    40–4, 46, 48
  intensity in agriculture, 81
  productivity by sectors, 30, 33;
    growth of, 33, 39–42; in
    agriculture, 78–81, 86–9, 102;
    in services, 142–6
land leasing, 86
land ownership, 85–6
land tenure, 85
logistic pattern, 9–11, 15–8, 49, 273
  and technology, 35–6
  in agriculture, 33–4
  in industry, 32
long waves, 20

mechanisation process, 72–6
  in agriculture, 93–8
merchants, role of, 103
mobilisation of resources by
  inflation, 244–7
modern economic growth, 18–20,
  275
  onset in Europe, 20
monetary expansion and inflation,
  238
multiplier, 156
multiplier–accelerator model, 170–2

neo-classical theory of growth, 6,
  60–8
  for Taiwan, 223–5
  limitations of, 65–8

per capita income differences, a
  modern phenomenon, 3
Phillips curve, 156, 248–9
population growth, 57–9, 98, 102–3
  endogenous, 56–8
  exogenous, 59
price flexibility, 54
  and interest rate, 157
production function, 62
productive capacity, 7–10, 272
  increase of, 9–10, 13, 158–9
  utilisation of, 8, 153–8

rate of growth
  declining, 9
  determinants of, 10–14; classical,
    12–13, 53–149; income
    distribution, 14, 257–70;
    inflation, 14, 233–56;
    Keynesian, 13–4, 153–230;
    structural, 10–11, 27–50
  logistic, 9–10, 15–8
  natural, 164
  stability of, 165–70
  steady, 9
  Taiwan, 219–30
  warranted, 161–4
  see also economic growth
re-allocation effect, 40, 42–4, 47–8
rent of land, 94

S-curve, 16–17, 50, 273
savings, 61, 66–8, 155–6, 264–5
  and income distribution, 264–5
  and investment, 66–8
  in Taiwan, 222–4
  paradox of thrift, 156
Say's Law, 13, 53–4, 153, 159, 170
  reversal of, 160–1
service sector
  and growth slackening, 147–8
  demand for, 139–42
  growth of, 136–49
  labour productivity in, 33, 142–6
  non-market, 142
  price of, 145
  share in GDP, 138–9
  structure of, 136–7
social capability, 131, 277

soft landing, 287
structural determinants of growth,
    10–11, 27–50
  basic model, 38–44
  preliminary model, 35–8
  simulation of, 45–9
structural transformation, 27–35,
    273
  in Taiwan, 224–6
structure of production
  and growth of income, 35–50
  and income distribution, 265–70
  and income level, 27–9
subsistence level, 57

Taiwan experience, 218–30
take-off, 19, 106–7
taxes, 155–6, 186–7
technological progress
  capital saving, 111

causes of, 125–31
  in agriculture, 59, 89–93
  in China, 103
  in industry, 104–5, 108–25
  in Taiwan, 228
  labour saving, 111
  neutral, 110–1
technology, rigidity of, 157, 170
trade sector, 140
transport sector, 140
tropical development, 21–2, 276

unemployment, natural rate, 156

vent for surplus, 214–15, 228
virtuous cycle of export-led growth,
    230

Wagner's Law, 182–8